世界の村と街#1 エーゲ海の村と街　*Villages and Towns: Aegean Sea*

Villages and Towns
世界の村と街

#1

エーゲ海の村と街

Aegean Sea

企画・撮影：二川幸夫／文：磯崎新／解説・作図：鈴木恂／デザイン：細谷巖

Edited and Photographed by Yukio Futagawa
Introduction by Arata Isozaki
Articles and Drawings by Makoto Suzuki
Designed by Gan Hosoya

A.D.A. EDITA Tokyo

"Villages and Towns #1 Aegean Sea"
Copyright © 2016 A.D.A. EDITA Tokyo Co., Ltd.
3-12-14 Sendagaya, Shibuya-ku, Tokyo 151-0051, Japan
All rights reserved. No part of this publication may be reproduced,
stored in a retrieval system, or transmitted,
in any form or by any means, electronic, mechanical,
photocopying, recording, or otherwise,
without permission in writing from the publisher.

Copyright of photographs
© 2016 GA photographers
English translation: Lisa Tani

First published in 1973
Revised edition published in 2016

Printed and bound in Japan

ISBN 978-4-87140-454-9 C1372

目次
Contents

P.10 非透明性の空間―――磯崎新
Non-transparency of the Aegean Space *by Arata Isozaki*

25 第1章〈ミコノス島〉
Part One : MYKONOS

26 ミコノス―――鈴木恂
Mykonos *by Makoto Suzuki*

52 ミコノスの道と広場―――鈴木恂
Streets and Plazas of Mykonos *by Makoto Suzuki*

81 第2章〈サントリーニ島〉
Part Two : SANTORINI

82 サントリーニ―――鈴木恂
Sanatorini *by Makoto Suzuki*

108 サントリーニのテラス―――鈴木恂
Terraces of Sanatorini *by Makoto Suzuki*

129 写真説明
Pictures and Explanations

140 後記
Notes and Remarks

142 エーゲ海地図
Map of Aegean Sea

非透明性の空間────磯崎新
Non-transparency of the Aegean Space *by Arata Isozaki*

I

空気は，本当にその場所まででかけていって，吸ってみないとわからないものだろうか。

　エーゲ海の紺碧の空と海。幾重にもかさなりあって浮ぶ島々。そんな光景の敍述を幾つかの本で読みとり，写真を眺めたりしながら，私は，実は充分に理解したつもりになっていた。

　それには，私なりの理由もあったのだ。私は，日本の多島海と呼ばれる地域に連なる海岸でそだった。この海岸では島々は遠くにかすんでいるが，気候は比較的温暖であり，内海のために，海が荒れることもめったにない。その海岸の白砂に寝ころびながら，たとえば春霞のたなびいている島影のみえる水平線を眺めていたりすると，いつの間にかその光景がマラルメのうたった牧神の午後の舞台のように思えてくることもあった。そして背後のはまゆうの草むらから，突然，ニンフがあらわれてくるにちがいないといった想像さえめぐらすこともできたのだ。

　のちに，瀬戸内海の上空を飛行してみて，島々のひろがりが，エーゲ海の航空写真にそっくりにみえたことも，あの少年時代の思い込みをいっそう固めることだけに役立ったようだ。ただ，日本のこの海域にむらがる漁師町の民家は，そまつな板壁で，黒い瓦をのせていた。ときには板葺きの屋根に小石をのせたまんまのものも多かった。この黒っぽいシルエットだけのような集落は，入江の深部に群がるように，ひそかにおかれるといった，たたずまいをもっていた。

　その集落は，青黒く澄んだ水面に，沈むようにつきでている岬の裏側などに，ほとんど明確な輪郭線をもたず，ただ自然の内側に，消滅していく瞬間だけを待っているような表情をしているのだが，私は，おそらくエーゲ海域では，そんな岬の突端に，ポセイドンの神殿が，白大理石で建てられ，あたりの海を睥睨している，そんなことぐらいが違うのではないかと思っていたふしもあったのだ。

I

Maybe we never get to understand an atmosphere until we really visit the place and breathe it.

　Deep blue sky and sea of the Aegean. Islands floating in numerous layers. After reading depictions of such sceneries in several books and looking at photographs, I had in fact felt like I fully understood.

　And that for a reason of my own. I was raised on a coast facing an area called the archipelago of Japan. This coast, although giving onto a misty view of faraway islands, has a comparatively mild climate and faces an inland sea with very few storms. As I lay on the white sand of the beach and stared at the horizon where silhouettes of islands were veiled in spring haze, there were moments when that scenery appeared to me as a setting for Mallarmé's poem "The Afternoon of a Faun." And I would let my imagination run and be so sure that all of a sudden a nymph would emerge from a thicket of crinums behind me.

　When later on I flew over the Seto Inland Sea and found that the expanse of islands there looked exactly like in the aerial shots of the Aegean, it certainly contributed to consolidating my boyhood illusions, despite the fact that fishing villages that cluster around this marine area in Japan were clad in shabby board walls and roofed with black tiles—many of them even had a bare, wood-board shingle roof with stones placed on for weight. This type of settlement with dark silhouettes was usually a clustered presence placed secretly deep inside a bay.

　On the crystalline surface of blueish black water or behind a cape that protrudes as if it were sinking, those settlements, showing hardly no clear outlines, had an expression of being blankly waiting for the moment they would disappear in the wilderness. I somehow believed that in the Aegean, a temple of Poseidon built with white marble stood at the tip of such cape and lorded over the sea, and that that was about it in terms

さらにこのような類推に拍車をかけたのは，神々の物語である。神といっても，古事記などという正史に登場するような日本の神々ではない。岩石や湧水や山頂など，みわたすかぎりの自然が所有する普遍的とみていいような光景の細部に，無数の神が宿ってしまっているような，土着の思考の生んだものである。それはエーゲ海域が，多数の神々のドラマで覆われていることに通ずるものがある。島々はこの神々の居住地であり，事件の舞台でもあった。風景がこの連想を触発する。たとえば，航海するにつれて，次々に特徴をもった島の姿があらわれてきたとき，それは神の名前をもって記憶するのがもっともいい。これらの海域では，あきらかに神が人間に近づき，人間と交接し，そして飛び去り，生き残っていくのだ。私にとって，風景のなかに土着の神々が住みこむことが当然の事実であったので，エーゲ海域のあらゆる細部までが，既にそこを訪れる前から，身近に感じられ，疑うべき異和感が，ほんのひとかけらもないものと映っていたのだろう。

　にもかかわらず，空気を吸ってみるまでは，場所の深部にひそんでいる眼にみえない形質のようなものの理解には到達しないということは，エーゲ海域を実際に横ぎり，それを幾度か繰りかえすにつれて，明瞭に浮びあがってくる。モンスーン地帯の一部をなしている日本の瀬戸内海の光景は，みわたすかぎり微粒子が充満しており，これがひきおこしてるグラデーションによって，はじめて奥行きが感知できるような質感におおわれている。すべての輪郭がもうろうとゆらめいている。あいまいに溶け合っている。突きぬけるような直線的な透明性はどこにも見あたらない。

　エーゲ海の東岸イオニアの都市ミレトスに住んだタレスが，水がすべてのものの根源的な実体であると指定したことは，自然科学と哲学がまだ区分を明らかにする必要のなかったギリシア文化の創生期における決定的な名言であったとい

of difference.

　Moreover, such assumption came to be reinforced by the stories of Gods. Not the kind of Japanese Gods referred to in the official history of the *Kojiki*, the Records of Ancient Matters, but Gods as a product of indigenous minds—countless Gods living in the details of universal landscapes owned by the vast wilderness such as rocks and springs and mountaintops. And it has something to do with the Aegean region being abound with dramas of numerous Gods. Islands are where these Gods abide, the settings for various events. The landscape evokes such imageries. For instance, when on a cruise a series of characteristic islands emerges, it is best to remember them under the names of Gods. In this area, Gods undoubtedly approached humans, coupled with humans, then flew away and kept on living. For me, indigenous Gods dwelling within the landscape was a matter of course: every detail of the Aegean felt familiar even before my actual visit and looked so completely devoid of any skepticism.

And yet the fact that an understanding of something like a trait that is invisible to the eye and lingers at the depth of a place is unattainable until one comes to physically take in the atmosphere became gradually clear with each actual crossing of the Aegean. The scenery of the Seto Inland Sea of Japan, which is a part of a monsoon zone, is inundated with fine particles as far as the eye can see, covered in a texture that can only be detected through gradation caused by those particles. Everything has a silhouette that shimmers as in a fog. And ambiguously blend in. Clear-cut linear transparency is nowhere to be found.

　Thales who lived in Miletus, an Ionian city on the eastern coast of the Aegean, asserted that water is the prime substance to every matter—a crucial predication at the dawn of Greek culture when it was not yet necessary to differentiate between natural science and phi-

われているのだが，タレス流にいうならば，日本のその地方において，水が，微粒子状をなして，空間を濃く満たしているのである。水が空間に充満するとは，すなわち水蒸気の存在が決定的になっていることを示している。空気のなかの密度だけでなく，手にさわるあらゆるものに及ぶわけで，砂をすくうとじっとり水気をもっており，濶葉樹の葉はその表相がつねになめらかに潤っているのだ。ところが，エーゲ海においては，水はそれほどの浸透性をもたない。分離し，空気中から析出され，あの透明な地中海の海水となって，底部に溜っているようにさえみえる。

　この島々は険しい山地あるいは丘で，ほとんど岩盤が露出し，耕作可能地は，わずかな表土が窪地にたまった部分だけである。その裸の山地が，わずかにオリーブを栽培できるにすぎない。そのような土地も，夏期にはいると，完全に乾燥して，ほとんど砂漠に近い有様になるのである。

　ニンフ達が水あびし，牧神がまどろんだ草叢も，日本の土地がしめすむんむんするような腐蝕土の嗅いでなく，乾燥地の草が特徴的にしめすように，葉の表面が，かたくちぢこまり，刺をもち，ときにオレガノやエストラゴンのような芳香をはなつスパイスをみのらせはするが，肌ざわりが荒く，かさかさしてしまっている。

　おそらく，そのかわりに，というべきだろう。このエーゲ海の空はあくまで透明なのだ。水蒸気をふくまず，ぬけるような碧がその裏側にみえる。空と海とが，同質の碧でありながら，光線の反射角だけで存在を区別する。逆光線のなかにはいった島は，濃紫色にかわる。こんな光景のなかでは，日本の風景が普遍的にみせているような，微粒子の濃度で位置の関係を判別するといった認知の方式は，うまれてこないはずである。透明であるために，距離にかかわりなく物体は明視される。そこには，透視されたときにあらわれる縮尺された，比例の関係だけがあらわれるだろう。それが幾何学の世界になる。物体は明視される度合いを

losophy. As Thales would put it, tiny particles of water thickly fills the space in that region in Japan. Water filling a space suggests that the presence of water vapor is decisive. The latter involves not only its density in the air but also all tangible things: sand scooped in the hand being damp and humid; surface of broadleaf tree leaves being always smooth and moist. But in the Aegean, water does not have that much permeability. It even looks as if it were separated, precipitated from the air and pooled at the bottom of that transparent Mediterranean as sea water.

　These islands consist of rugged mountains or steep hills where bedrocks are mostly exposed, with limited arable land where scarce topsoil is deposited in depressions. Only olive trees can barely be cultivated on those naked mountains to a small extent. Moreover, the land dries up completely in summertime to look almost like a desert. Unlike the steamy smell of humus of the Japanese soil, the meadow where nymphs have bathed and the faun has dozed off implies, as typically shown in grass in arid terrain, prickly leaves with curled stiff surface and occasional spicy flavor like oregano and tarragon, mostly dried out and rough to the touch.

　Probably 'in exchange for that' would be a better expression—the sky over the Aegean is consistently transparent. Free of water vapor, bottomless azure is visible from beneath. While the sky and the sea share the same type of azure, their presence can be distinguished exclusively by the angle of reflection of a ray of light. A backlit island changes its color to dark purple. In a scenery like this, a formula of discerning the relationship of positions by the density of fine particles that is universally observed in Japanese landscape would never be devised. By virtue of transparency, objects are clearly visualized regardless of distance. The only thing that emerges there is the scaled-down proportional relationship that becomes apparent upon transparent viewing—the outcome is a world of geometry. Objects

変えずに，ただ距離に換算されるような大きさの差としてみえるのである。

　エーゲ海域の空気そのものが，その場所を内側から支えている眼にみえない形質を形成するのに，決定的な役割をしていたのだということが，私にはその空気を吸いこみ，肌で岩石や，草花などを感じとることによって，はじめて理解できはじめる気がしはじめたのだ。

　それには，私の思いこんでしまったギリシアにたいする固定観念がからんでいるというべきだろう。

　パルテノンに結晶したようなドーリス人の生みだした完璧なプロポーションに支えられた建築のうむ秩序感。ピタゴラスからユークリッドにいたる幾何学体系の純粋性。そして，プラトンが「ティマイオス」のなかで，唐突に，この宇宙を構成する四元素が，正多面体をなしているという説明をはじめるといった，すべての事象を，可視的形態に還元するような透明性。あるいは，本来超越的な属性が与えられるべき神々の姿態をさえ，眼の前に実在する人間をひたすら描写することによってだけ表現してしまうような明視性。それに，ミレトスの人ヒッポダモスが創始した格子状の道路割りをもつ都市計画の整合性。これらのギリシア文化の特性のように思われている諸属性が，うみだされていった地域にたいして，私は日本の水蒸気の充満した空気のなかで，たしかに背景になった光景が若干の類似点をもっていた，それだけの理由で，強引な類推をしていたのである。古代のギリシア人達は，自然のなかに，第一原質のようなものを捜していたのだが，その第一原質に，常に思考が還元されていき，同時に，全宇宙にまで演繹できるような整然とした秩序をえがき得たことを理解するためには，あまりにもひとつの抽象的思考としてそれをのみこんでしまっていた気配があった。

　たとえば，エーゲ海にのぞんだ絶壁のうえにつくられてい

are visible as mere differences in size that can be converted to distance while keeping the degree of clarity of visibility intact.

　I started to realize that I might be able to understand that it was the very atmosphere of the Aegean which played a decisive role of shaping the invisible characteristics that support the place from inside, only after I have inhaled the atmosphere and felt the touch of rocks and flowers there.

And it eventually had to do with my personal assumption about certain Greek stereotypes.

　Sense of order demonstrated in architectures supported by perfect proportions created by Dorians that was embodied in the Parthenon; purity of the systems of geometry from Pythagorean to Euclidean; and transparency that reduces all events to visible forms, as Plato had all of a sudden started to claim in his Timaeus that the four elements that constitute this universe are regular polyhedra; or clarity of visibility that can express even the depictions of Gods—who are supposed to have transcendental attributes—through a blind devotion to portraying actual persons in sight; then finally, consistency of urban planning featuring grid-patterned road networks, a creation of Hippodamus of Miletus. For the simple reason that the Japanese landscape in an atmosphere filled with water vapor as a backdrop had in fact a few points in common with a region where emerged various attributes that are considered as characteristics of Greek culture, I have drawn an overreacting analogy between them. While the ancient Greeks searched for the primary element in the natural world with their mind constantly reduced to that primary element, they succeeded in drawing a systematic order that would even make the entire universe the subject of deduction. I have so much swallowed it as an abstract idea that it kept me from understanding it.

　For example, looking at the Acropolis of Lindos built

るリンドスのアクロポリスの列柱が，夕日で，黒い長い影を階段のうえにおとしている光景をみていると，ここには，空間のなかに，本当に線が引かれ，影が，黒一色につぶされているのを感じることができる。ぼやけたり，かすんだりすることはない。何も混入されてない，硬質で，ほとんど真空といっていい程に乾燥しているからだろう。

その明確な輪郭線をもった影を感じとっていると，古代ギリシア人達のあくことない第一原質への還元の努力が，当然のものように思えてくる。陰翳と呼びうるような，あいまいな気配はどこにもない。明視される。かりかりに研磨される。鉱物性の結晶が組みたてられる。岩盤の露出した，不毛な山塊と，白大理石の列柱とは，硬い影を投げ合うことによって，このような透明な空間のなかで，はじめて結びつくのである。

ぬけるような空をしていても，日本の内海にはこのような透明な空気がない。私は，この青空を，もう一度，正方形に切り抜く必要を感じる。その奥にあらわれる幾何学的な透明性をもった空間。おそらくそのようにして，はじめて2000年以上も前に，エーゲ海域のうみだすことのできた空間の形質に接近できるのではないか，と私には思えてならないのだ。

青空のなかに，さらに正方形をぽっかりと切り抜かねばならぬ，と感じたのは，私がはじめてエーゲ海を旅して，もういちど日本の空気を吸いこんだときに，ふっとよぎった幻想なのだが，二度，三度と同じ場所を訪れなおしてみて，この正方形の透明空間の存在だけは，ふりはらうことができないだけでなく，ますますその輪郭を明瞭にしてしまいつつある。私にとっては，エーゲ海域の形質を理解する原像になってしまったのだというべきだろう。

II

露出した岩塊，オリーブ，紺碧の空と海。こんな自然の光景以外に，もはやエーゲ海域では，古代ギリシア的な空間

atop a mural precipice overlooking the Aegean as its colonnade casts long, dark shadows on the stairs at sunset, there is a feeling that this space is literally striped with shadows daubed in black. None of these lines are blurry or dim. Certainly because they are solid, free from impurities, and almost as dry as in vacuum.

As I perceive those shadows endowed with clear contour lines, the ancient Greeks' inexhaustible effort for the reduction to the primary element seems only natural. There is not the faintest hint of vague presence that may be called a nuance. Clarity of visibility. Polished to a crisp. Assemblage of mineral crystals. The barren mountain mass with exposed bedrocks and the colonnade of white marble bond together only when they throw solid shadows to one another in this transparent space.

However deep and blue the sky might be, there is no such transparent atmosphere in the Japanese inland sea. I feel the need to cut a square out of this blue sky once again, and reveal a space with geometric transparency. I cannot help but think that that is the only way to approach the characteristics of space that the Aegean region managed to create more than 2000 years ago.

This urge for cutting a square void out of the blue sky is a fantasy that crossed my mind when I came back from my first trip to the Aegean and breathed air in Japan. Having visited the same place on several occasions, not only the presence of this square transparent space cannot be dismissed, but its contour is becoming clearer than ever: it is to me an archetypal image for the understanding of the Aegean characteristics.

II

Exposed bedrocks, olive trees, deep blue sky and sea. Besides such natural sceneries, it is difficult to detect an ancient Greek space in the Aegean today.

Of course one can visit the National Archaeological Museum in Athens. There is the hill of Acropolis that continues to dominate this city with the same sense of

を感知することは困難なのだ。

　もちろんアテネで国立博物館を訪れることができる。この街を古代と変らずにそのスケール感で支配しつづけているアクロポリスの丘がある。デルフォイの神域，スニオン岬，リンドスのアクロポリス，エピダウロスの劇場がある。しかし，このような古代の断片は，たんなる発掘品であり，廃墟であり，痕跡にすぎないのではないか。廃絶した文明がその残骸だけをみせているといってもいい。

　プラトンやピタゴラス，フィディアスやイクチノス，ホメロスやソフォクレス達がえがこうとした空間を，私は彼らがのこしていった断片を寄せあつめ，あのエーゲ海域の空気の実在感だけをたよりに，想像しなおしているだけではないのか。彼らが生きていた時代が所有した空間の形質は，おそらく彼らの日常を充たし，どこにでもみつかり，無意識の行為にまで浸透していただろう。それが崩壊し，みうしなわれ，当然のことながら，彼らの文明の消滅とともに，消えうせたというべきだろう。

　たとえばこの海域の東南端にあるロードスは，十字軍の基地になっていた。当時は，その全島が主にフランスの騎士達によって統治されていた。それ故，古代ロードスはそのまま放置され，港街が騎士達の手によって建設されている。街の中心にある城館は，わざわざフランスから技師がよびよせられ，ゴシック風に建設された。

　この城館の呼びものになっているのは，いま玄関の正面に据えられているラオコーンの像である。トロイ落城の際，その神宮ラオコーンが，蛇に巻かれて死ぬ，あの断末魔をえがいたヘレニズム期の傑作彫刻である。美術館に改造されているわけだから，この島で出土したラオコーン像がかざられるのは当然なのだが，実はここにあるのは，たんなる模造品にすぎない。本体は，ヴァチカンに送られてしまったまんまである。

　そういえば，この城館の中庭はローマ風に手がいれられ，

scale as in the ancient times. There are the sanctuary in Delphi, Cape Sounion, Acropolis of Lindos, and the theater of Epidaurus. Still, these fragments of antiquity are unearthed articles and ruins that are mere traces—the remains of an extinct civilization.

　Am I only picking up the debris of spaces drawn by Plato, Pythagoras, Phidias, Iktinos, Homer and Sophocles to try to re-picture them relying just on the sense of reality in the atmosphere of the Aegean region? The characteristics of spaces that belonged to the period when these people were alive, would have most probably filled their daily life, been ubiquitous, and prevaded even the unconscious behaviors. When that collapsed and came to be lost, it was only natural that everything vanished with the demise of their civilization.

　For example, Rhodes at the southeastern end of this region had been a Crusader base. Back then all of the island was governed by French Knights. For this reason, the ancient Rhodes was left intact, as the Crusaders built a new port town. The palace castle in the center of the town was build in a Gothic style by engineers brought all the way over from France.

　This palace's highlight is the statue of Laocoön placed in front of the entrance today. It is a sculptural masterpiece of the Hellenistic period depicting the last agony of the Trojan priest Laocoön as he dies wrapped around by serpents at the fall of Troy. Considering that the building has been converted to a museum, it would be legitimate to display the statue of Laocoön which had been unearthed in this island, but in fact the one shown here is only a replica. The original was sent to the Vatican and kept there.

　As I recall, this palace's inner courtyard was renovated in Roman style, with arcades orderly lined with Hellenistic marble pieces, that are also modern-day replicas. After a long Turkish rule, Rhodes had once again fallen into the hands of Italy. This museum even boasts a pompous bronze plaque embedded on the wall

廊下には，ヘレニズム期の大理石像が整然と並べられてはいるが，それもやっぱり現代の模造である。トルコの長い支配の後に，ロードスはふたたびイタリアの手に移る。この美術館は，ムッソリーニが改築したむねをれいれいしくブロンズに鋳込んで壁にはめこんでいる有様だ。

　街の公館はほとんどムッソリーニ・ローマのスタイルをしている。その間に鉛筆のような尖塔をもったモスクが点在する。メッカの方向に軸をむけるため，ほとんどのモスクは，道路割りから，奇妙にずれた配置になっている。さらにはギリシア正教の教会堂も割りこんでいる。

　この混淆をいかに理解するべきなのだろう。ヘレニズム期以後に，数えきれない程の他国の様式が流れこみ，絶え間なく通過していった。そのあげくに，やっと古代ヘレニズムの最盛期の彫像がもどってきたというのに，それが模造品であったとは。

　それはロードスの街だけがみせる喜劇的な現象ではない。都市と名づけられているほとんどの街が，この海域ではまったく同様の状態になっている。混淆のあげくに，様式そのものまでが風化してしまったのだ。

　こんな混淆し惨落した光景に背をむけるとすれば，サントリーニとかミコノスといった，土着の形式以外に何も異物の浸入した形跡のないまちを訪れるより他にない。

　ここでは，文明と呼ばれ得たもの，様式として定義され得たものとは無縁である。いわば歴史的な時間から絶縁しているというべきだろう。かりに過去においてそのまちの附近に都市の存在が確認されていたとしても，ミコノスの目の前に横たわっていたデロスのように，略奪され，破壊され，大理石の破片だけになり，何ひとつ連続性を認めることができない。

　忘却されてしまい，日常の生活の内側ではかすかな痕跡さえ残されてもいないのだ。

stating that Mussolini has renovated the building.

　The majority of the town's administrative buildings are in Mussolini's Roman style. Then there is a scattering of mosques with pencil-like minarets. Most of them are positioned strangely off the street networks, because a mosque's axis has to face toward Mecca. There are also Greek orthodox churches that are slot in the townscape.

　What to make of this indiscriminate mixture? Since the Hellenistic period countless foreign styles have poured into the island and passed through it incessantly. And when a sculpture from the best period of the ancient Hellenism was returned, all they were given was a replica.

　Such comic phenomenon is not typical of Rhodes. The majority of towns called 'city' in this region fall under the exact same circumstances. After all the mixing, the style itself has weathered away.

　If we were to turn our backs to such scene of mixture and distress, we are left with no other option but to visit places such as Santorini and Mykonos where there are no traces of impurities in their indigenous styles.

　They are immune from what was called a civilization and what was defined as a style, insulated from the so-called historical time. Even if in the past the existence of an ancient city was confirmed in the vicinity of a town, as in the case of Delos situated right in front of Mykonos, it would have already been plundered and destroyed into fragments of marble, to the point that continuity on the island is nowhere to be found.

　All is lost in oblivion, with not the faintest trace being left inside people's lives.

　Thus it may be assumed that Santorini and Mykonos have been independent from all kinds of historic events and styles, and that people there began their lives in a corner of pristine nature and built their own settlements. There can be found evidences of indige-

だから，サントリーニやミコノスは，あらゆる歴史的な事件や様式とかかわりなく，まったく白紙のまんまの自然の一隅に，生活が開始され，みずからの集落をつくりはじめたとみなしてもいい。ここには住居をかたちづくる土着の形式を認めることができる。しかし，この形式は，技術の系や様式に転化する見込みがなく，閉ざされたままになっている。それぞれの時代の文明はみずからの様式をもったのだが，それは，展開し膨大な量の同型のものを再生産しながら，いつの間にかその内側にひそむ形質を析出しはじめ，遂には究極の一点にむかって収斂を開始する，このような自己運動を経ていくものだ。ところが，このまちまちにみえる土着の形式は，みずから使用する技術を最小限におさえ，同時にあつかう素材も固定し，反復を繰り返してはいるが，様式の自己運動に転化する程の活力をひそませていない。ひたすら限定された枠組みのなかにおさめられている。いわば，閉鎖系のモデルをみているような状態になるのである。

私の興味は，このように自然発生的にうまれてきたまちが，おのずから生成させていった空間が，かつてこの海域をおおい，その後も，絶大な繁殖力で，世界中に伝播していったヘレニズムが所有したものと，同質なものかどうかという点にあったというべきだ。

そして，このまちにふみこみ，さまよい歩いているうちに，冷徹な稜線が物体の輪郭をかたちづくっていたはずの光景が，いっこうにみあたらず，それだけではなく，あらゆる物体が急にその緊張をゆるめてしまい，細部は溶けて行き，ある種の甘美な芳香までがただようような，そんな空間のなかに置かれている自分を発見してしまった。やっとつかみとり得たかも知れないと思っていた透明な秩序感をみいだせることができず，私は，いらだたしい異和感にさえおそわれたのである。

nous styles that shaped those houses. However, these styles are most unlikely to sublimate to any system or style of technology and remain closed. Civilizations had their own styles in their times, but as they developed and reproduced their clones in huge quantities, deposition of characteristics that hid inside began in the process, leading to the final convergence to an ultimate point. Such is the usual process of self movement. But although the seemingly varied indigenous styles limit the technology that they use to a minimum as well as fixing the materials they use and repeat it over and over again, they do not have any dormant dynamism powerful enough to sublimate themselves to the self movement of style. They are consistently kept within a limited framework, which makes us feel like looking at a closed system model.

My interest was in whether or not those towns that grew spontaneously and their spaces that were generated autonomously are of the same nature as the Hellenistic attributes that had once covered this region and have later on spread across the world with tremendous fertility.

Then, as I set foot in one of the towns and wandered about, not only did I realize that the scenery in which cold and bitter ridge lines supposedly shaped the contours of objects was nowhere in sight, but I also found myself in the middle of the kind of space where every object suddenly released its tension, details melted away, and something like a sweet aroma scented the air. Not being able to uncover the transparent sense of order that I thought I came to grasp at last, I was even seized by a frustrating feeling of uneasiness.

III

And I had every right to feel uneasy. The thickly whitewashed spaces of this town are essentially different in character from those ancient Greek spaces that were organized with the intention of staying true

III

異和感をおぼえるのが当然かも知れない。純白の石灰汁の厚塗りされたこの街の空間は，古代ギリシアの，あのあらゆる物体の背後にまで，透明な論理をつらぬきとうそうと意図しながら編成されていた空間とは，本来異質なものなのだ。

そもそも，古代ギリシア的と呼ぶべき空間の形質が，エーゲ海域全体に浸透していたと思いこんだ方がおかしかった。

私がギリシア的なものと考えた空間の形質は，たしかにエーゲ海域の自然とかかわり合うことによって形成されたことは事実であろうが，実はBC13世紀頃にこの海域に進出し，アッティカ地方を中心に定着したドーリス人の手になるものであった。いうならばエーゲ海域の全体のなかで，ある時代，ある地方に偏在したひとつの種族が基本的につくりあげていったものであった。

今世紀の初頭に始まったサー・エヴァンス達による発掘によって，ここにドーリス人達の侵略の前に姿を消してしまったひとつの文明があったことを私たちは知っている。クノッソスの宮殿がそのクレタ文明の最大の遺構なのだが，いま，若干の復元のなされた発掘跡を訪れると，あの大理石を研磨することによって，整然とした秩序形成を意図していったギリシア人の空間とはまったく異質で，渾沌とした不透明な空間が存在していたことを知ることができる。

クノッソスは，なだらかな丘陵のうえにつくられているので，全体の階層は複雑になる。平面をみると1層か2層にみえるけど，地形に応じて層が重なり，実は4層以上にわたっている。そのうえ，必要に応じて部屋をつぎたしたため，相互に脈略なしに連結している。しかも何度かの地震で崩壊し，そのたびに再建されているので，統括している秩序はみつからない。

深く屈折して下っていく階段室を降りていくと，その上部から，太陽光が，幾段かに屈折してふってくる。この階段をすくなくとも3層は下り，まっくら闇の狭い廊下にみちびか

to the transparent logic all the way through the back of every objects.

To start with, my notion of the characteristics of so-called ancient Greek spaces permeating the entire Aegean waters simply proved to be wrong.

Despite the fact that the characteristics of spaces that I thought were Greek have indeed come to be shaped by being involved with the wilderness of the Aegean, they were actually devised by the Dorians who had expanded into this region by 13th century BC and settled down around the Attica region. They were basically created in all of the Aegean region by a single tribe that was eccentrically located in a certain area at a certain period of time.

Owing to excavations conducted by Sir Evans that began at the outset of this century, we now know that there had been a civilization which vanished prior to the Dorian invasion. The palace of Knossos being the largest archaeological site of Minoan civilization, a visit to the slightly restored site reveals the existence of chaotic, non-transparent spaces that are totally different from those spaces by the Greek who intended to create methodical order by polishing marble.

Since Knossos is built on top of a gently sloping hill, the overall stratum becomes complex. Plan-wise it looks to be single or double-layered, but in fact the layers are superimposed following the site topography for more than 4 levels. Also, rooms were added when and where necessary, resulting in unrelated linking with one another. Furthermore, houses were rebuilt each time they collapsed in an earthquake, so there are no presiding orders that rule them.

Deeply winding staircase descends as sunshine pours in, several times refracted on the way. Climbing up these stairs for at least 3 levels, we are guided to a pitch-black, narrow corridor that bends a few times and leads to more steps in descent. All of a sudden, just when we thought we were climbing down from ground

れ，2度3度と折れ曲り，またステップをおりる。すると，最初地上から降りていったはずなのに，ふたたび地上の光線のさし込む部屋にでてしまうのだ。

　迷路としか表現できない。しかも立体的に交錯した迷路である。その迷路の闇に深くしずみこむと，それは冥府の一部にさまよい込んだ気持さえするのだが，逆に外光のさしこむ部屋は，はなやかな気分につつまれ，まったく陽気な壁画が壁面を彩っている。こんな屈折した明暗が，その迷路の細部にまで浸みわたっているのである。

　このクノッソス宮殿は，ギリシア神話に，迷宮（ラビリントス）として登場する。ミノスの王が，建築家であり技術者であり発明家であるダイダロスに命じてつくらせた宮殿である。そしてアテナィの王子テセウスが，アリアドネのたすけを借りて，その奥に住んだミノタウロスを退治したあの宮殿なのである。

　おそらくギリシア人達にとって，この迷宮は彼らの意図した透明で整合性をもった空間の対立物，いわば反世界であったと考えられないか。非透明でおどろおどろした，闇におおわれてしまっているような空間，そこは，半獣人ミノタウロスのすみかとしてはうってつけの場所であろう。ミノタウロスがテセウスに退治されるという神話は，とりもなおさず，アテネが代表する透明なアッティカ的な空間が，非透明なクレタ的な空間，すなわち東方的な性格のエーゲ海域に浸透していた空間を否定しきろうとする歴史的な過程をいいあらわそうとしていると読んでいいだろう。とにかく，これ程対立的な形質をふくんだ空間は他に類例がないからだ。

私がサントリーニの街をあるいて感じた異和感は，ここにはアッティカ的と呼びうるような空間が微塵もなく，おそらくクノッソスにみられるような東方的で迷宮的な空間だけが復活していたためであろう。そしてミコノスで感じた，甘美な芳香は，ここには整合性や透視性にうらづけられた計画性

---

level in the first place, we wind up reaching once again a room with natural light at ground level.

　It is nothing other than a labyrinth—one in a three-dimensional web. Whereas being enclosed in darkness in the depth of that labyrinth feels like being lost in a part of the underworld, a room with exterior light feels festive, with cheerful murals adorning its walls. Such wry contrast of light and dark pervades all through the details of the labyrinth.

In Greek mythology, this palace of Knossos is mentioned as the Labyrinthos. It is a palace that Daedalus—architect, engineer and inventor—was ordered to build by the King Minos, and the very place where Prince Theseus of Athens with the help of Ariadne killed the Minotaur that dwelt in the depth of the labyrinth.

　Possibly for the Greek people this labyrinth was their intended spatial opposition to transparency and consistency, a sort of antiworld. Non-transparent and macabre, it certainly was a space shrouded in darkness that is appropriate as a dwelling for the half-man, half-bull Minotaur. The myth that the Minotaur was killed by Theseus might as well be interpreted as an attempt to illustrate the historical process of the transparent Attican space represented by Athens trying to completely deny the non-transparent Minoan space, that is, space that saturated the Aegean region which was rather Oriental in character. In any case, a space that embraces this much opposing character is extremely unique.

The uneasiness that I felt while walking the streets of Santorini was probably due to the absence of any sort of Attican space and the fact that only the Oriental, labyrinthine spaces seen in Knossos have managed to come back to life. And the sweet aroma perceived in Mykonos probably had to do with the complete lack of planning backed up by consistency and transparency,

がまったく見当たらず，そのかわりに，屈折し，溶融し，不定形が不定形をうんで，やはりクノッソスの壁画のような，偏平な陽気さにあふれていたこともからんでいよう。

　ヘレニズムは，ひとつの古典主義として，世界中に伝播し，いまだに生命力を保持しつづけている。恐らく，すべての事象を完璧な整合性に到達するまで論理的な追求をとめないというような，ひとつの様式が確立されていたためだろう。様式はそれが生命を得るためには，社会的な要因もふくめて，ひとつの制度を際立せねばならない。古典主義は，そのような制度を確立する典範となったといいかえてもいい。

　そのヘレニズムが消滅し，さらに残骸のうえをいくつかの様式が通過したあげく，これも風化しつくしたとき，いわばまったくの白紙還元のなかから形成されはじめた集落が，自然発生的な空間形成をするのは当然のことだ。私にとってとりわけ興味深いのは，ここには古典主義的な，つまりアッティカ的な性格がまったく見当たらず，まさにそれが対極と措定していた不定形な非透明性の空間があらわれていたということだ。

IV

直径30キロに及ぶ海中の大クレーターの一隅が破れ，海水でみたされると，それは巨大な湾となる。サントリーニに近づくとき，船はこのクレーターにはいり，湾のもっとも奥にある船つき場の手前に碇泊する。いわば，火口壁の内側に進出しているのだ。彎曲した絶壁，その噴火がつい先日であったかのように，その絶壁は焼けただれた火山性の礫が露出している。当然ながら，その表面はもろく，いまにも雪崩のように崩壊する気配をみせている。おそらくBC1500年頃のクノッソス宮殿をおそった大地震と，それによる崩壊が，この海中火山の爆発と関係あるといわれたりするだけあって，その火口壁は，爆発がつい先日の事件だったかの

and alternatively with distortion and melting away where the amorphous creates the amorphous, and the fact that it was filled with flat cheerfulness as in the murals of Knossos.

　Hellenism has spread throughout the world as classicism that still maintains its vitality to this day—presumably because a style had already been established in which pursuit of logic would never cease until all events reached a perfect consistency. A style has to establish a system, including social factors, in order for it to have a life. In other words, classicism became a norm for establishing a system.

　When that Hellenism disappeared and several other styles passed through its remains and ultimately weathered away to naught, it was only natural for these settlements that started to form themselves from an entirely clean state to form spaces in a spontaneous manner. What is especially interesting for me is that there is no sign whatsoever of classicist, that is, Attican characteristics, and that there emerged amorphous, non-transparent spaces that were predicated as the exact opposite.

IV

A giant undersea crater with a diameter of some 30 km partially fails and fills with seawater, and it becomes a huge bay. Approaching Santorini, ships enter this crater and anchor short of the dock at the innermost part of the bay, in the inside of the crater wall. As if an eruption occurred just days ago, the curved wall exposes burnt volcanic rock. Its surface is naturally brittle, ready to crumble like an avalanche any moment. As it is said that the great earthquake at around 1500 BC that hit the palace of Knossos and its subsequent destruction was associated with this underwater volcanic eruption, its crater wall reveals freshly burnt surface as if the explosion were a very recent event.

　The settlement is built on the top of this steep cliff, almost hanging out toward the bay. Needless to say,

ように，なまなましく焼けた肌をさらしているのだ。

　この集落は，その絶壁の頂部に，湾に向かってのりだすようにつくられている。もちろん平坦な土地はない。崖のいっかくをけずりとり，洞穴をうがち，テラスをかまえ，折り重なるようなつみあげられかたをしている。特徴的なのは石灰汁の厚塗りで床，壁，道路といわず人工物のすべてをおおいつくしていることだ。そのために，遠望すると，この街は断崖の頂部に真白にかぶせた残雪のようにさえみえる。

　ひとつひとつの住戸が次々に建設されていく。決して計画的に割りつけられたものではない。ランダムな集合である。偶然にえらばれた特殊な地形のうえに，まずひとつの住戸がおかれる。その結果をみたうえで次の住戸がかさねられる。しかも地形のうねりにそってつくられているので，各戸のレベルがすこしづつ喰い違っている。屋根が展望できるテラスになり，それが隣家のテラスと数段の階段で直結される。ロバだけが乗りものになっている街路が，それらのテラスの間をうねっていく。水平な線は何ひとつ感じられず，いつの間にかメビウスの輪をたどって歩くような気分になる。基本的にすべての窓が海にむかってひらいている。いうならばこのメビウス的な空間を形成させているのは，それぞれに独立した部屋が，窓をもち，海と太陽を眺めとりいれることを確実に保持しながら，つねに他を意識し，地形の変化に対応しながら，自分の位置を設定しているという，単純な原理だけを守っているからに他ならない。海を眺める窓をうがつという，明解な方式だけを存在させながら，自在な集合をうみだしている。

　このような集合状態を明確にさせるために，石灰汁が塗られているとみてもいい。床，壁，天井，塀，テラス，階段，屋根，街路面，つまりあらゆる表面が，すべて白一色に塗られている。毎日のようにバケツに水で溶いた石灰を，いたるところかまわず，区切ることもなく塗りつづける。そのために，空間にみえるすべての物体が癒着して，連続体に化し

there is no flat land. People carved into a corner of the cliff, bore caves, installed terraces and piled up houses in an overlapping manner. Characteristically, every man-made features from floors, walls to roads are thickly whitewashed. As a result, looking from afar, this town looks like some lingering snow on a white-capped cliff.

　Houses have been constructed one by one. In a layout that is far from being planned out. The complex is random. It all begins with a house being placed on a particular kind of topography that was chosen haphazardly. Looking at the result it produces, the next houses are superimposed. Because they are built following the earth's undulation, the level of each house slightly differs from one another. The roof becomes a terrace with a view, and comes to link directly to the next-door neighbors' terraces through a few steps of stairs. Streets, where the only means of transportation are donkeys, wind through these terraces. With not a single line that is horizontal in sight, it eventually feels like walking on a Moebius band. All the windows are basically opened facing the sea. What shapes this Moebius band-like space is, as it were, no other than the fact that it is exclusively committed to a simple principle in which houses have independent rooms with windows in order to maintain without fail a visual introduction of sea and sun while being always conscious of others and responding to geographical changes for the purpose of setting up their own positions. A free and flexible cluster is created by focusing only on the straightforward method of opening a window for a view over the sea.

　We may as well see that whitewash is applied in order to make such state of cluster clear and explicit. Floors, walls, ceilings, fences, terraces, stairs, roofs, roads—every single exterior surface is whitewashed. Almost daily, people keep on painting everything everywhere with lime dissolved in water in a bucket. So all objects that are visible within a space are glued together

ていく。個別につくられた住居が，立体的にみずからのもっている床面を交錯させているうちに，その単一のシステムが，外へ外へとひろがり，石灰汁で連結され，ついに，ひとつの量塊にみえてくる。そして，各戸がもつ窓や部屋は，あらかじめつくられた巨大な量塊をそれぞれがくりぬいていったのではないかと思える程に，一体化してしまうのである。

ミコノスにおいても，住戸の形成過程は同質のもののようにみうけられる。ここでは，ひとつのせまい入江の奥につくられた漁港を中心に街が展開している。彎曲した入江の奥のかたちにそって，港にひらいた広場がある。それが要になって，周辺をとりまくゆるやかな丘にむかって，すべての街路が扇状にひろがっている。丘のうえには，独特のかたちをした，童話の世界にあるような風車が並んでいる。扇状の道路は必ずしも規則ただしくひろがらない。たどたどしく，ギクシャクしながら，もつれ合っている。そのもつれ合った節々に，ちいさい辻ができる。広場というにはあまりに狭く，まがり角という程そっけないものでもない。日本の街がかつてもっていたような辻にもっとも近いというべきだ。ここに，店がでる。オリーブの樹が，1本か2本，ぽつんと，それ故にかぎりなくシンボリックに植わっている。その白っぽい緑をした葉の他は，すべてが純白なのだ。ただ背後の空だけは，例の抜けるような碧である。

街路網全体は，いくつもの辻が分節をつくっているようにみえるのだが，ほとんどが等質で，看板やみせの飾りつけを記憶しないかぎり，特徴をもって区別することはできそうもない。そのなかをさまよい歩くと，完全に方向感覚を失いはじめる。面的にひろがっている網目にからみとられてしまうと，あのバロックの奸計のあふれた迷路の庭園を歩くようなもどかしさがうまれてくる。しかしここには奸計の破片もみあたらず，ひたすらイノセントな努力だけで，常々と組みたてられてきたことが，無器用な，それでいて唐突なうね

to turn into a continuum. As a house that has originally been built independently interlocks its own floor surfaces in a three-dimensional manner, that single unit of system expands outward, connecting with others through whitewash to ultimately look like one large mass. Then, each house's windows and rooms come to be so well integrated to the point that one might think that each of them was separately carved into an existing enormous mass.

In Mykonos the formation process of houses seems to be similar in character. Here, the town is developed around a fishing port at the back of a narrow cove. There is a plaza opening to the port along the shape of the innermost section of the curved cove. From this plaza as a center, all the streets fan out toward the surrounding gentle hills. On the hills are windmills with their unique shape right out of a fairytale. Fan-shaped streets are not necessarily laid out systematically. They run erratically and awkwardly, tangling with one another. And created at the nodes of those entanglements are small crossroads. The latter being too narrow to be called a plaza and not so blunt as a street corner, they are closest to the 'tsuji (crossroads)' that has used to be found in Japanese cities. This is where the street stalls are set up. One or two olive trees grow in an infinitely symbolic manner by the way they are planted. Apart from their whitish green leaves, everything else is pure white, against a backdrop of the usual bottomless azure of the sky.

Although the entire street network appears to be articulated by a number of crossroads, most of the streets are so homogeneous that it is almost impossible to distinguish the characteristics of each street as long as one does not remember signboards and store decorations. Wandering about these streets, we begin to feel totally disoriented. Once entangled in the net that expands two-dimensionally, the experience becomes

りかたのなかにうかがわれる。サントリーニの街路では，海がひらけるテラスがぽっかりとあらわれるので，方向はくるわない。しかし絶え間なく変化するレベルによって，高さの関係がいつも見失われていく。ミコノスでは，レベルが変らないかわりに，方向が不明になる。いずれにせよ，おそらく古代ミレトスがもっていたような計画的な整合性はどこにも見当らない。アポロンの祭壇のような，アゴラのような，象徴性をもった核が不在なのだ。ひたすら住戸がひとつづつ自らの存在を明示し，そのうえで等質なひろがりをたかめ，遂には相互に溶融して一体化してしまう。内部に，明視できるヒエラルキーをもたない。全体の空間が，そのために分節化することもなく，したがって文脈が形成されていない。すべてが発生状態のまま，ちょうど熔岩が凝固した，その停止の状態を再現しているかのようだ。

　このふたつの集務の形成のされかたが，空間にヒエラルキーをつくらず，分節化せず，単純な集合状態そのままであり，いうならば，自然がその活動の過程で析出し凝固した物質そのままの姿をしていることは，クノッソスの神殿が，数世紀にわたって，幾度かの崩壊をくりかえしながら，集積をつづけていったことと，いちじるしく類似しているのだ。そのような類似点が，迷路の空間となってあらわれたとみるべきか。

　古代ギリシアが生みだした透明な空間は，ここではきれいさっぱり忘却されてしまっている。同時に，はるかに遡った東方の文明がうんだ，さわやかで，甘く，陽気な気分が復活しているのだ。この街の住民にとって，古代ギリシアのアッティカ的な透明性と求心性をもった空間など，必要なくなっているといっていい。

　いま，ふたたび渾沌状態に陥った現代都市の生活者にとって，文明の死滅のあとにうまれた，ひそやかな原初的な非透明性の世界への回帰は，彼岸の存在として限りない魅力をもっていよう。しかし，エーゲ海域のこれらの街々を巡

frustrating, like walking a maze garden full of baroque schemes. But here, not a single fragment of scheme can be found: what have been built with only innocent efforts are shown in the awkward, yet sudden undulations. On the streets of Santorini where gaping terraces that open to the sea pop up here and there, our sense of direction never gets lost. On the other hand, the continuous level changes make us lose track of the height relationships. In Mykonos levels never change but orientation gets lost. In any case, the calculated consistency that the ancient Miletus most probably had is nowhere to be found. There is an absence of a symbolic core, like Apollon's altar or an agora. Each of the houses single-mindedly devotes itself to clearly demonstrate its own presence, on which basis a homogeneous expanse is enlarged and ends up fusing with one another to become unified. Inside, there is no hierarchy that is clearly visible. Therefore, articulation of the entirety of the space never happens, neither does the formation of any context. Everything stays as it was when it emerged, like reproducing the halted state of lava when it has just congealed.

The way these two settlements were formed without creating a spatial hierarchy or any segmentalization and maintained a simple state of aggregation and thus retained the exact shape of congealed materials that nature deposited in the process of its activities is strikingly similar to the way the palace of Knossos has continued to accumulate after repeated destructions over several centuries. We might as well assume that it was this similarity that manifested itself as the labyrinthine space.

Here, the transparent space that the ancient Greece had created is lost in oblivion, as if it had never existed. And at the same time, the brisk, sweet, jovial atmosphere created by Oriental civilizations from way back is revived. The residents of these towns no longer need the ancient Greek, Attican spaces with transparency

り歩いて，彼らが，いとも簡単に，パルテノンやホメロスやプラトンを忘れてしまっている事実をみて，私はいいしれない恐怖感におそわれたのだが，いったんこの非透明性の空間に抱かれてしまうと，あらゆる疑問や設問をうしなわせ，思考を停止させ，紺碧の空と海と白色の壁と天井で充足できるのだと思えるようになる。それだけのあまさをもったヴェールでこの街の空間はつつまれているのである。

and centrality.

    Today, for a dweller of a modern city which has once again slid into chaos, a return to a world of quiet, primordial world of non-transparency that was born after the death of civilization has an endless charm as a presence of enlightenment. However, walking through those Aegean towns I came upon the fact that people have so easily forgotten about Parthenon, Homer and Plato and felt terrified beyond words. But once wrapped within this space of non-transparency, all doubts and questions go away, thoughts come to a standstill, and we are made to feel that deep blue sky and sea and whitewashed walls and ceilings are all that it takes to achieve sufficiency. It is a veil with that much sweetness that envelopes the spaces in these towns.

第1章〈ミコノス島〉
MYKONOS

ミコノス───鈴木恂
Mykonos *by Makoto Suzuki*

キクラデスの島々は乾いた黄色である。その街や集落は輝くほど白いキューブの群であり，エーゲ海の青に対照してある。

　灌木のまばらに残る薄緑の丘，耕やされた葡萄畑の濃い緑色は，ごく限られた島の部分を覆う。キクラデスの島では，港の街と山上の街が比較的はっきりと上下に別れてつくられているが，いずれの場合も平地の少ない島の地理的条件によって，街や村は斜面を利用することになる。

　ミコノスは，もちろん港の街の類系に入り，サントリーニは山上の街の特異な例といえるだろう。しかし，平坦地に近いミコノスも絶壁の頂きのフィラの町も，全体的には斜面に重なり合う堆積された家々の群として捉えられる。

　一般的に，漁業や商業的活動で栄えた街は，港を中心にして，それを囲む斜面につくられている。また外敵からの防禦を要した街や，農業を主とした村は，山上や山腹に発展している。しかし，オィアに見るような山上の漁村や，ミコノスのような農業も盛んであった港町などもあって，一概に云いきれない。

　街や集落の高低の位置選択は，島のデザインにかかわることである。そのデザインはもっと広い理由，自然条件の強弱，生産や交易の手段，防衛や攻撃の機能，神話や宗教，呪術や伝統の広大なフレームなどへの，生活を通した人間からの解答の総体と考えてよい。そしてその解答が，キクラデス諸島の場合，斜面に置かれたことで，視覚的に解りやすい答として表出されているということなのではなかろうか。

　ミコノスの街は，二つの入江にはさまれた低い台地にその中心がある。この台地は，せいぜい5，6mの丘で斜面というほどの勾配もないが，街の全体は緩く盛りあがっていて，遠くからでも街の大きさや家々の密集した状態が解る。数年前までは，この台地に集中した街は固まって見え，点在する風車とコントラストを見せていたが，近頃は，東の丘に家々が分散して建てられて，街が一回り大きくなった感じがする。

　最も旧くからある街区は岬の台地の中央の部分で，その広さは2ha程度であろう。これは目印になるような教会で示すと，東は入江の中ほどにあるキリアキ教会，南はカテドラル，北西は岬の先端にあるパラポルティア教会が囲む三角形の地区ということができる。

The Cyclades are dry, yellow patches of islands. Towns and villages there are clusters of sparkling white cubes that contrast with the blue of the Aegean.

Light green hills with sparse shrubs and the thick green of cultivated vineyards cover very limited areas of the islands. Although in the Cyclades harbor towns and hilltop towns are relatively separated up and down, both are subject to geographical conditions and have to make use of hillsides.

Mykonos obviously falls into the harbor town category, while Santorini is a rare case of hilltop town. But both the nearly flat Mykonos and the clifftop settlement of Fira can be seen as clusters of stacked houses overlapping along the hillside.

Generally, towns that thrive on fisheries and commercial activities are built on slopes surrounding the harbor. On the other hand, towns in need of protection from foreign threat and farm villages are developed either on the hilltop or the hillside. However, there are exceptions such as the hilltop fishing village in Oia or the harbor town of Mykonos where farming was also thriving that defy generalizations.

The choice of high or low position of towns and villages affects the design of an island. And that design is the sum of answers given by the humans through their living to much broader reasons such as the strength of natural conditions, methods of production and trade, defence and attack functions, and the huge frames of magic rites, tradition, mythology and religion. In the case of the Cyclades, these answers are expressed in a highly visual manner, by being placed along the hillsides.

Tucked between two bays, the town of Mykonos centers around a low plateau. The latter being no more than 5 to 6 m high with not much of an inclination as a slope, somehow the entire town looks slightly raised, and the size of town and density of houses can be distinguished from afar. Until a few years ago this area around the plateau looked clustered in a contrast with the scattering of windmills, but recently, with houses being built dispersedly on the eastern hill, the town seems to have grown in its size.

The oldest quarter is located at the center of the plateau of the cape, covering about 2 ha. Plotting the area with landmark churches—Kyriaki Church in the middle of the bay area on the east; the Cathedral on the south; and Paraportiani Church at the tip of the cape on the northwest—

この非常に旧い街区は，あるものは数百年を経ているという。その後発展した街区は，東の港を囲む方向と，風車のある南の岬を回ったアイバスの入江の方向とに，伸びている。この両翼に加えられた街は，住居の仕組みや要素が同じであり，同じような規則を守り，似たような群形をもっているが，街は全く異って感じられる。われわれがこの二つの街区を連続して歩くことで，空間の決定的な差異を感じるだろう。このことは，われわれに，集合して住むための濃密な空間が失ってはならない幾つかのものについて示唆を与えてくれる。

　確かに，ミコノスの街を訪れた人々が，無目的に歩き集まる場は旧街区であり，そこに生活する人々が，美しい街として誇りをもっているのも旧くからあった街の区画なのである。

　したがって，ミコノスについて記録する場合，どうしてもこの三角形の地区についてになるだろう。そして，もう少し範囲を絞るなら，その重心の辺りの，二つの三角形のゾーン，丁度1ha程度の範囲としてもよい。このように区切っていく地区が三角の形状をもつのは，地形的な影響からではなく，道のネットワークによるからだ。つまり，道が三叉路を交点として展開されていることによるのである。

　ミコノスの住居群は，見事にくっつき合っている。少なくとも外見上1戸の家をそのグループの中から区切り別けることは出来ない。それほど緊密に一体化しているが，そのグループの総体が，ヴィジブルな骨格をもっている訳ではない。ミコノスにはメインの通りも，中心になる公園も，広場もない。いわゆる街の中心やセンターはなく，背骨に例えられる際立った道もない。こうした街の特徴と，この住居のグループや街路のネットワークは，大いに関係があるだろう。道については後述するが，最近では旅行者が増加したため，夏期のみ賑うことになった港の広場も，街の焦点というより，旅行者の量に対応する港の広さに依ってなのである。

　住居は，ただ集まることで，すでに全体をつくり出しているといってよい。隣り合って置かれることで，有機的な総体となるような，個と総体の関係にある。このような部分と全体の即時的な関わりを，個に当たる住居の側から見てみよう。

前述した三角地区をみると，住居のグループは様々な形で結ば

shows a triangular area.

Some blocks in this extremely old quarter is said to be several hundred years old. Later on, the area was expanded toward east surrounding the port and toward the bay beyond the cape on the south where the windmills are. The new town added to both wings features the same structures and elements of houses, observes the same kind of rules and has a similar formation type as the old town, but feels completely different. Walking through these two areas, we feel a definite spatial distinction. And this fact gives us an indication of things that a dense space for collective living must never lose.

It is indeed in the old town that people who visit Mykonos would wander about and gather. It is also the beauty of the old town that the residents feel proud of.

As a result, a document on Mykonos will inevitably be about this triangular area—or if we were to focus a little more, about a 1-ha area around its center composed of two triangular zones. The reason why urban zones are always triangular when drawing lines is not topographical and is rather attributed to the street networks. In fact, streets are laid out so they intersect at three-fork junctions.

Houses in Mykonos are spectacularly stuck together. At least from outside it is impossible to distinguish a house from the group it belongs to. They are so closely integrated, yet the entirety of the group has a visible framework. In Mykonos there are no main streets, no central parks, no plazas. The so-called downtown or town center is inexistent, and so are major roads that can be compared to backbones. There is no doubt that such characteristics of this town have much to do with the clustering of houses and its street networks. Putting aside the streets that will be discussed later, the plaza at the harbor, which becomes crowded exclusively during summer due to the recent increase of tourists, is on account of the area needed for the harbor to accommodate the volume of tourists, rather than being the town's point of focus.

A simple gathering of houses is enough to create a whole. By being placed adjacent to one another, the houses become an organic whole. Let's have a look at this immediate relationship of the individual parts to the whole from the point of view of the parts—the houses.

Observing the aforementioned triangular area, one can find that houses within a group are connected in various man-

ミコノスの街路のネットワーク　　Street Networks of Mykonos

れているのがわかる。戸数は5，6戸から10戸位まででそれ以上は並列形か線形をとるグループに限られるようだ。これは道に接する接し方からの限界である。前庭やパティオは，この場合数が少ないし，外と内を結びつけるスペースとして利用されていない。すなわち，直接出入口が道に接することが原則になっている。そこでは人の家の前とか，人の家の裏口の横とか，人の家の階段を数段拝借することに関係なく，道に接する戸口をもつことが重要なのである。

　住居は平均して2階建てであり，1階は居間，食堂，厨房，及び物置き等に使われ，2階は全面的に寝室である場合が多い。1階と2階は外にある階段によって結ばれる。だから1階2階共に道に接することが必要になる。この重要な上下の動線が外に出ることで，幾つかの興味ある結果を住居内部にも外部としての道にも，もたらすことになる。一つは道に対して，プライベートな部分が突き出ることによって，道がその意味を個化することだ。その第二には，その突き出るものが階段，バルコニー，物置，そして草花などに限定されることで，グループの家々から出されたものが同じ種類のファサードをつくっていくことである。

　したがって，個から突き出た要素の機能的同一性と，共通である場に露出した最もプライバシィの濃い部分の使用のされ方が示す多様性と個性。それがこの単純な仕かけの見えない役割りであり，道を媒介にしなくては成り立たない空間の意味になっているのである。

　だから道は，この街で規則としての公共性を示すものではない。セミ・パブリックというより，よりプライベートに近い側で捉えているといってよい。彼等の道に対する概念は，そうした意味で，われわれの道のそれとは違う。それは内と外の概念も含めた，個とグループの連帯関係の概念の違いにも関連していることを示すだろう。

　港からこの地区に入ると，そこはすでに内側の感じがする。日中のほとんどは彼等の居間が，そこに伸びてきているのを感じる。彼等が夜寝る前にバルコニーから向いのバルコニーへ挨拶を送るそんな会話も感じる。これらの機能を秘めたインサイドの親密な空間を，この細い曲りくねった道に，われわれが感じるとき，それがミコノスの道と家のデザインの原点のように

ners. A group is composed of typically 5 or 6, up to 10 households. Groups made up of 10 or more seem to always take a parallel or linear formation. This limit is determined by the way a house shares a border with the road. In this case, there are only few front yards and patios, and they are not used as a space to link the outside with the inside. In fact, the principle here is that a door has to be tangent to a street. What counts is to have a door that opens to a street, regardless of it being placed in front of someone's house or next to someone's house's back door, or having to borrow a few flights of stairs of someone else's house.

　In average, a house is two-storied, with the living and dining rooms, the kitchen and storage on the 1st floor, and all the bedrooms on the 2nd floor. The two floors are connected by exterior stairs. Hence the need for both floors to be tangent to the street. By placing this important vertical circulation outside, some interesting consequences are brought to both the inside of the house and the street that is the outside. One such consequence is that, as a private element protrudes into the street, its meaning is individualized by the street. Another consequence is that, by limiting the things that protrude to items such as the stairs, balcony, storage and flowers, all those things that are placed outside the houses of a group eventually create a certain type of facade.

　Functional co-identity between elements that protrude from individuality, and diversity and distinctiveness shown by the usage of the most private parts that are exposed to shared spaces, are the hidden roles of this simple mechanism, representing the meaning of space that is bound to be mediated by a street.

　Thus a street in this town is not something that demonstrates a rule as a public aspect. It is regarded more private than semi-public. Their notion of a street is, in that sense, different from ours. It also indicates an association with the difference in the notion of joint relationship between the individual and the group including the notion of inside and outside.

　Entering this area from the harbor, one already feels like being inside. For most of the daytime it feels like being within an extension of the residents' living rooms. It feels like someone is sending a goodnight message from the balcony to someone on the balcony across the street. And when we feel in these narrow, winding streets the

思えてくるのである。
　純白に塗られた道と家は，また住居の集合体に同化を計るかのようである。白は，この社会では個を目立たせるための色ではなく，皆がそれを，日々常に塗ることは，道と家を，家とそのグループのつながりを保ち，外から決定されそうな境界や区画を拒否する行為なのではないか。
　かって，海から帰る人々にとって，青に対する白，黄色い島影に村する白は，帰りつく街の喜びであった。その同じ喜びが，日々に道と家に塗られる白い色にこめられてはいないか。白い色には，もう一つの効果が見出せる。それは，狭さや，隙間，裏面，そうしたものを消す方法としてである。われわれが思いもよらない60cm幅などという狭い道が，光の拡散で明るい道に変わる。隙間やコーナーや隅を，気分の良い開いた壁に錯覚させるのである。すなわち白い色は，二つの効果，密住の方法と連帯の方法とに大いに加担しているように思える。

　もう数年前になるが，この街に居て，道や広場を実測していたことがある。滞在したのは11月，次の連絡船が来るまでの1週間ほどであった。肌寒い風の吹く荒れたエーゲ海の11月ともなれば，旅行者もいないひっそりとしたミコノスに還っていた。
　しかし，そのようなミコノスが，本来のミコノスで，夏の旅行者で賑わう街はミコノスらしくないというのではない。多少の時間滞在すれば，この街は古くからすでに外来者に開かれた街ではなかったかと思われてくる。それは，個人の部分も街全体としても，同じように開放的なスケールをもっているからだ。エーゲの海洋文化圏の中央に位置し，常に歴史的出来事の道筋にあった島の街として，多分古来コミュニケーションには開かれていたといえるだろうと思う。このような外来者を区別しない島の歴史も，この街のつくりに，良い意味のデザインを残すことになったのではないだろうか。

intimacy of an inside space that harbors such functions, it seems as if it were the origin of the design of streets and houses in Mykonos.

　Painted in stark white, streets and houses appear as though they are trying to integrate to the residential ensemble. In this society, white is not a color to emphasize the individual: when people use the color on a daily basis, is it not an act of keeping the streets and the house, the house and the group connected, as well as rejecting any boundaries and zonings to be defined by outside forces?

　At a time in the past, for those coming home from the sea, the white against the blue, or the white against the yellow island hue used to represent the joy of returning to their hometown. It may be that the same joy is implied in the daily coloring of white on the streets and houses. There is another effect that can be found in the color white: a method of erasing such things as smallness, gap and backside. Diffusion of light turns a narrow street with an unthinkable width of 60 cm into a bright street. It creates the illusion of pleasantly open walls in place of gaps, angles and corners. That is to say, the color white seems to take a considerable part in two effects—methods of dense living and joint living.

It has already been several years that I have stayed in this town to measure its streets and plazas. It was in November, and about a week until the next ferry arrives. Chilly November wind blew over the stormy Aegean, and calm has returned to Mykonos as all the tourists had left.

　I am not claiming that that is the true nature of Mykonos and that a busy town with summer tourists is not its usual self. Spending a certain amount of time there, one realizes that this town had most probably been open to visitors from outside since old times, because it has an open scale both in terms of individual parts and the town as a whole. As a town on an island that has always been found along the paths of historical events and located in the center of the Aegean maritime cultural region, it is only natural to think that it has been, since the ancient times, open to communication. Such history of indiscriminating visitors from outside has certainly left design marks in a good way on the makeup of this town.

思えてくるのである。

　純白に塗られた道と家は，また住居の集合体に同化を計るかのようである。白は，この社会では個を目立たせるための色ではなく，皆がそれを，日々常に塗ることは，道と家を，家とそのグループのつながりを保ち，外から決定されそうな境界や区画を拒否する行為なのではないか。

　かって，海から帰る人々にとって，青に対する白，黄色い島影に村する白は，帰りつく街の喜びであった。その同じ喜びが，日々に道と家に塗られる白い色にこめられてはいないか。白い色には，もう一つの効果が見出せる。それは，狭さや，隙間，裏面，そうしたものを消す方法としてである。われわれが思いもよらない60cm幅などという狭い道が，光の拡散で明るい道に変わる。隙間やコーナーや隅を，気分の良い開いた壁に錯覚させるのである。すなわち白い色は，二つの効果，密住の方法と連帯の方法とに大いに加担しているように思える。

　もう数年前になるが，この街に居て，道や広場を実測していたことがある。滞在したのは11月，次の連絡船が来るまでの1週間ほどであった。肌寒い風の吹く荒れたエーゲ海の11月ともなれば，旅行者もいないひっそりとしたミコノスに還っていた。

　しかし，そのようなミコノスが，本来のミコノスで，夏の旅行者で賑わう街はミコノスらしくないというのではない。多少の時間滞在すれば，この街は古くからすでに外来者に開かれた街ではなかったかと思われてくる。それは，個人の部分も街全体としても，同じように開放的なスケールをもっているからだ。エーゲの海洋文化圏の中央に位置し，常に歴史的出来事の道筋にあった島の街として，多分古来コミュニケーションには開かれていたといえるだろうと思う。このような外来者を区別しない島の歴史も，この街のつくりに，良い意味のデザインを残すことになったのではないだろうか。

intimacy of an inside space that harbors such functions, it seems as if it were the origin of the design of streets and houses in Mykonos.

　Painted in stark white, streets and houses appear as though they are trying to integrate to the residential ensemble. In this society, white is not a color to emphasize the individual: when people use the color on a daily basis, is it not an act of keeping the streets and the house, the house and the group connected, as well as rejecting any boundaries and zonings to be defined by outside forces?

　At a time in the past, for those coming home from the sea, the white against the blue, or the white against the yellow island hue used to represent the joy of returning to their hometown. It may be that the same joy is implied in the daily coloring of white on the streets and houses. There is another effect that can be found in the color white: a method of erasing such things as smallness, gap and backside. Diffusion of light turns a narrow street with an unthinkable width of 60 cm into a bright street. It creates the illusion of pleasantly open walls in place of gaps, angles and corners. That is to say, the color white seems to take a considerable part in two effects—methods of dense living and joint living.

It has already been several years that I have stayed in this town to measure its streets and plazas. It was in November, and about a week until the next ferry arrives. Chilly November wind blew over the stormy Aegean, and calm has returned to Mykonos as all the tourists had left.

　I am not claiming that that is the true nature of Mykonos and that a busy town with summer tourists is not its usual self. Spending a certain amount of time there, one realizes that this town had most probably been open to visitors from outside since old times, because it has an open scale both in terms of individual parts and the town as a whole. As a town on an island that has always been found along the paths of historical events and located in the center of the Aegean maritime cultural region, it is only natural to think that it has been, since the ancient times, open to communication. Such history of indiscriminating visitors from outside has certainly left design marks in a good way on the makeup of this town.

ミコノスの港と街（部分）　*Port and town of Mykonos (partial)*

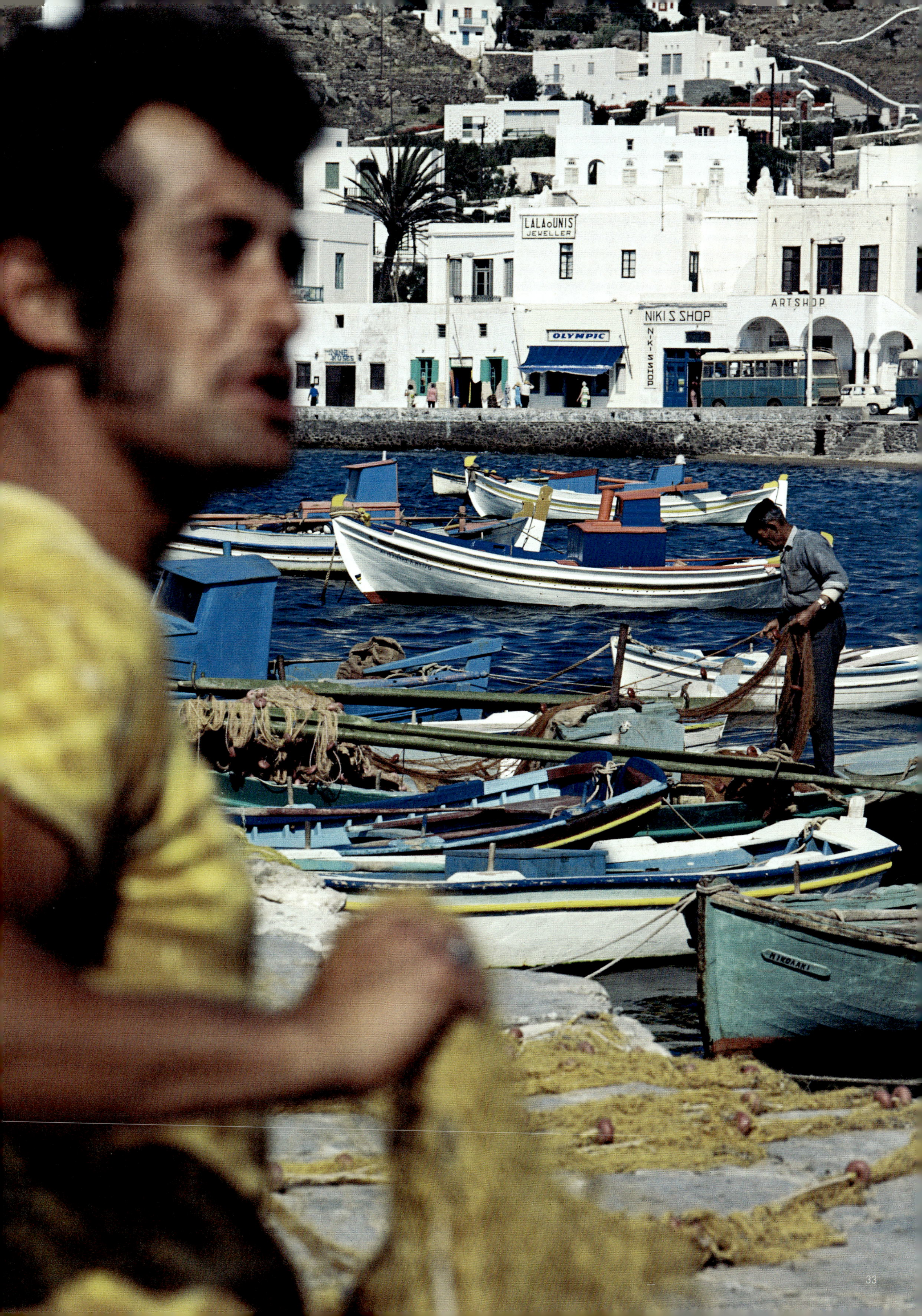
LALAOUNIS
JEWELLER
ARTSHOP
NIKI S SHOP
OLYMPIC

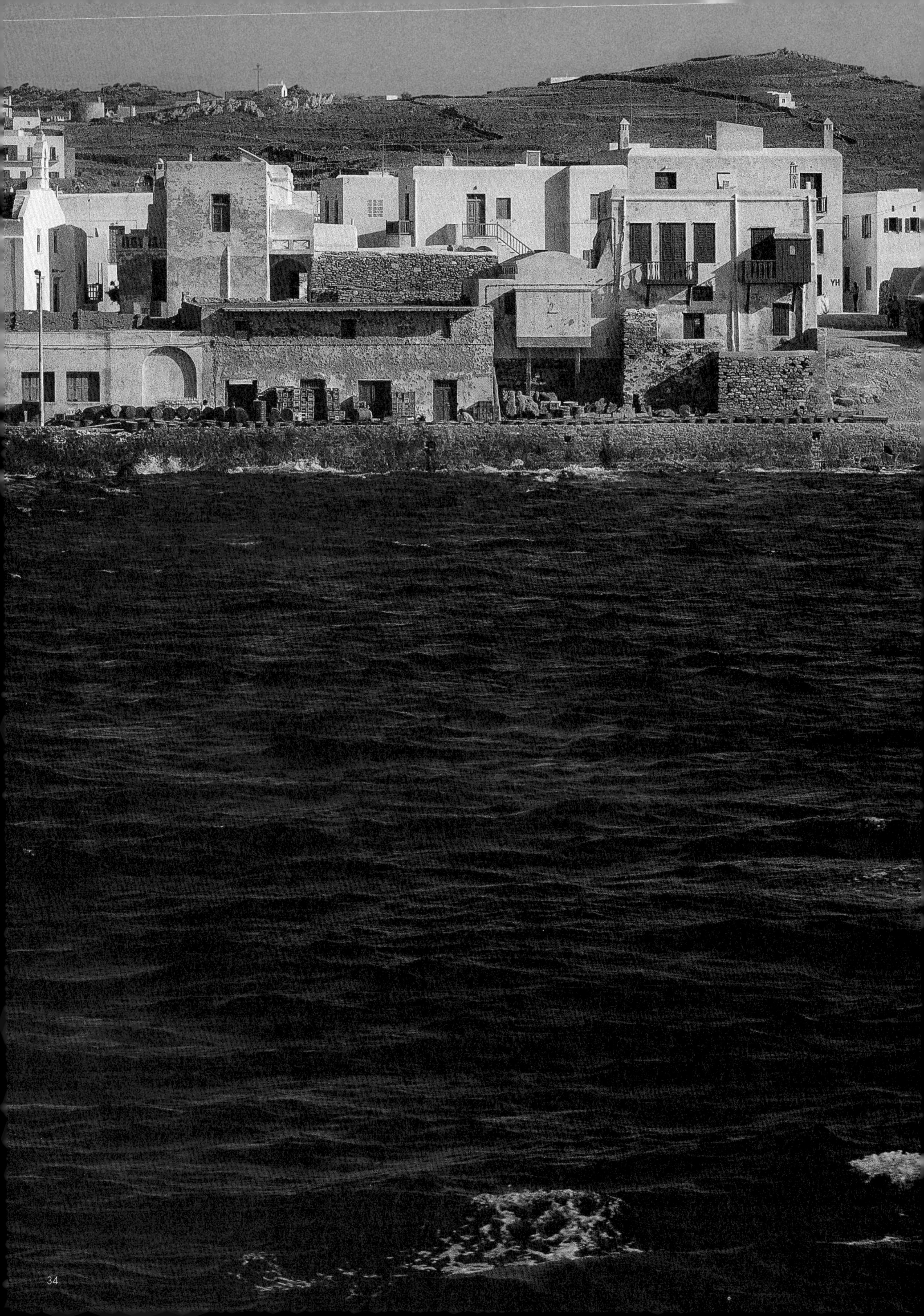
YH

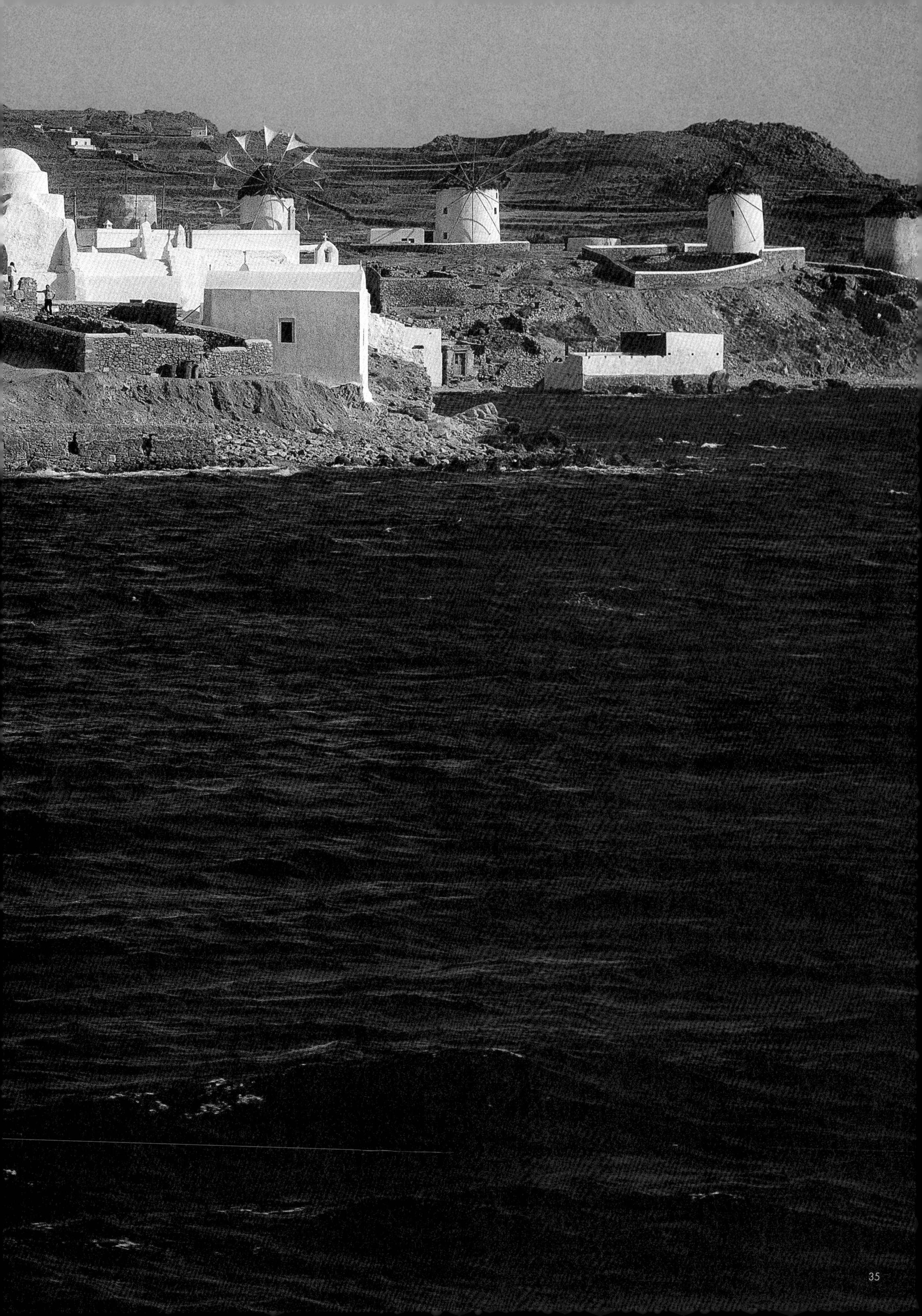

36

37

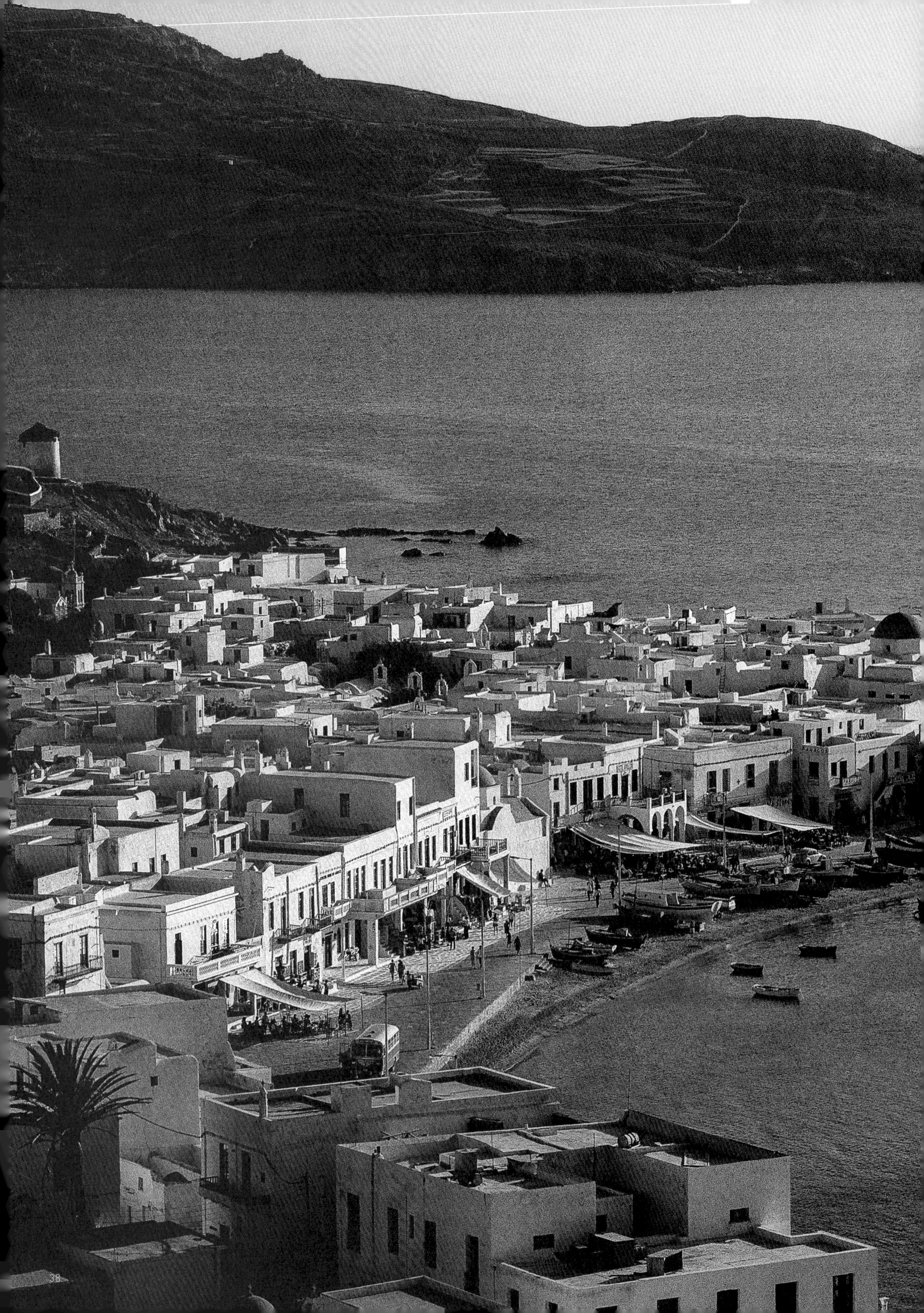

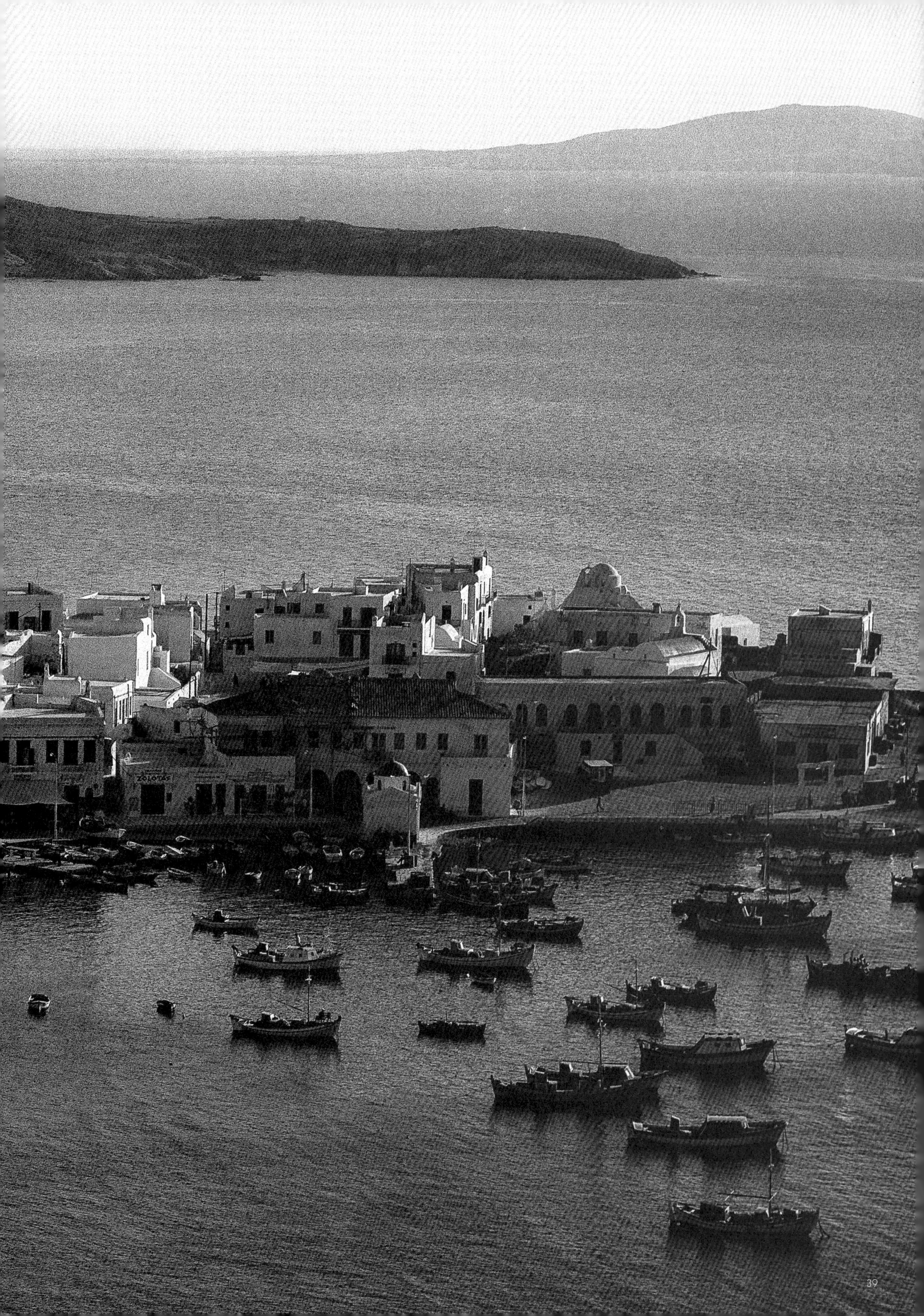
ZOLOTAS

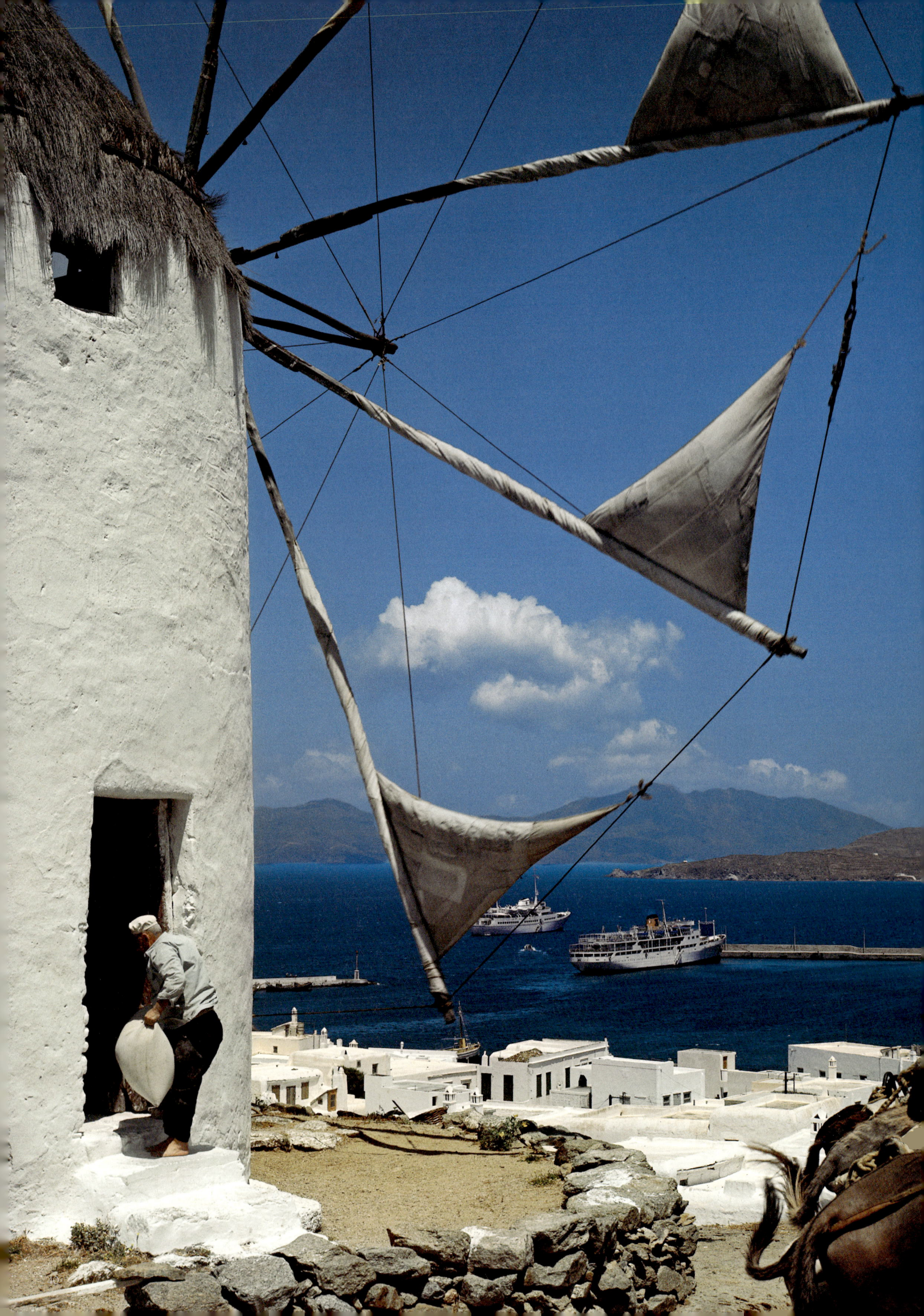

41

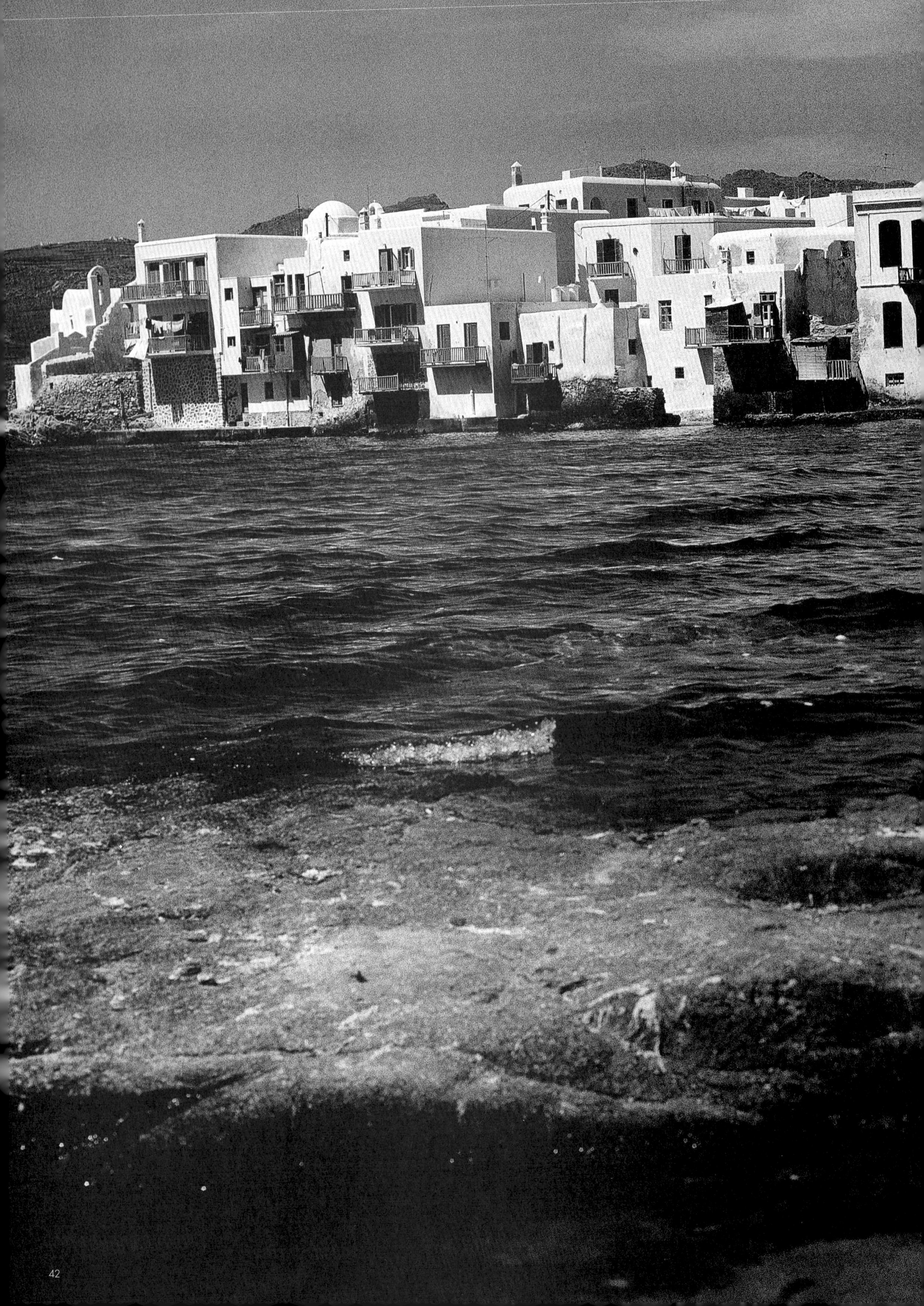

43

44

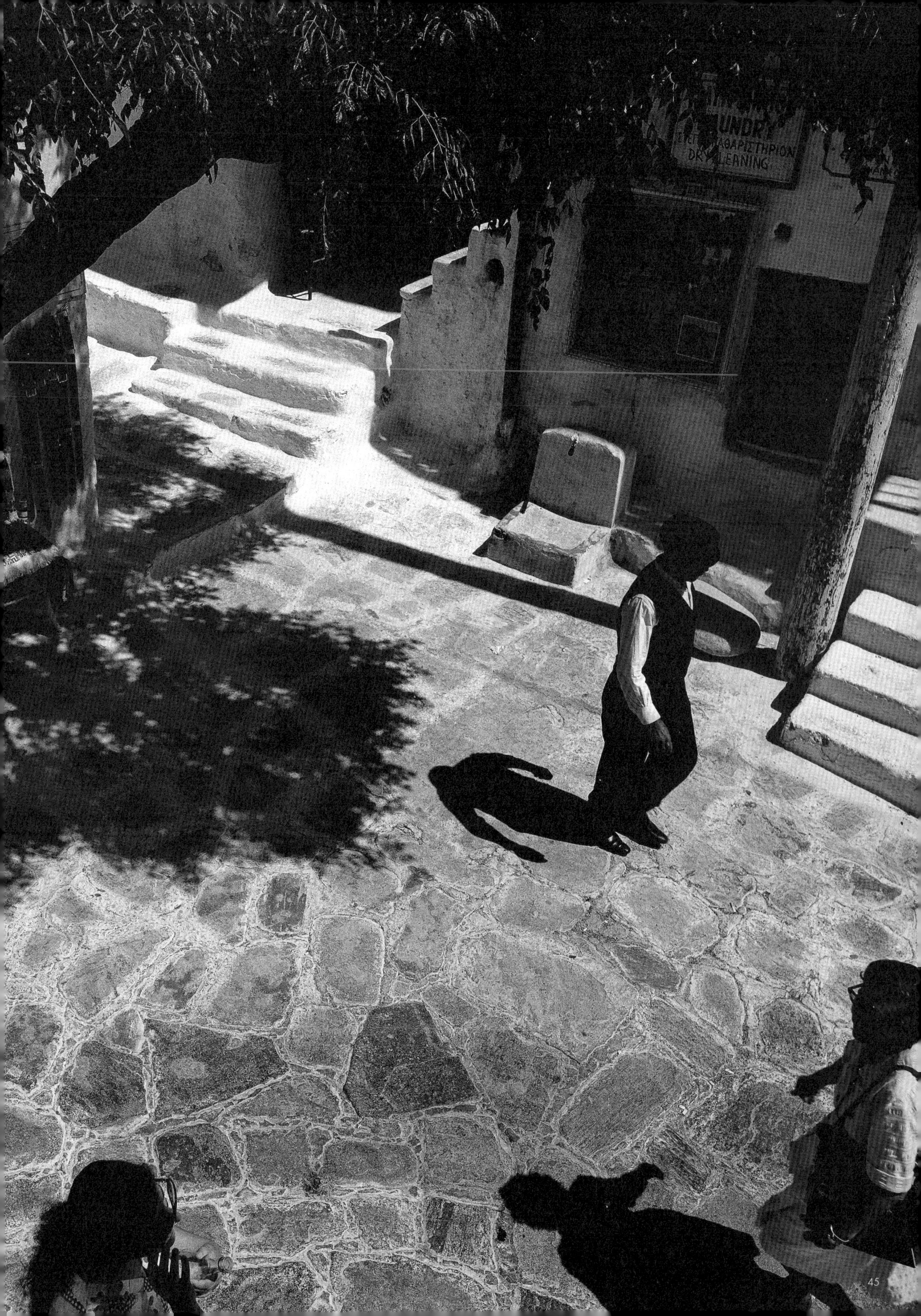

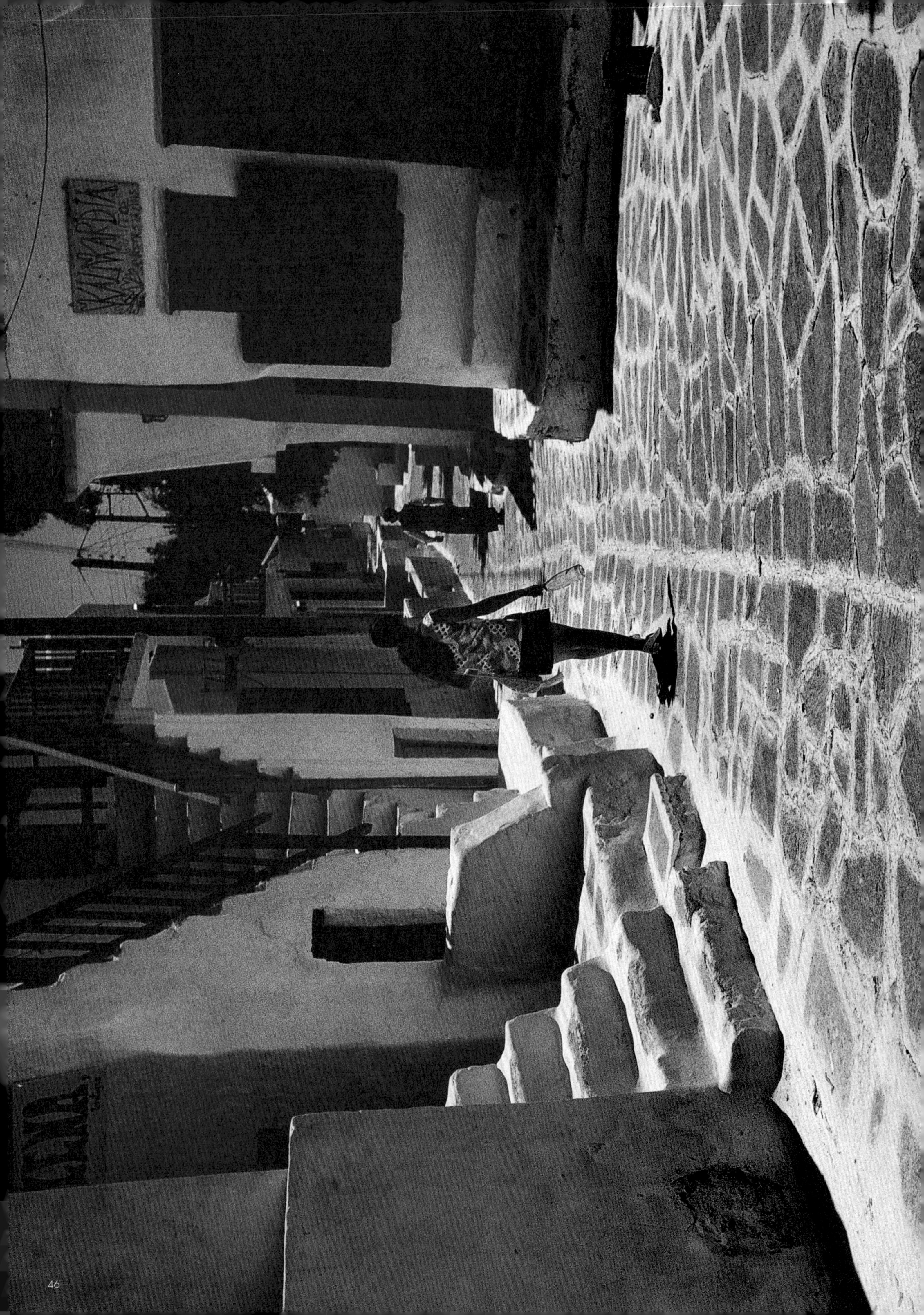

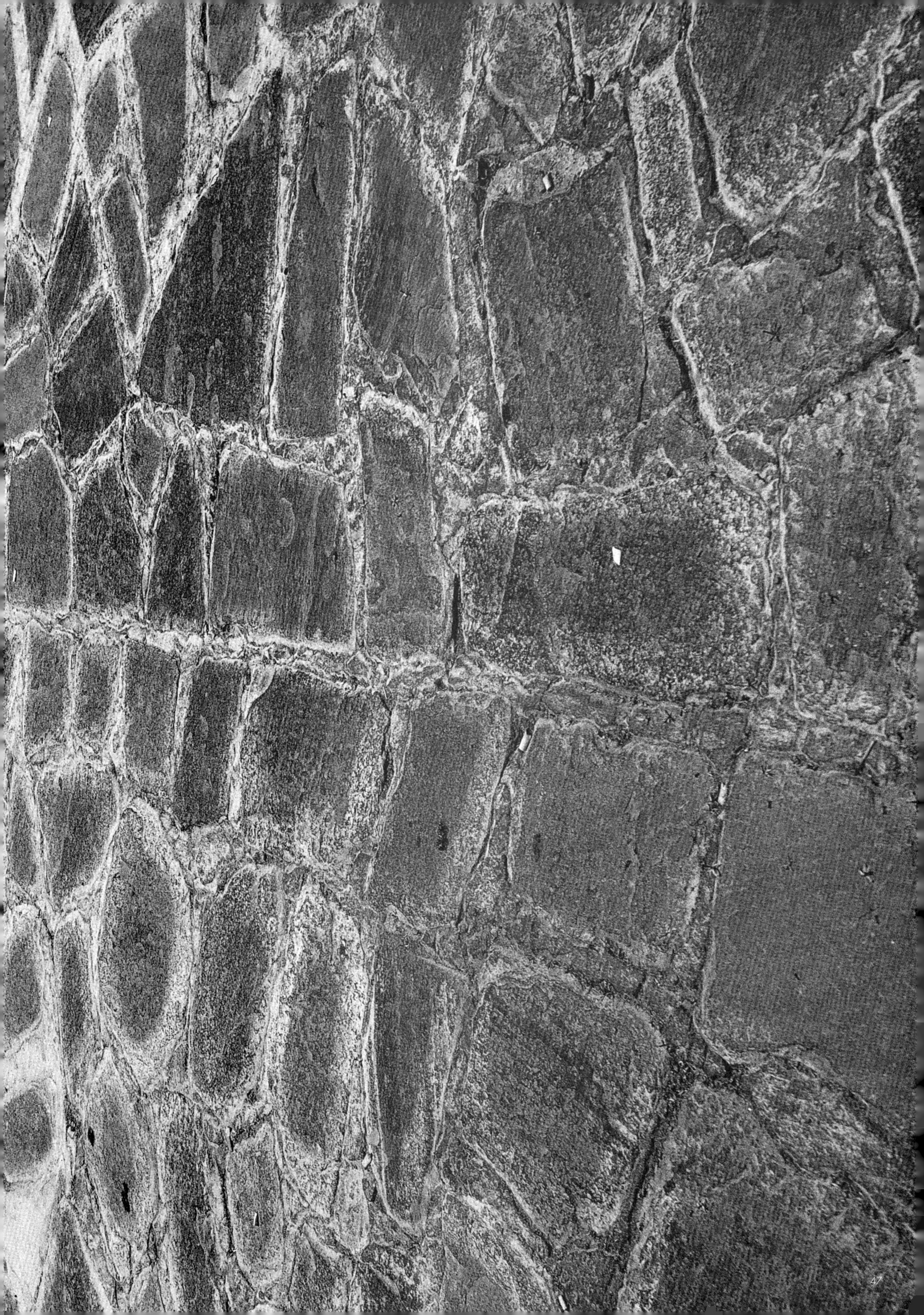

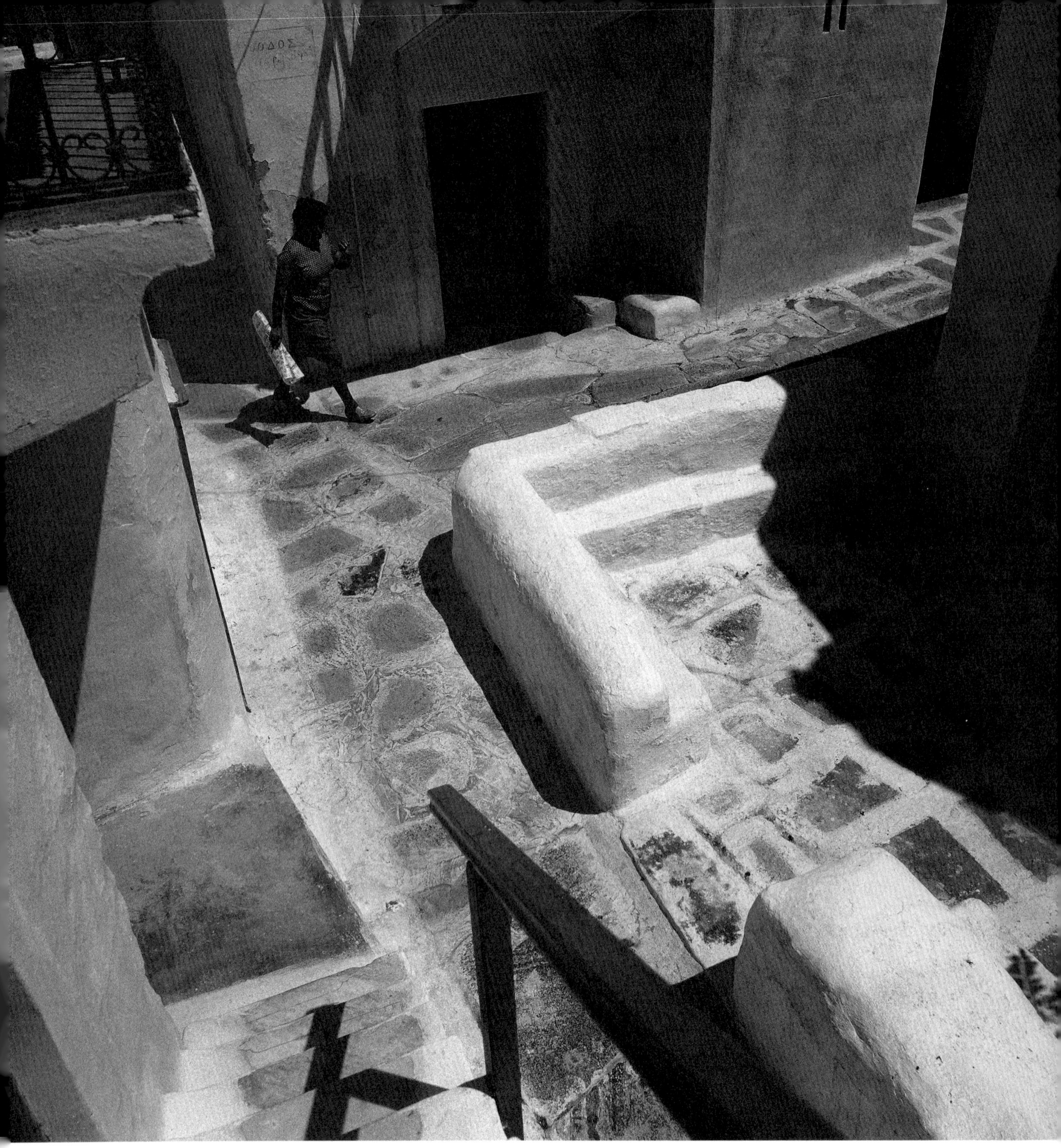

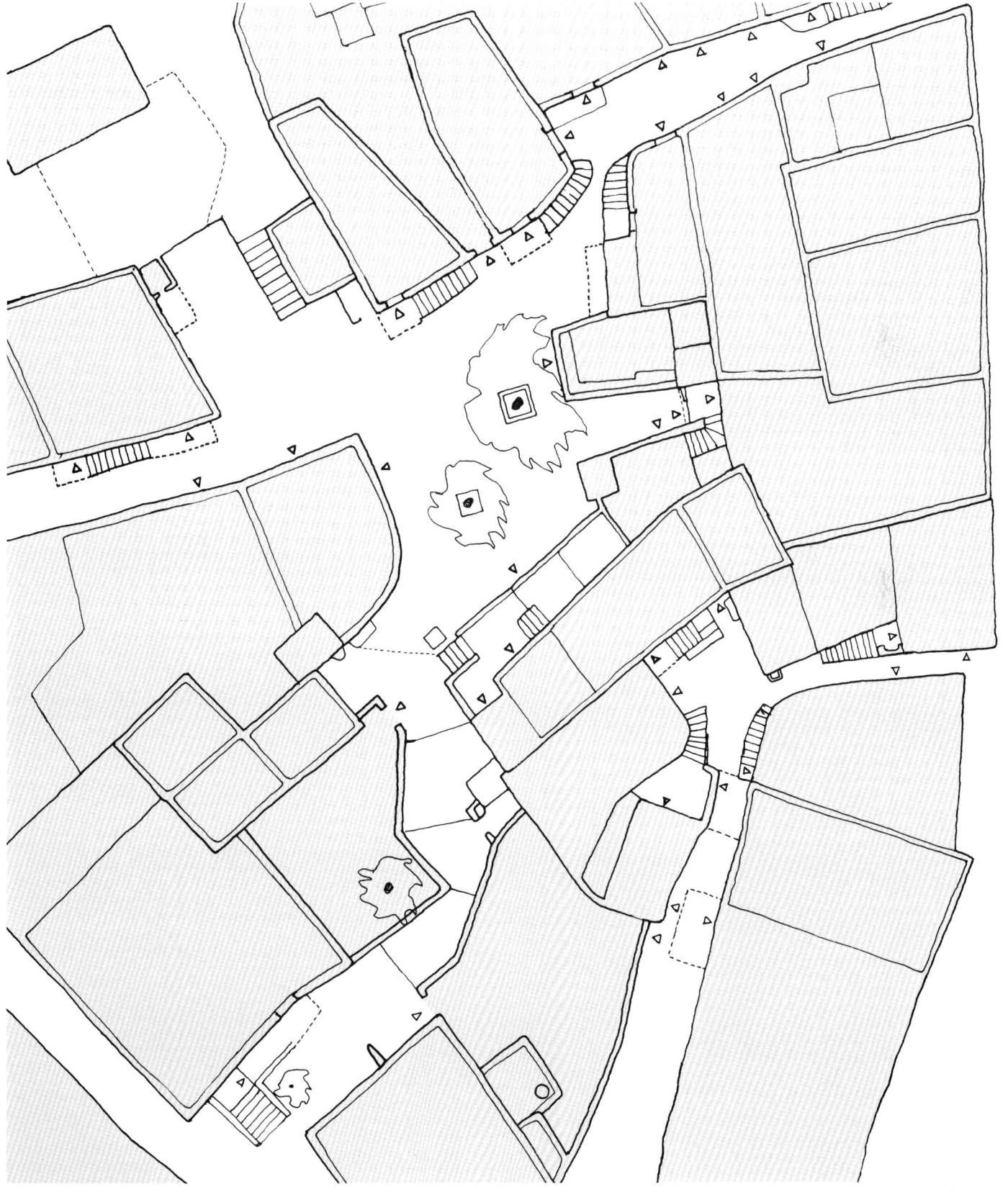

ミコノスの道と広場1　　*Streets and Plaza of Mykonos 1*

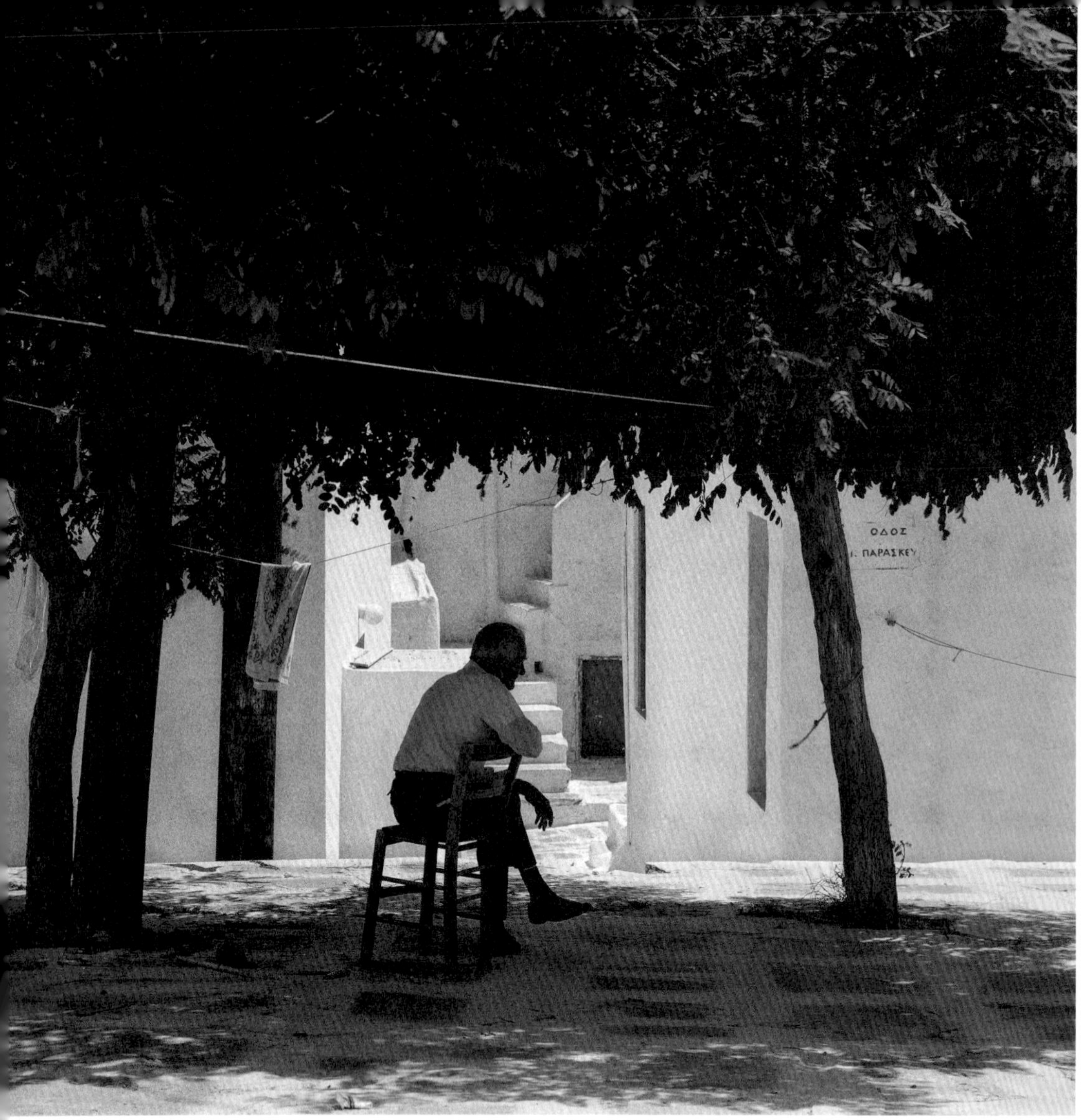
ΟΔΟΣ
ΠΑΡΑΣΚΕΥ

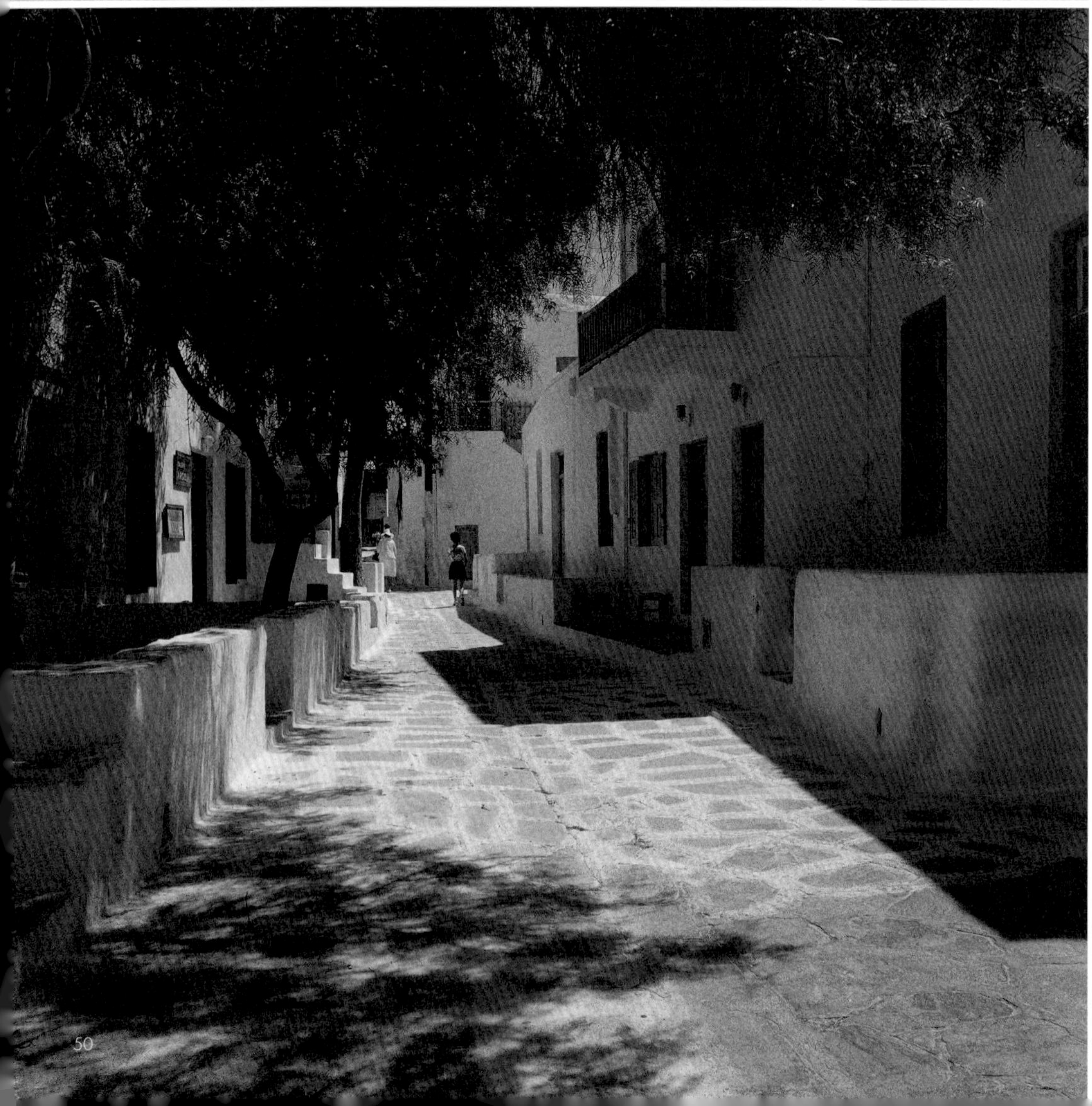

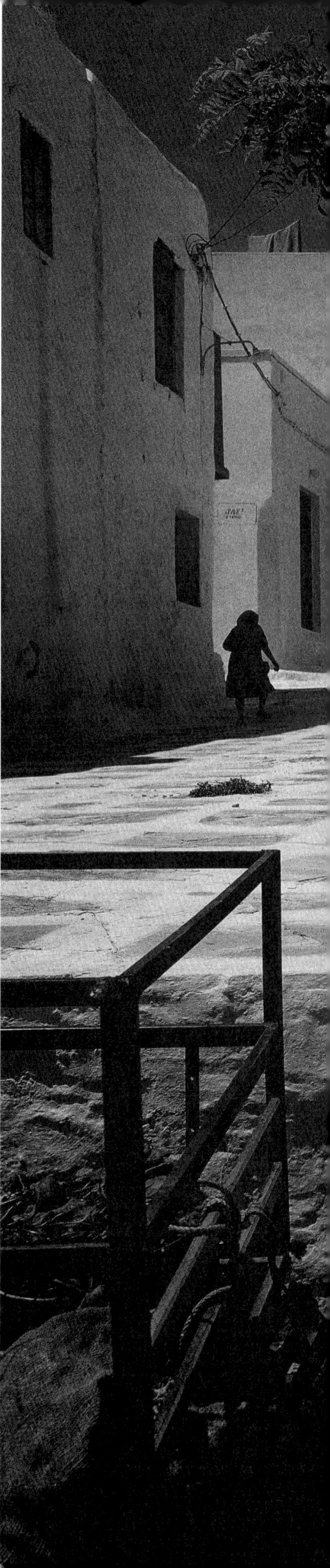

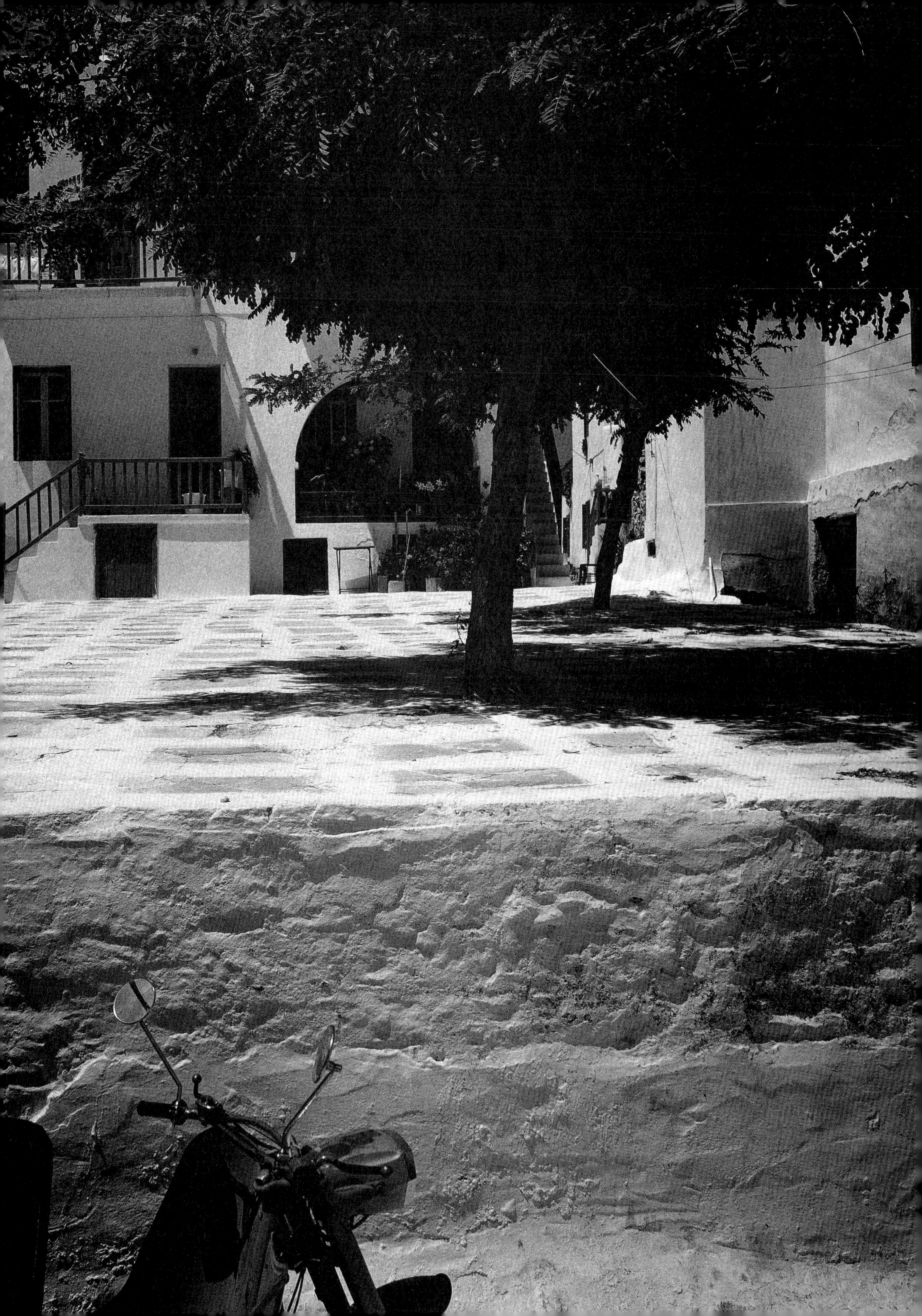

ミコノスの道と広場 ──── 鈴木恂
Streets and Plazas of Mykonos *by Makoto Suzuki*

300余におよぶといわれる教会は，4000人程度のミコノスの人口に比して非常に多い．しかし，どれも住宅程度の大きさか，それ以下の，例えば幅2m足らず，奥行きが5mといった小さなものまでが含まれる．

そのいずれもが，周辺の風景に対して際立った形態をしているというのでもなく，特別に，景観に対しての環境的配慮がされているのでもない．比較的新しいカテドラルや，パラポルティアのように幾つかの教会が重なり合って一つのモニュメンタルな規模と形をもったものもあるが，ほとんどは住居のグループのコーナーか，そのグループの中に取り込まれ，同じスケールで混じり合ってしまっているものが圧倒的に多いのである．

敢えてその違いを見分けるなら，ヴォールトの屋根や小さな鐘楼，長手が東西に向いているためにできる窓のない長い壁の特徴くらいなものだ．このような祈りの場の反集中的な，または反象徴的な扱いや，住居のスケールへの合わせ方，そして分散したそれらのポジションは，ミコノスにおいて教会のみに限らない．それはミコノスの町のフィジカルな構成に，共通した考え方として特徴付けられるものだ．教会の分散配置は，宗教上の慣習や，近隣の独特な生活的結び付き，漁民のコミュニティ，例えば同じ船に乗り組む人々の，船のまとまりの陸における表現として受け取れないこともないが，住居も含めて広場や道など，町を形成しているエレメントが，同じような集積の仕方を基本にしていることを考え合わせるとき，教会の分散のみによる単純な解釈はできない．

道や広場に見られる分散の構造は，教会のポジションに一致している訳ではなく，またそれはそれなりの独自な構成の原則が存るように思われる．迷路の町ミコノスといわれるように，広場と呼ばれる場は，厳密にいうと歩道のふくらみや，歩道の出合いの場として考えられる．道であることがより強い性格となっているひろがりに過ぎない．だから道によって，そのポジションは位置付けられ，分散することになる．

道は規則的といってよい位に三叉路の展開である．三叉路の交点は交りの方向や，出合う道の幅によって捩れたふくらみになる．しかし広場といわれる程度のふくらみは四筋以上の道の出合う点にしかない．古い街区の1ヘクタール程度の区域を例

Mykonos boasts some 300 churches, a significant number in proportion to its population of around 4000. However, most churches are the size of a house, including smaller ones with width less than 2 m and depth of 5m to cite an example.

None of them are shaped distinctively in regard to the surrounding scenery, or show special environmental concern to the landscape. With some exceptions such as the comparatively new Cathedral and Paraportiani made up of several churches overlapped to form a monumental scale and shape, most of them are incorporated into a group of houses or occupy a corner of it, as a great majority of them blend into those houses on the same scale.

If we were to look for distinguishable aspects, they are few: vaulted roof, small belfry, and the typical long, windowless wall that is a result of longitudinal sides facing east/west. Such examples of non-concentric or non-symbolic treatment of a place of prayer, the way they fit the scale of a house, and the dispersal of their locations do not apply only to churches in Mykonos. They may be characterized as a frame of mind that is in common with the physical structure of the town of Mykonos. The dispersed layout of churches can probably be understood as religious customs, linkage of daily life unique to the neighborhood, or an onshore expression of the fishermen's community—people grouped by the boat that they work on for instance—, but when we take into account the fact that elements such as plazas and streets including the houses that make up the town are based on the same type of cumulation, a simple interpretation by the dispersion of churches would not be appropriate.

The structure of dispersion found in streets and plazas do not match the locations of churches: it appears that there is a certain rule of its own. While Mykonos came to be known for its maze of streets, spaces that are called plazas are technically bulges of sidewalks and places where sidewalks meet. They are mere spaces with strong penchant for being part of a street. Hence their tendency to disperse, because their positions are determined by the streets.

It is almost a rule that the streets intersect in a fork. The point of three-way junction is a bulge twisted by the angle of intersection or by the widths of merging streets. However, a bulge large enough to be called a plaza has to be a junction of four or more roads. Let's take for example an area of about 1ha in the old quarter. There, around 50 spots,

にとってみよう。そこでは道の出合いの100パーセントに近い約50ヶ所が三叉路であり，交叉する点は2ヶ所しかない。そしてその2ヶ所は共に同規膜の面積をもつひろがりとなっている。

　この二つの広場は直接的な関連をもって結ばれているのではない。逆に，直線距離で50ｍの位置にある二つの広場は最も近い道を選んでも120ｍの迂回路をとることになる。多分このことは広場が，広場として意図的に置かれたのではないことを物語っているだろう。

外来者，特に四角い街区に生活しているミコノスの旅行者にとって，この道や広場は体験として楽しい。道を選びながら歩みを進め，思いがけなく出合う，道の左右はまるで同じような家々が並んでいるために，進んでいる方向は光と影によって判別する方がよく，広場や覚えやすいふくらみに出てはじめて自分の位置を確認するといった謎解きの楽しさなどが，確かにある。

　そして数日を経て，人々は歩きやすい三叉路や，親しみやすいコーナーを記憶しはじめる。ミコノスにおいて，道のシークエンスは常に三叉路の選択に節づけられていくことになり，この三叉路の分散が迷路のシステムを編んでいる訳だ。

　二つの広場は，実測のスケッチで示すように，規膜もプロポーションも似ている。しかし広場の性格に大きな差があって，北西の広場は明るくオープンな感じで，通りとしての要素が強い。歩道がそうであるのと同じ理由で，その広場も囲む家々の前庭のようなプライベートな使われ方をしている。東南の広場は二方を六つの教会に囲まれ，大きなパティオのように静かだが，より公共的な規則の内で使われているように見える。

　共通した点は印象的な木立だ。白く塗りこめられた囲みの中にある樹木は，唯一の自然の表象である。樹々の位置は自然のままの位置なのだろう。それが花壇や植樹ではなく，一本のそこに永くあった樹木としての価値を，その重厚な影によって印象づけている。

　樹木をさけることで広場ができ，樹木を残すことで道が集まったとすれば，それも広場の分散の一因と考えてよいだろう。

which is nearly 100% of the places where streets meet, are three-way intersections, with only the remaining 2 being crossroads. The latter 2 are spaces of about the same size. These two plazas are not connected in a direct relation. On the contrary, when trying to move between the two that are 50 m apart in a straight line, the shortest way one can take is a long way round of 120 m. This certainly illustrates the fact that none of these plazas was intentionally placed where it is as a plaza.

For outsiders, especially tourists living in square urban blocks, to wander the streets and plazas of Mykonos are pleasant experiences, choosing our way and walking down a street until it meets another. Since the streets are lined with similar-looking houses on both sides, it is safer to rely on sunlight and shadows to tell which way we are headed, and it is only when we come across a plaza or a familiar bulge that we can find our actual location—the experience is indeed entertaining, like solving a puzzle.

A few days into their stay people begin to remember walk-friendly forks and favorite street corners. In Mykonos, street sequence is constantly accentuated by the choice of road at a fork. In fact, it is this dispersion of forks that constitutes the labyrinthine system.

As shown on the measured drawing, the two plazas are similar in scale and proportion. Still, they differ in character: the plaza on the northwest feels open and bright, with more of an element of a street. For the same reason as the sidewalks are, this plaza is used in a private manner as if it were the front yard of those surrounding houses. The plaza on the southeast, enclosed by six churches on two sides, is as quiet as a vast patio, though it seems to be used within a more public set of rules.

One common feature is the impressive trees. Trees that stand inside the white-painted enclosure are the sole presentation of nature. The position of these trees suggest that they grew there naturally. Neither a of bed of flowers nor planted trees, they cast thick shadows that demonstrate the value of a tree that has been standing there all along.

If a plaza were a consequence of avoiding a tree, and streets converged as a result of keeping trees intact, these surely contributed to the dispersion of plazas.

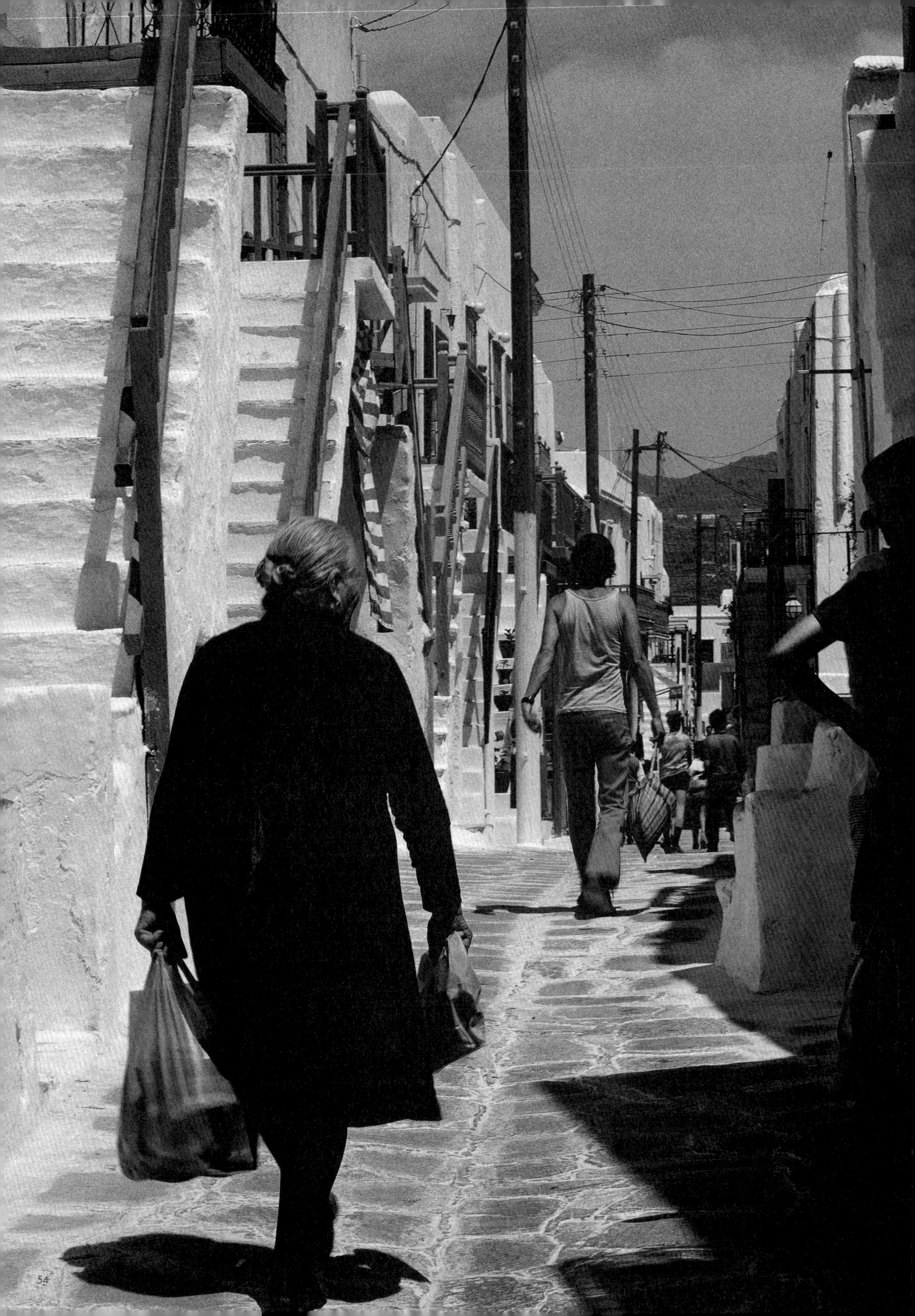

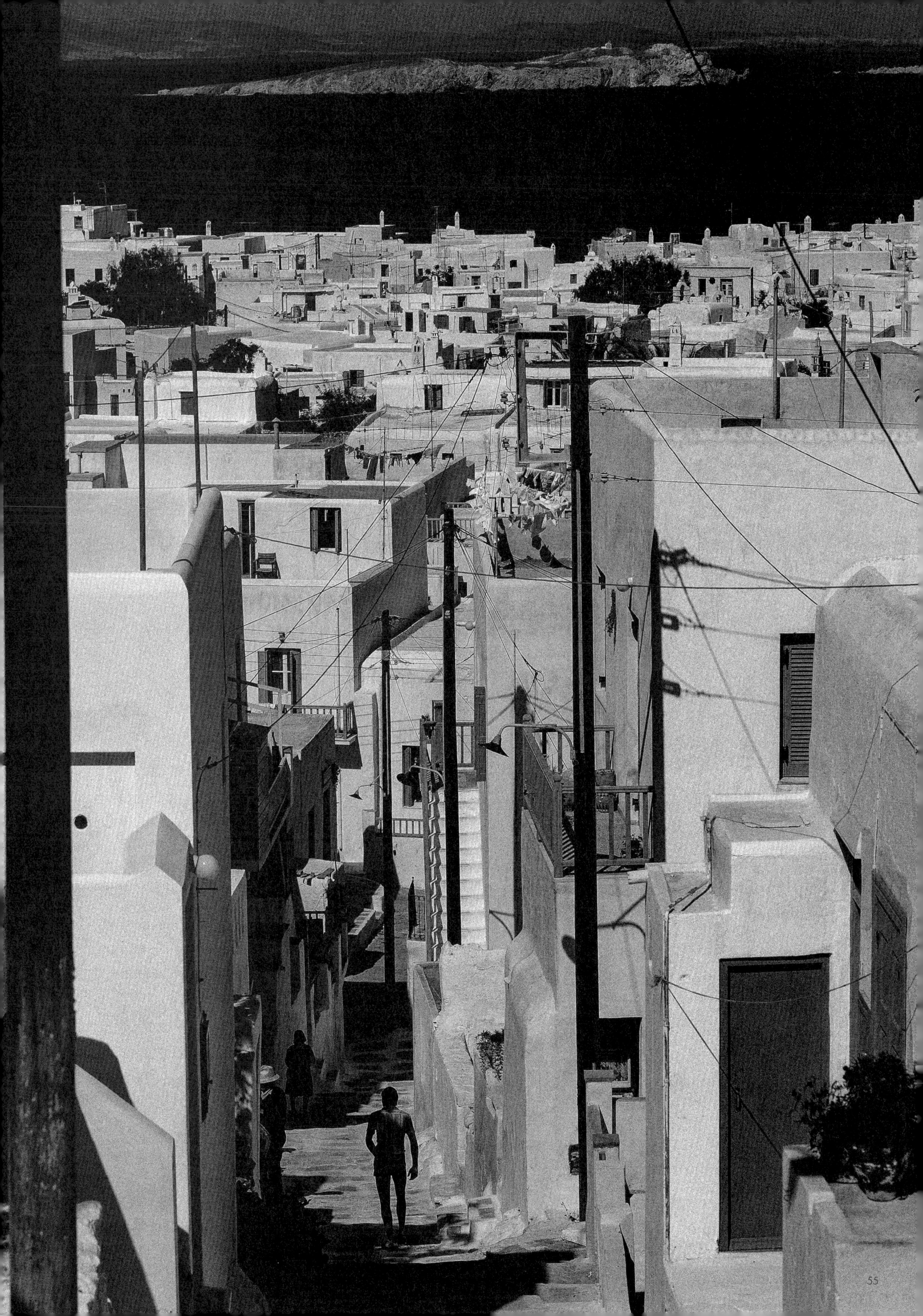

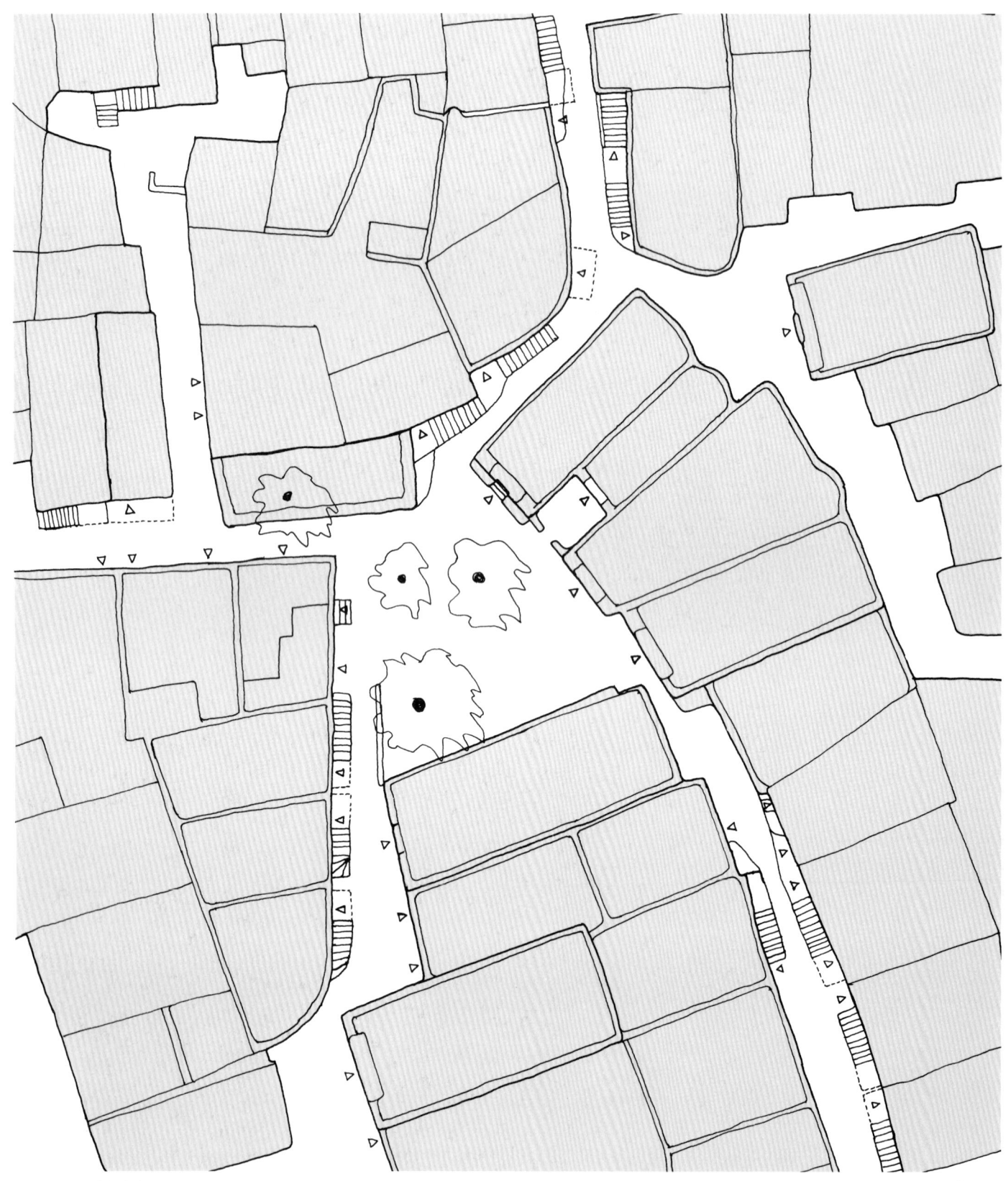

ミコノスの道と広場2　*Streets and Plaza of Mykonos 2*

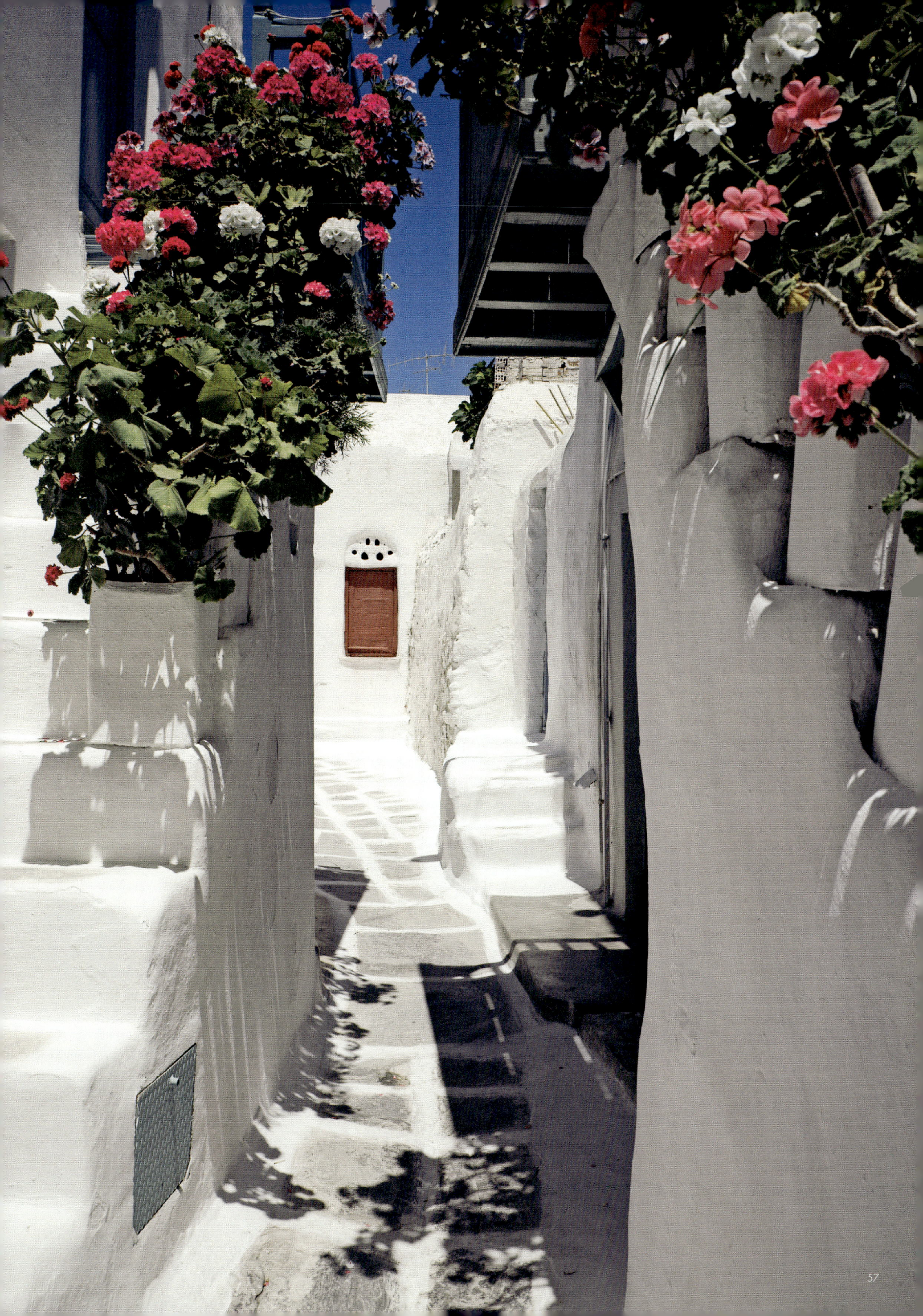

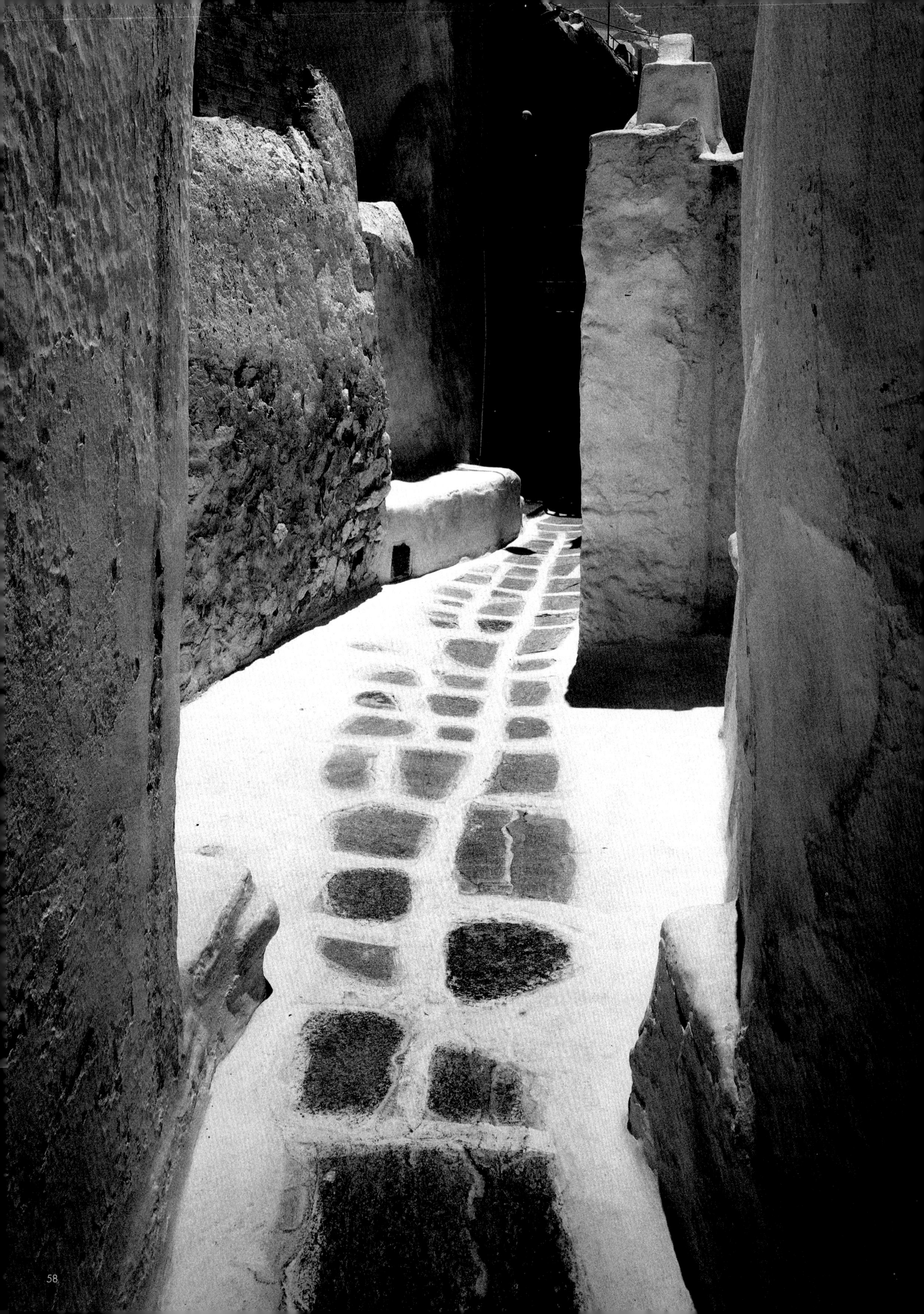

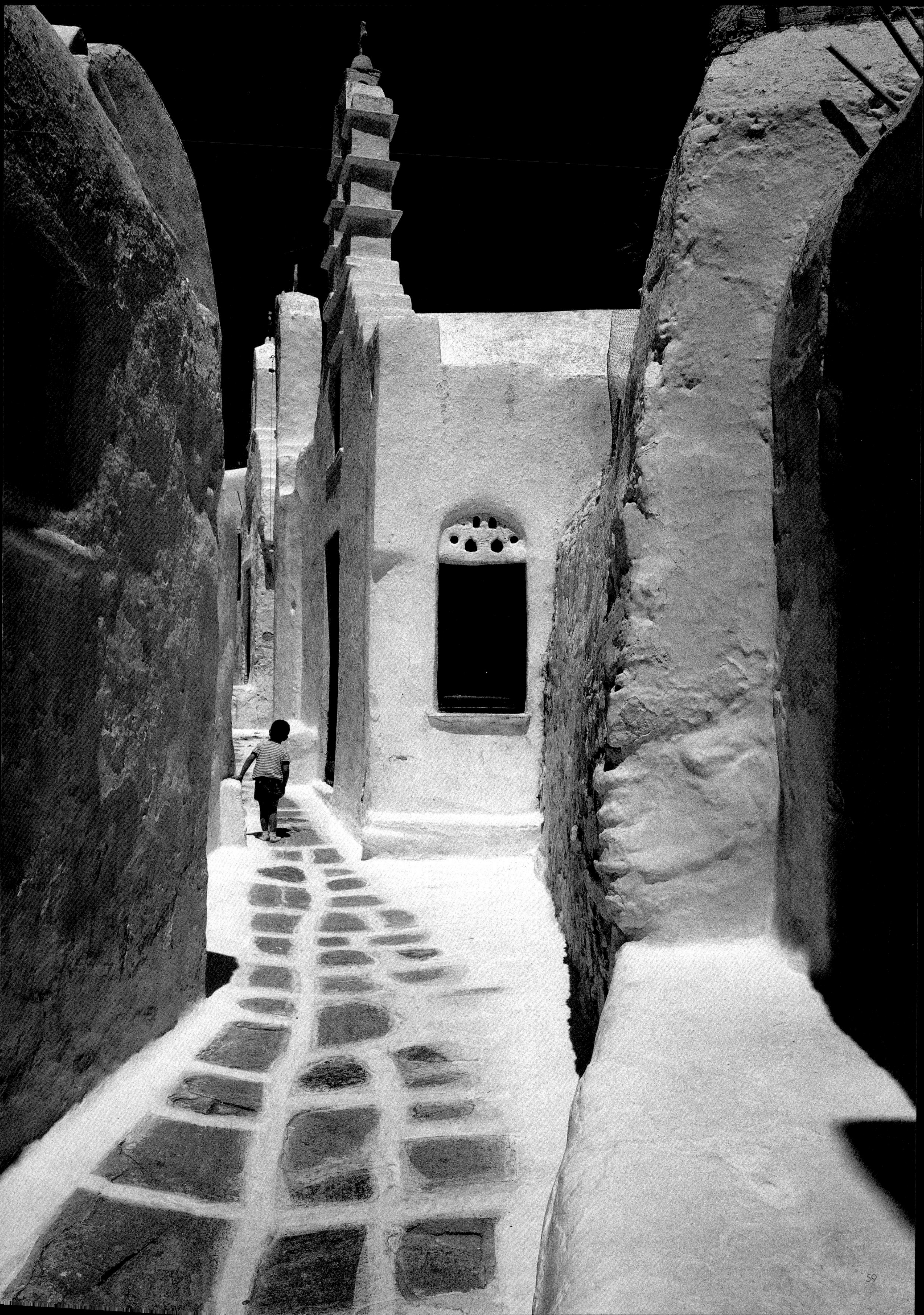

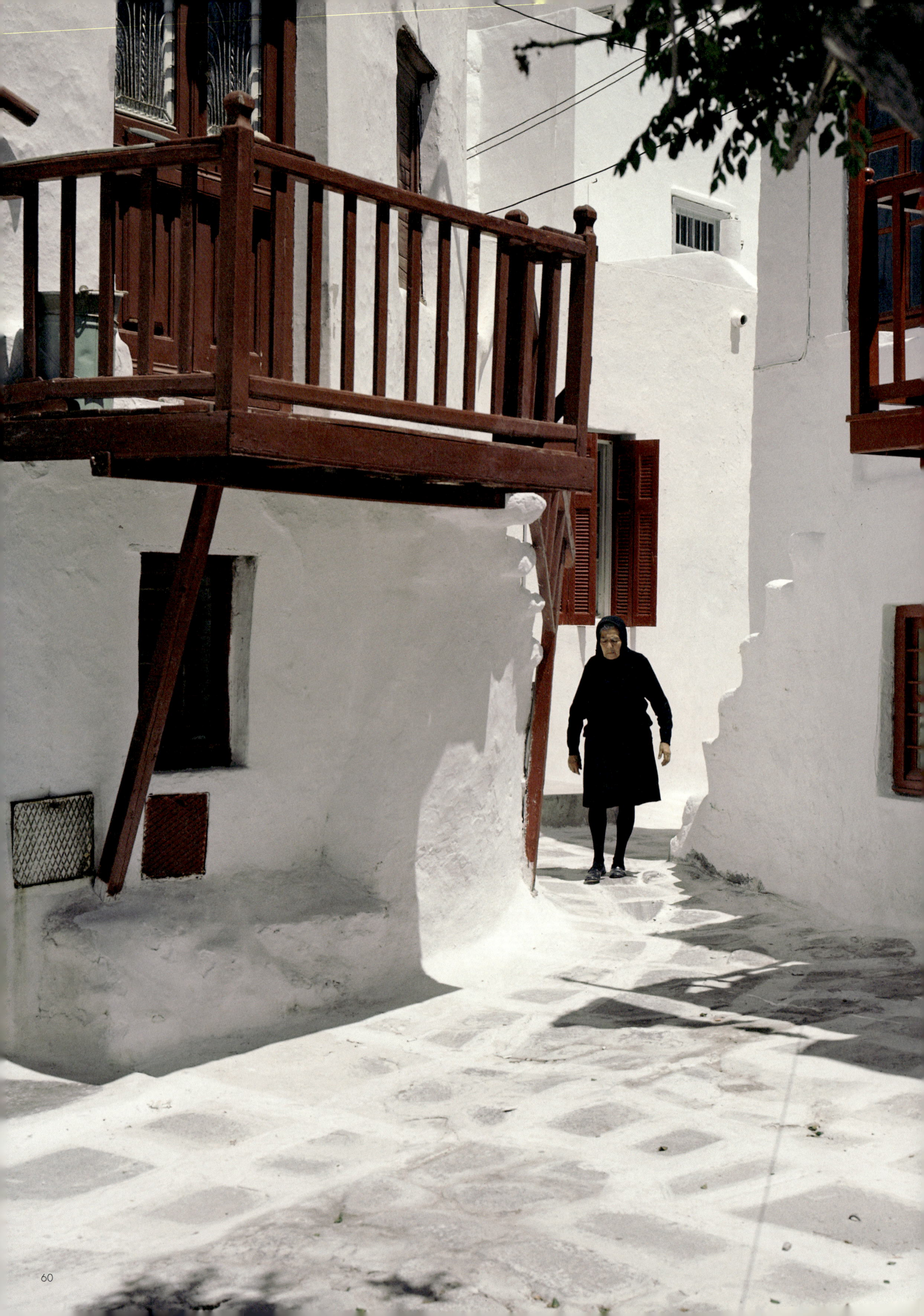

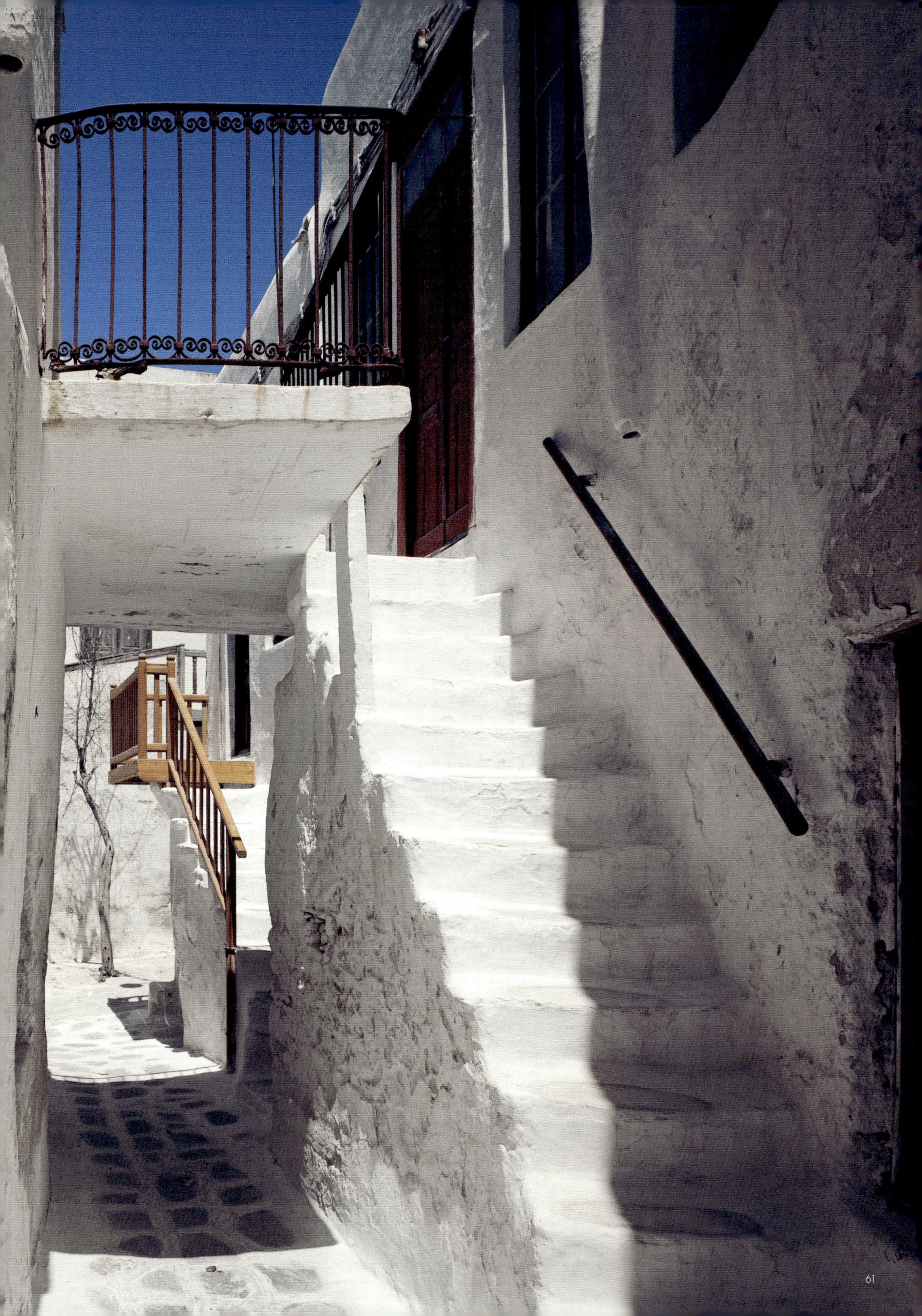

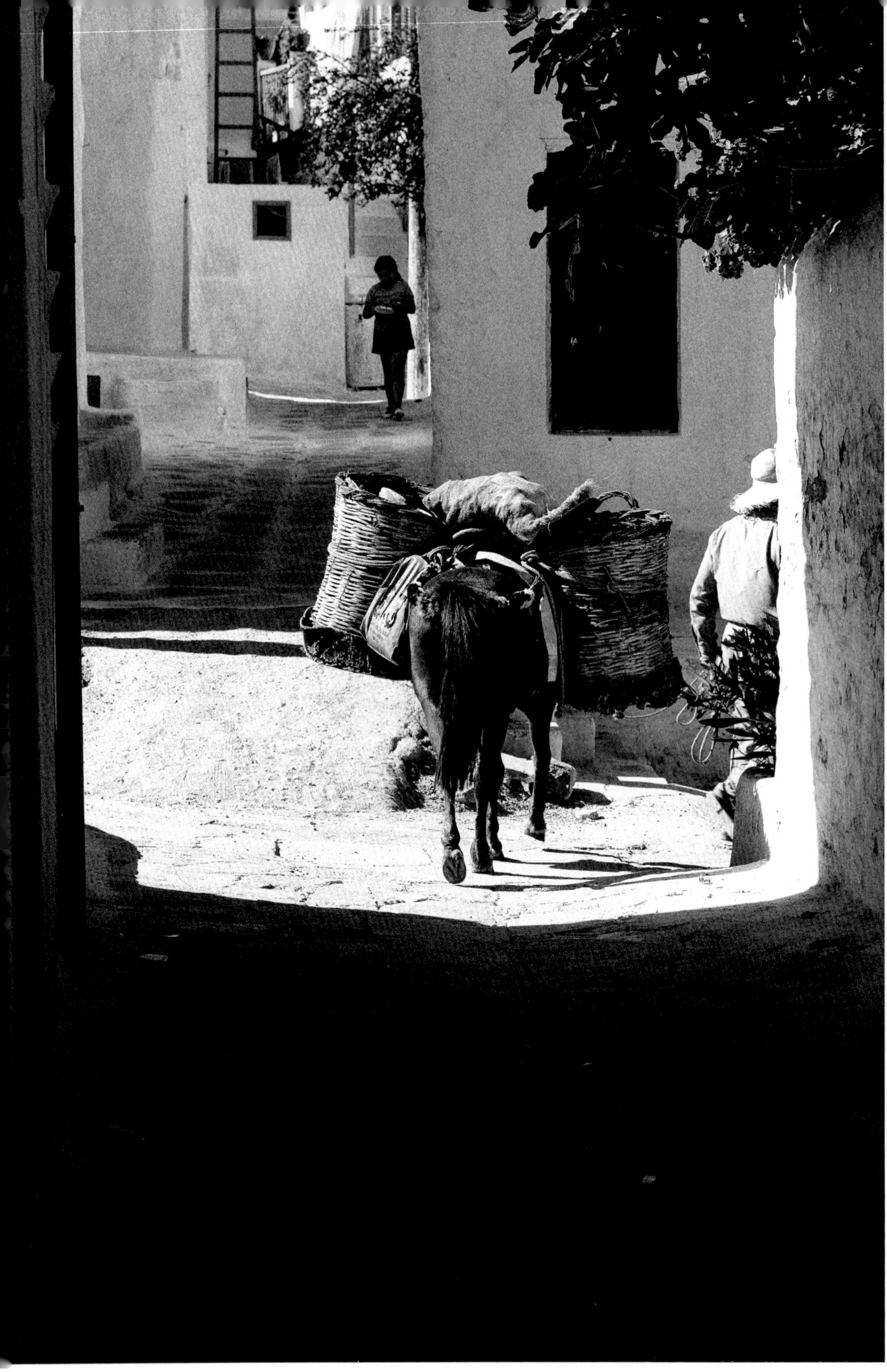
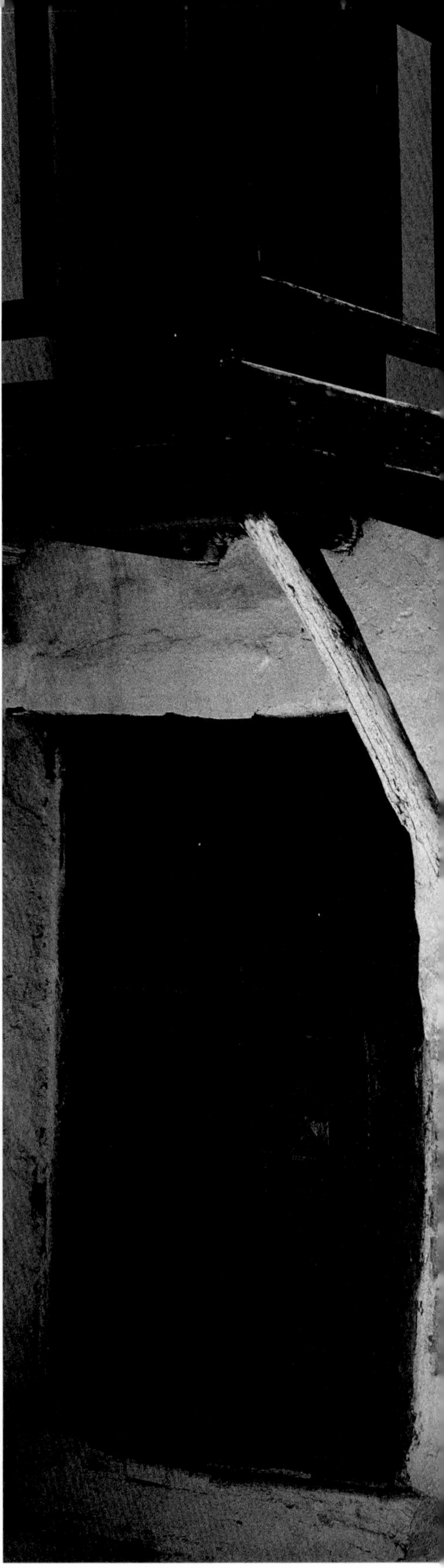

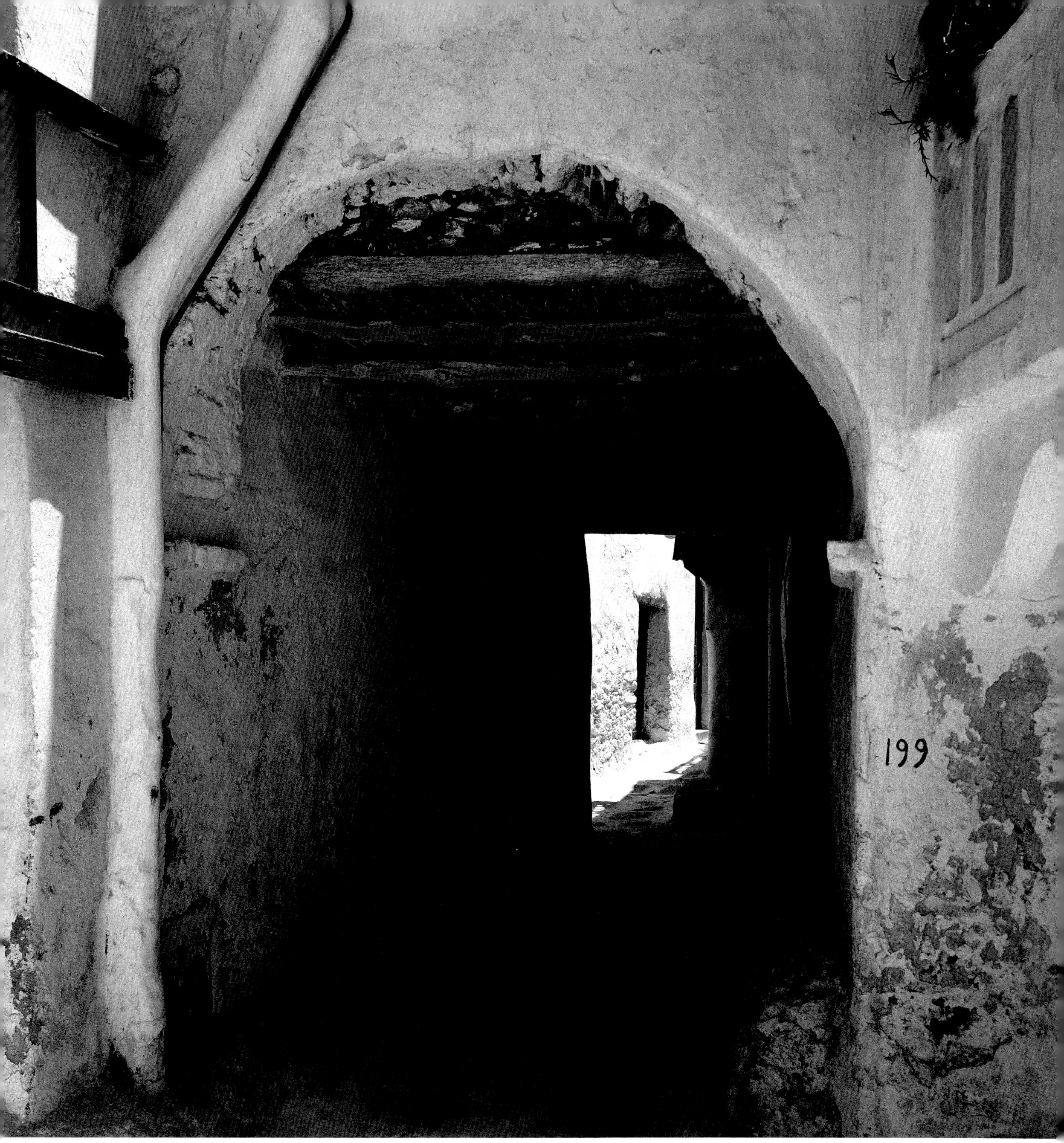
199

64

ΚΑΤΑΣΤΗΜΑ
ΝΕΟΠΕΡΙΔΜΟΥ
"Στὸ Γιῶργο"
ΓΕΩΡ ΚΟΥΦΟΥ

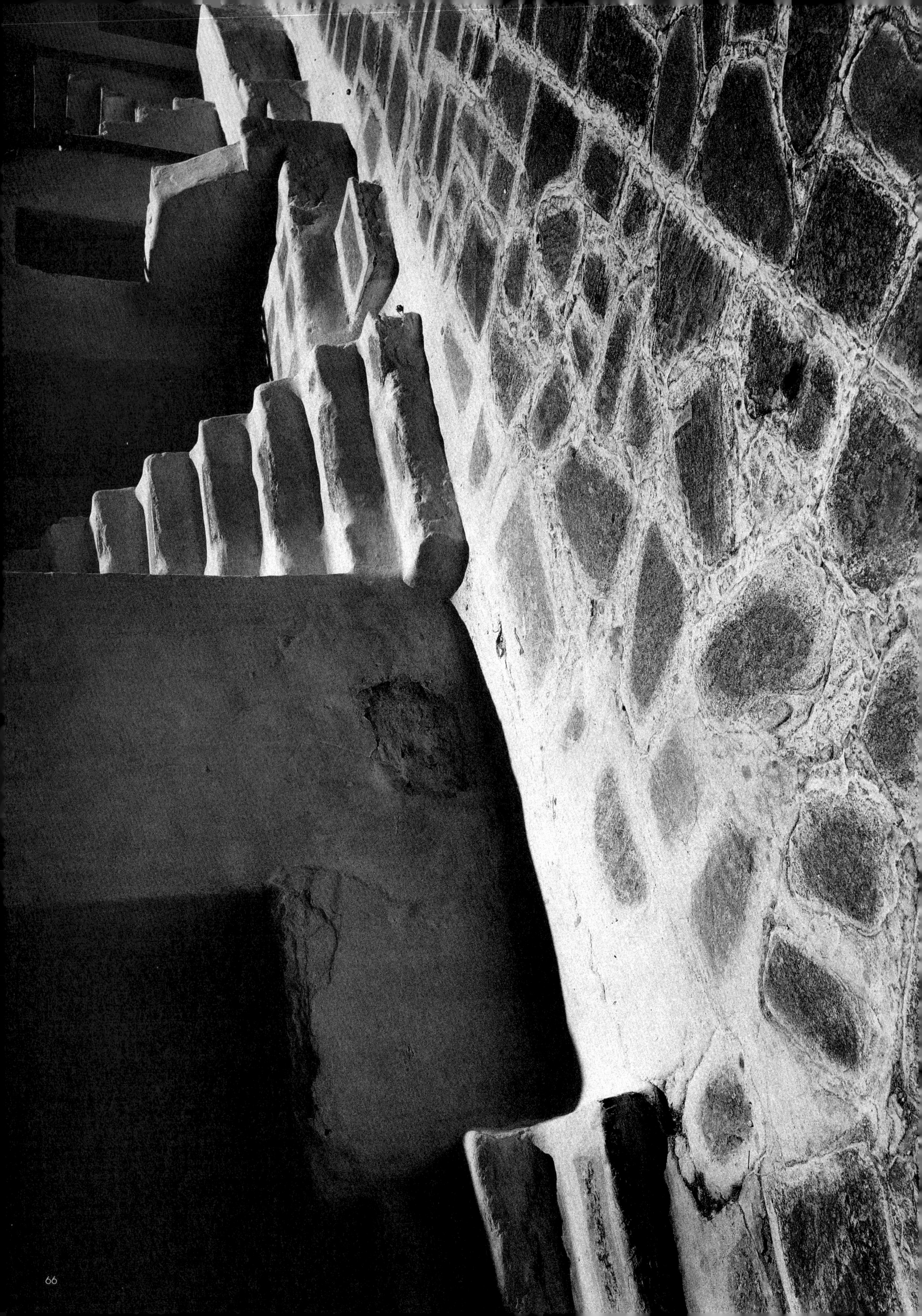

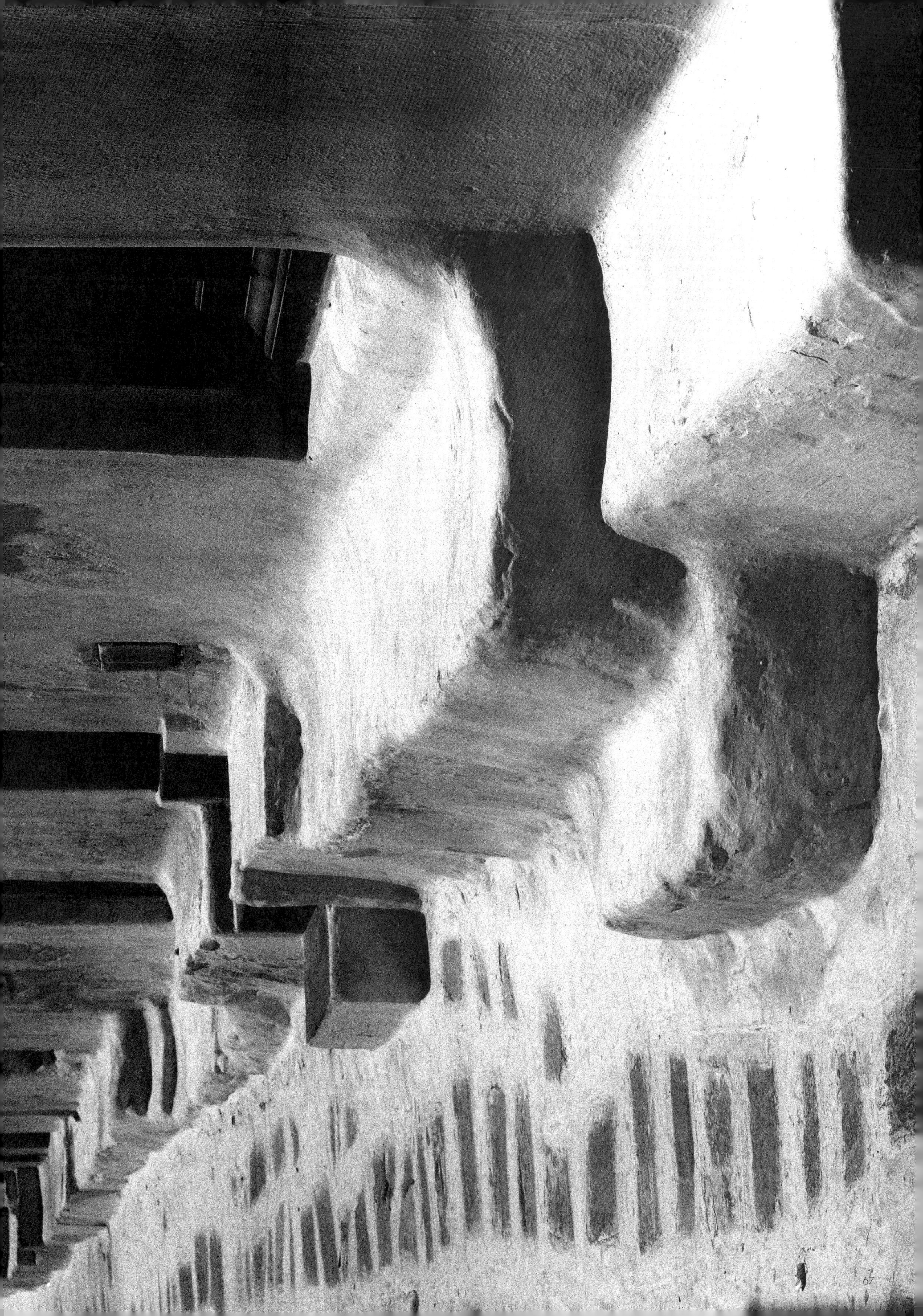

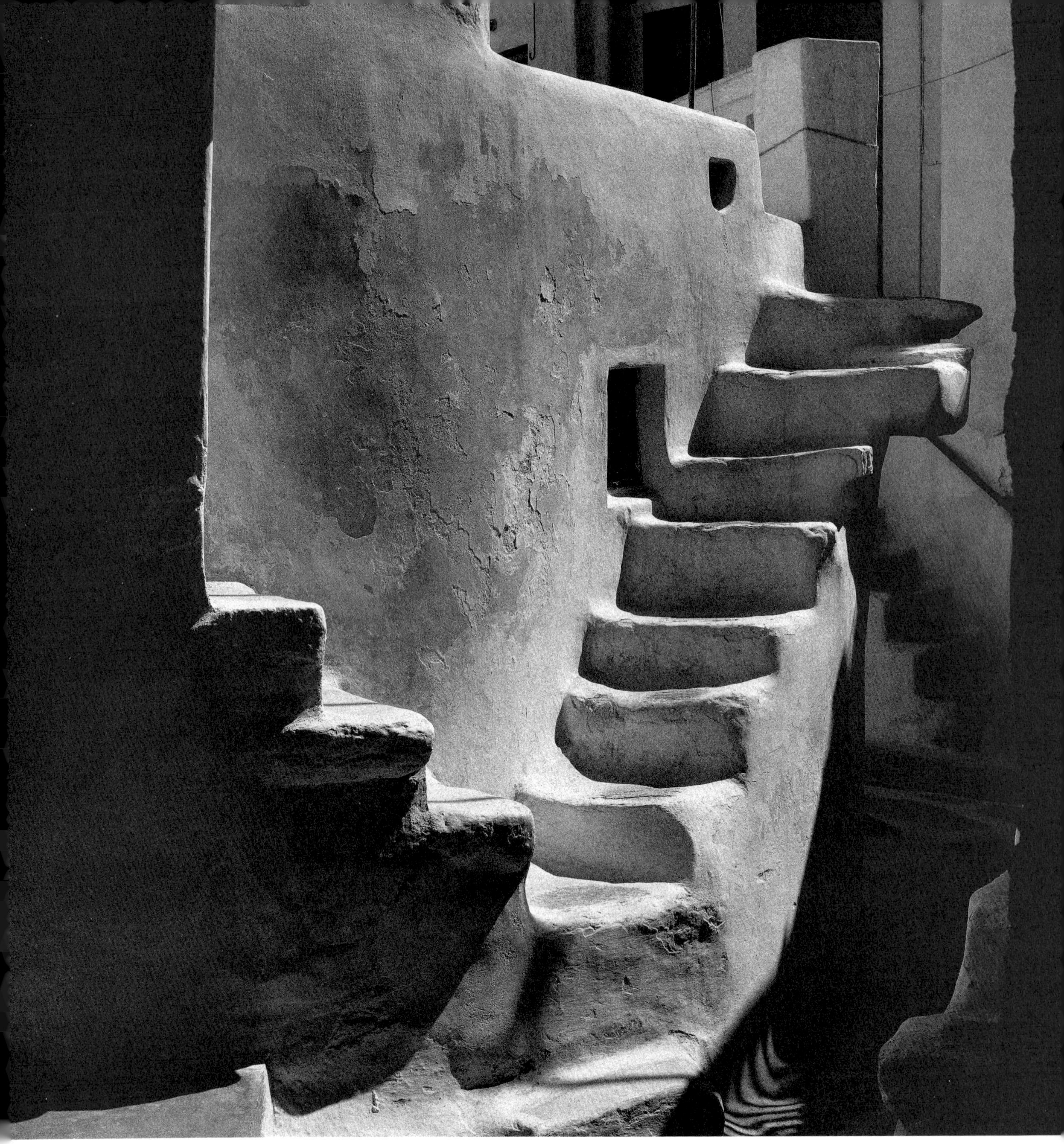

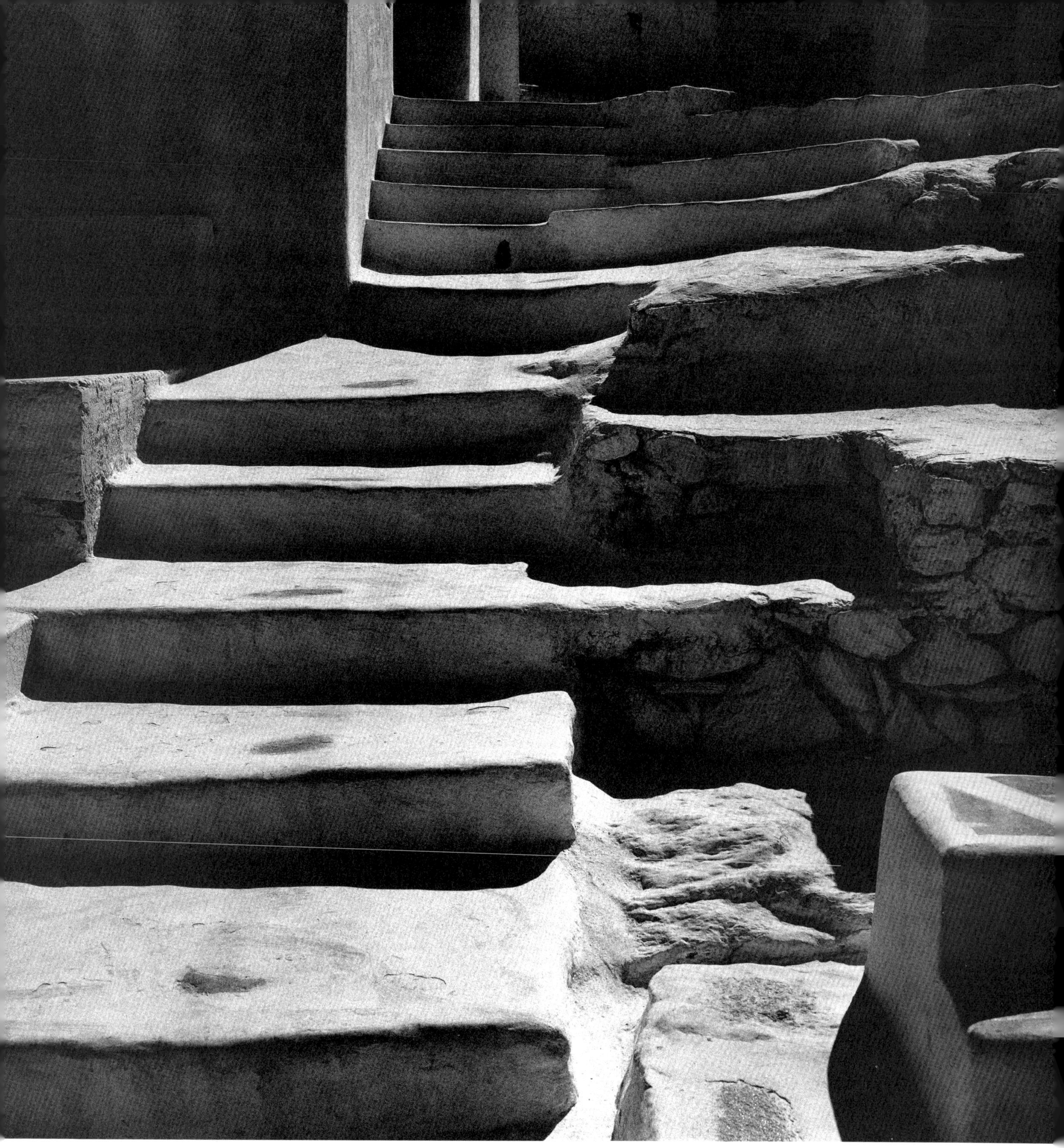

70

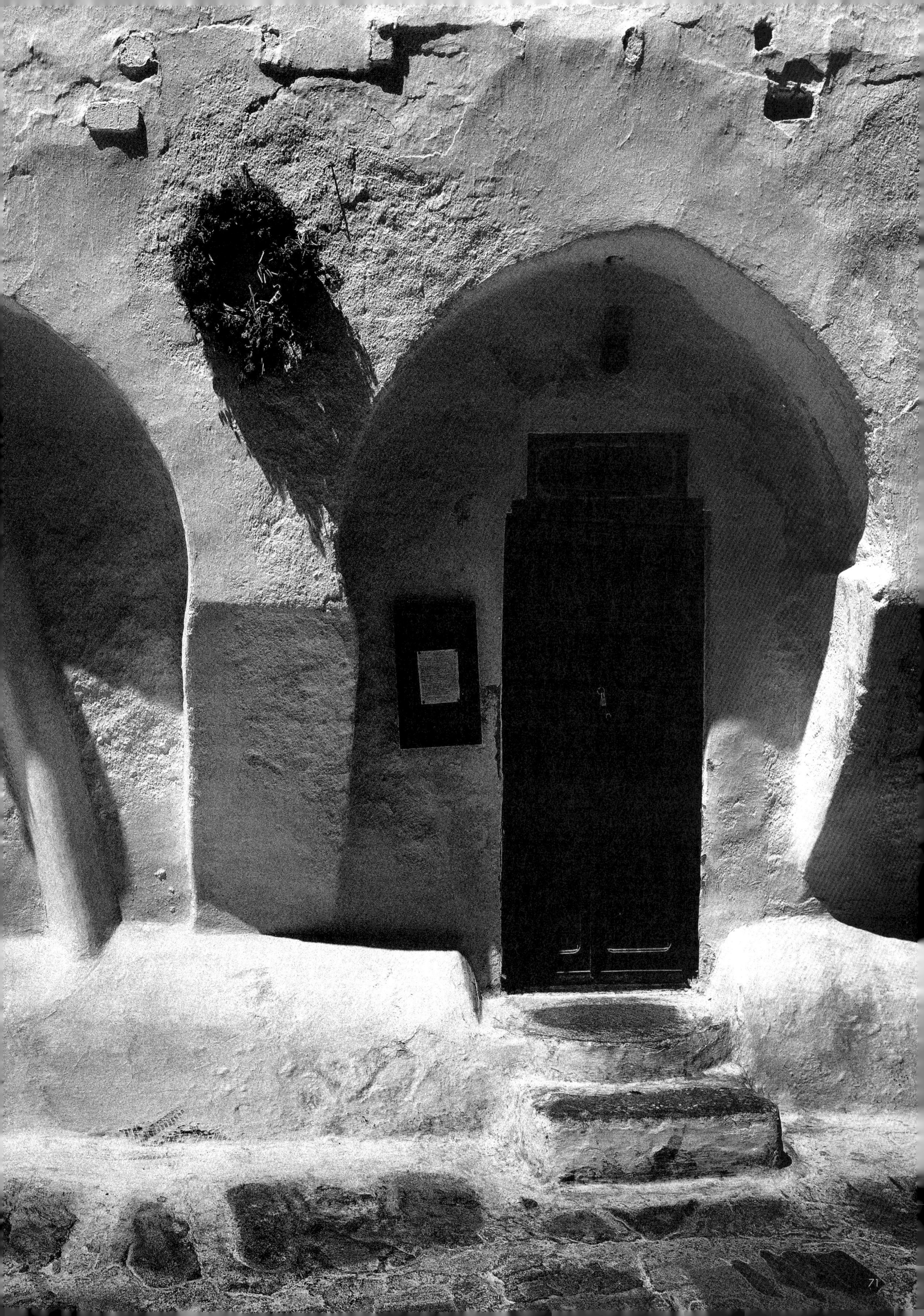

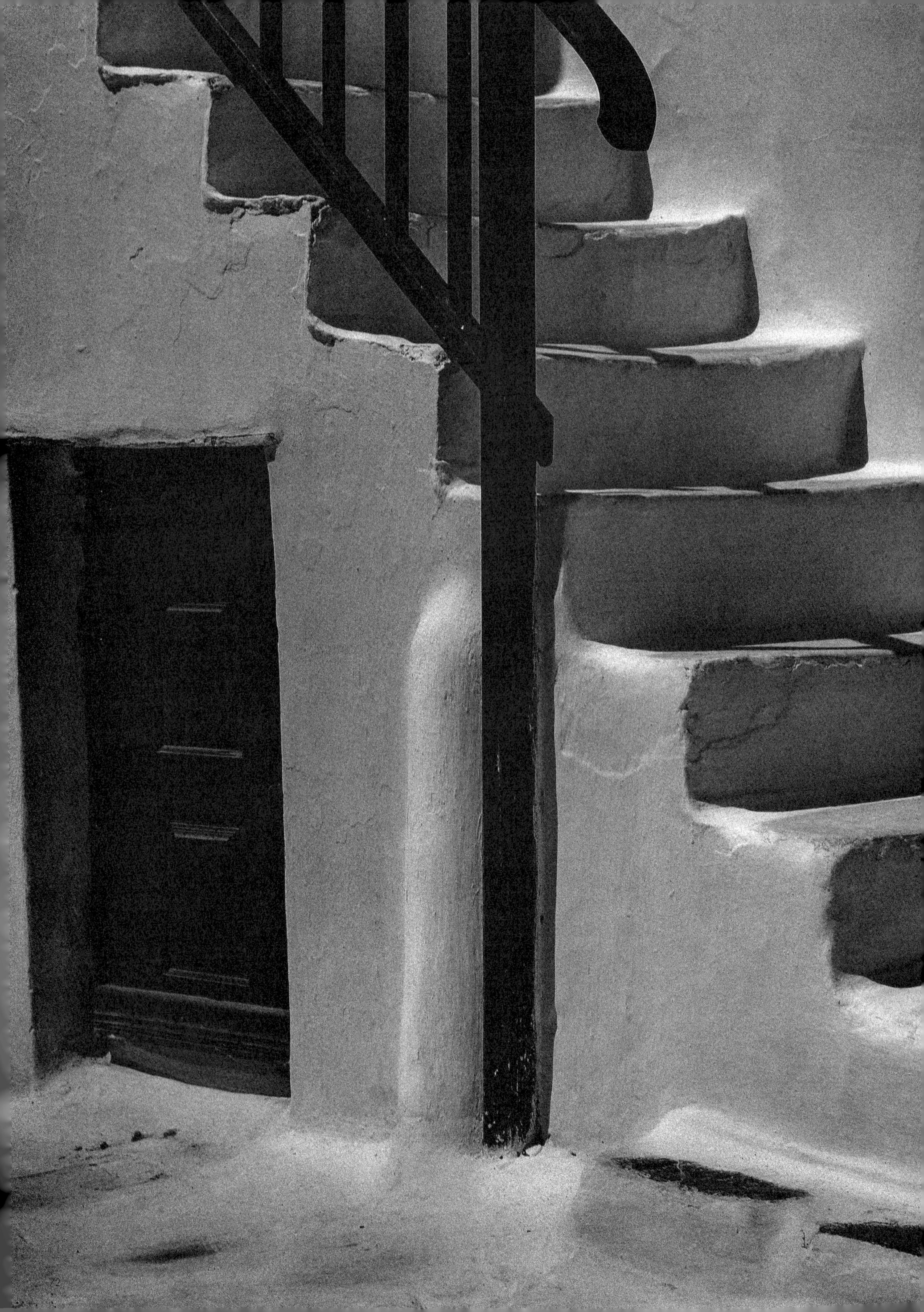

ミコノスの住居　*House in Mykonos*

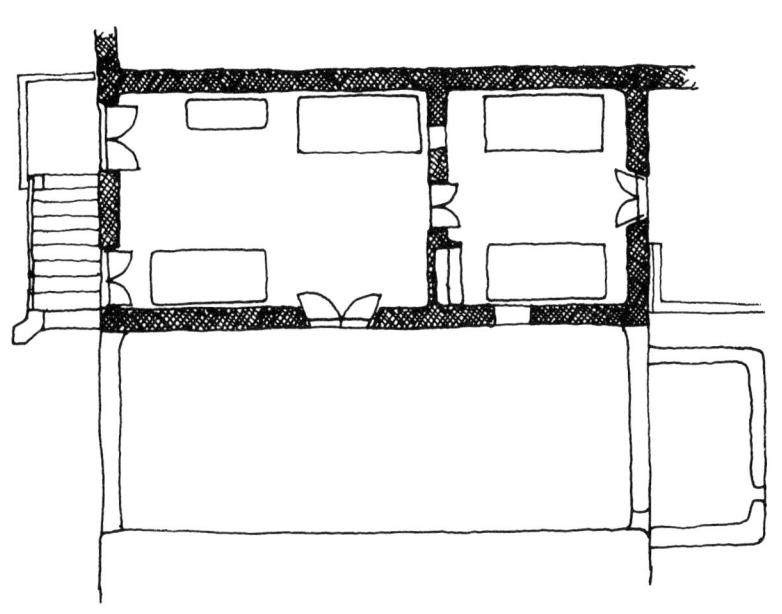

2階平面図　*Second floor plan*

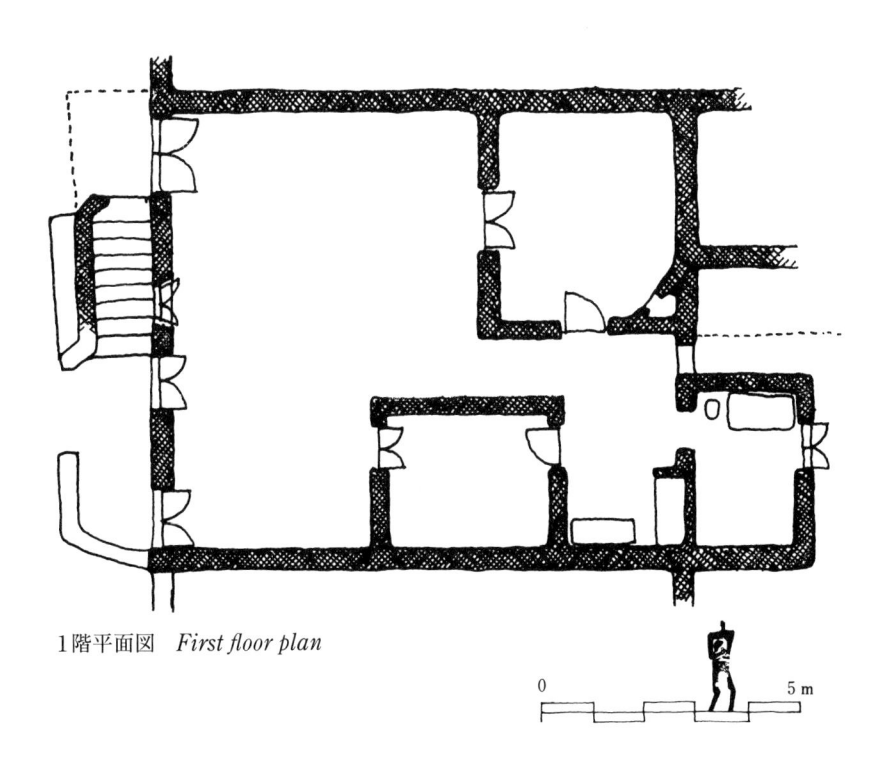

1階平面図　*First floor plan*

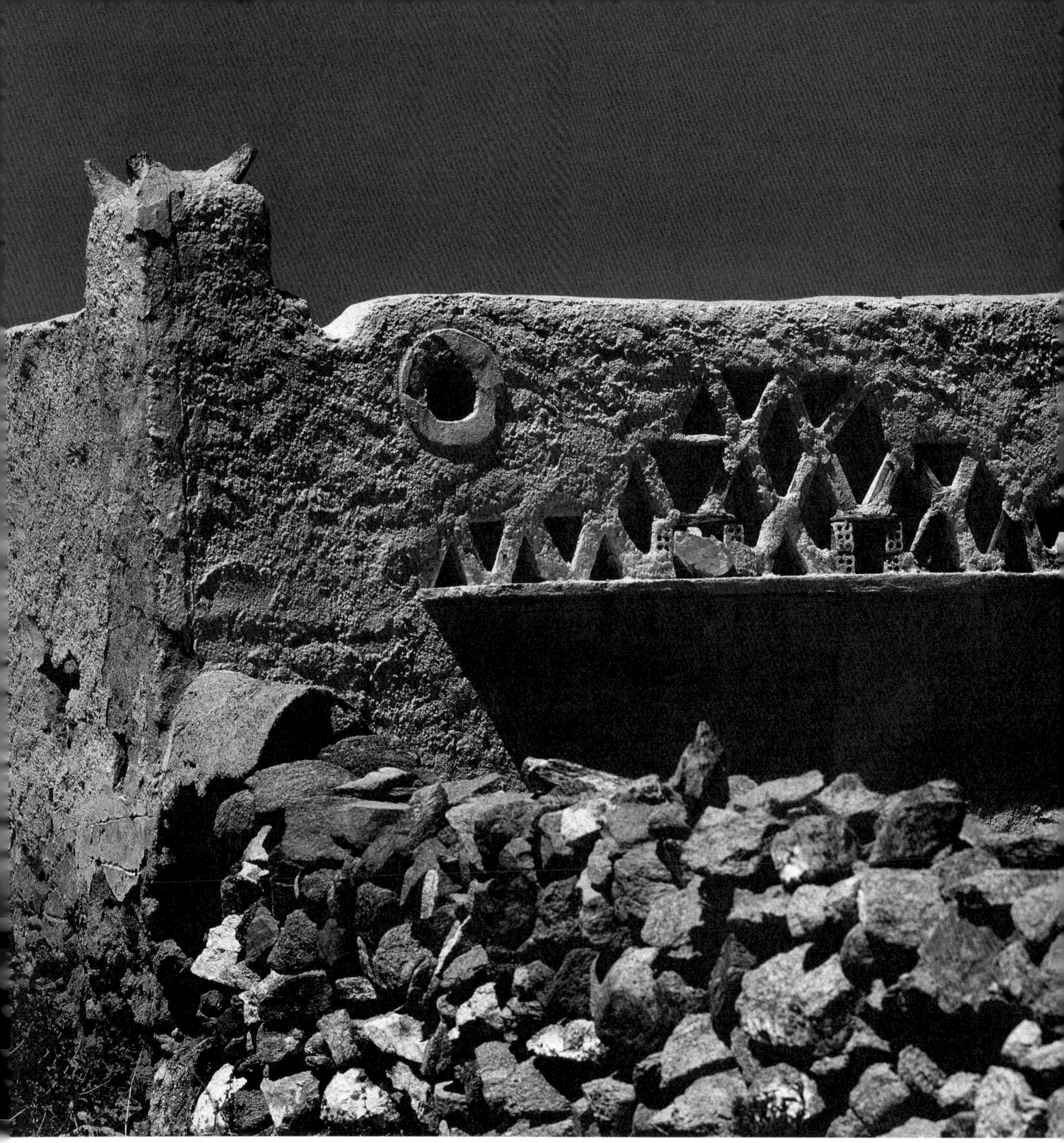

75

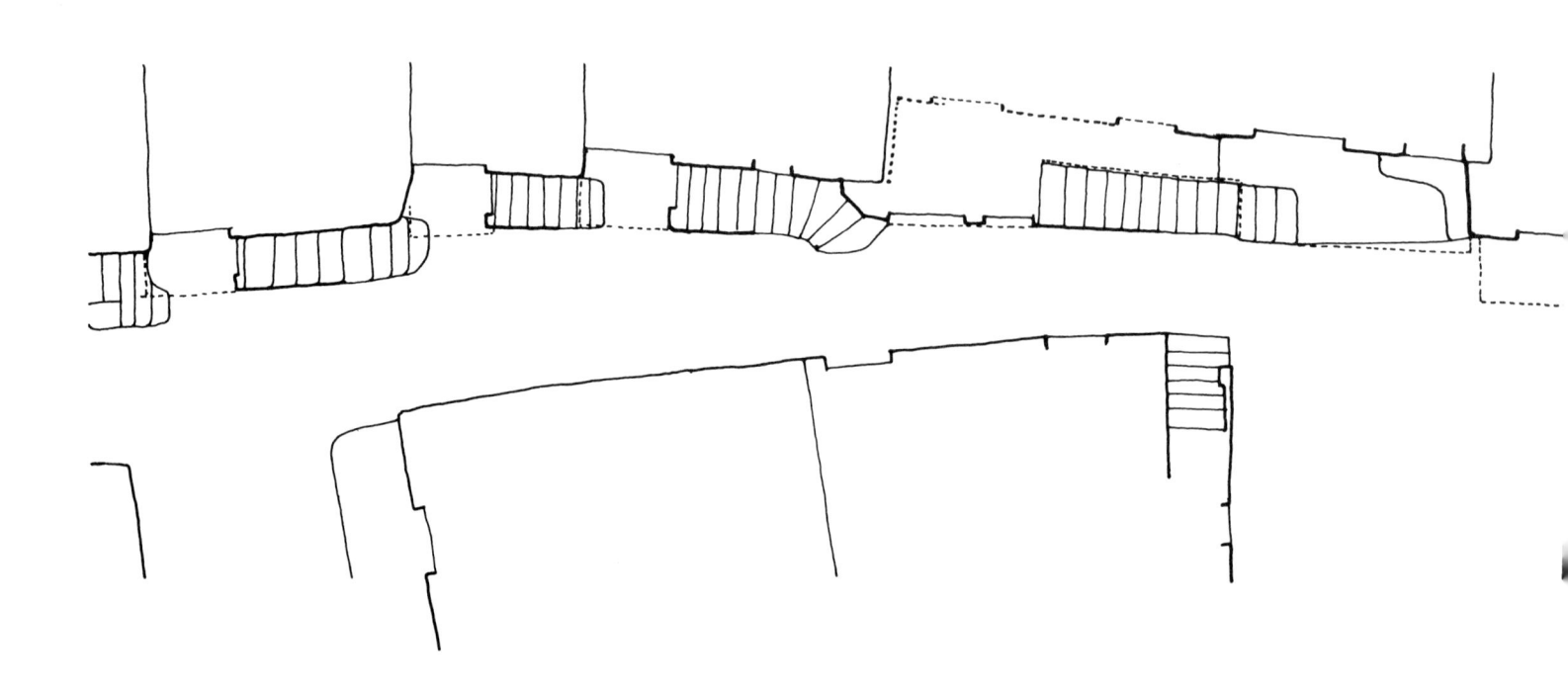

ミコノスの街路立面及び平面図　*Elevation and plan of a street in Mykonos*

0   10 m

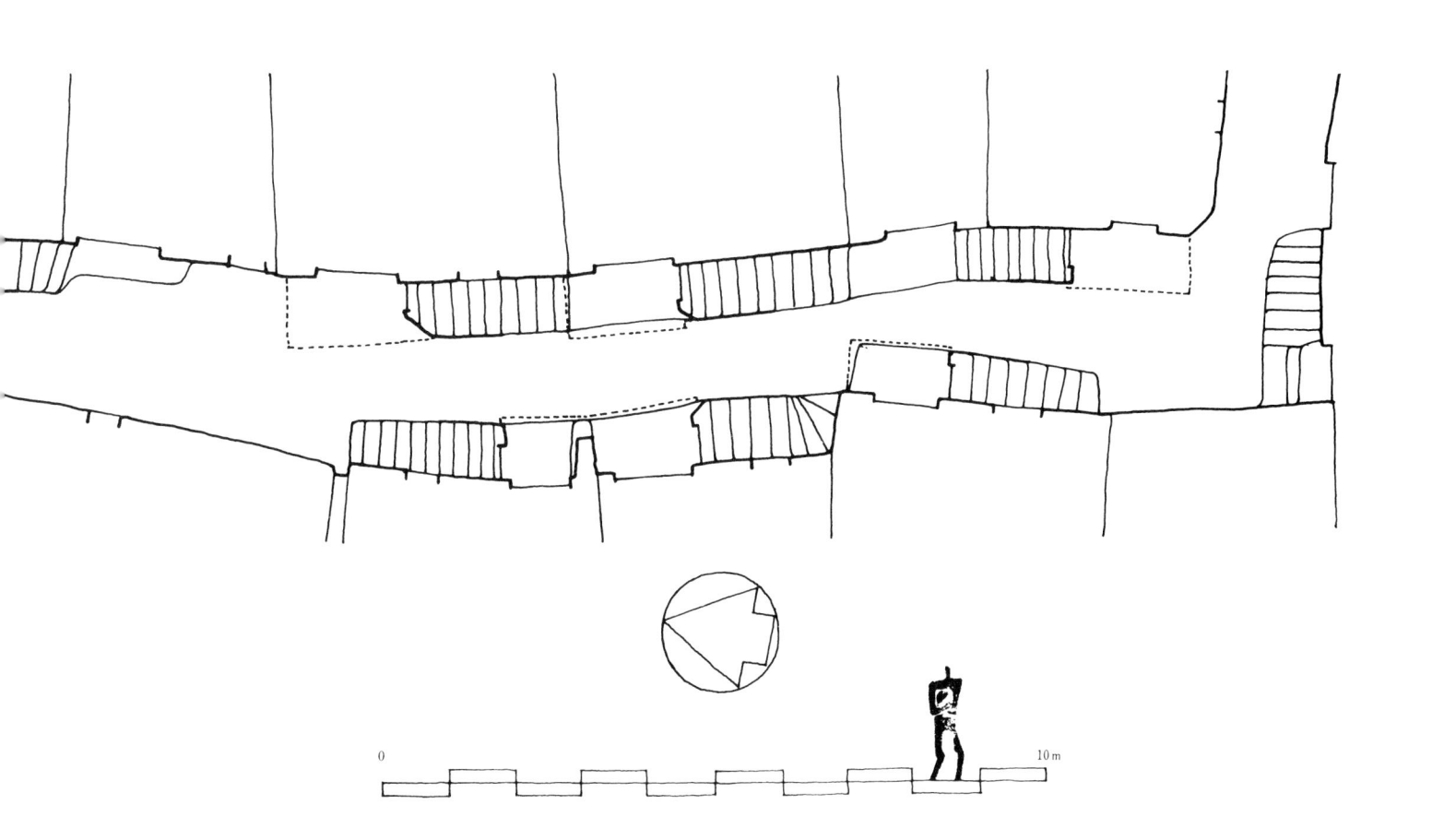

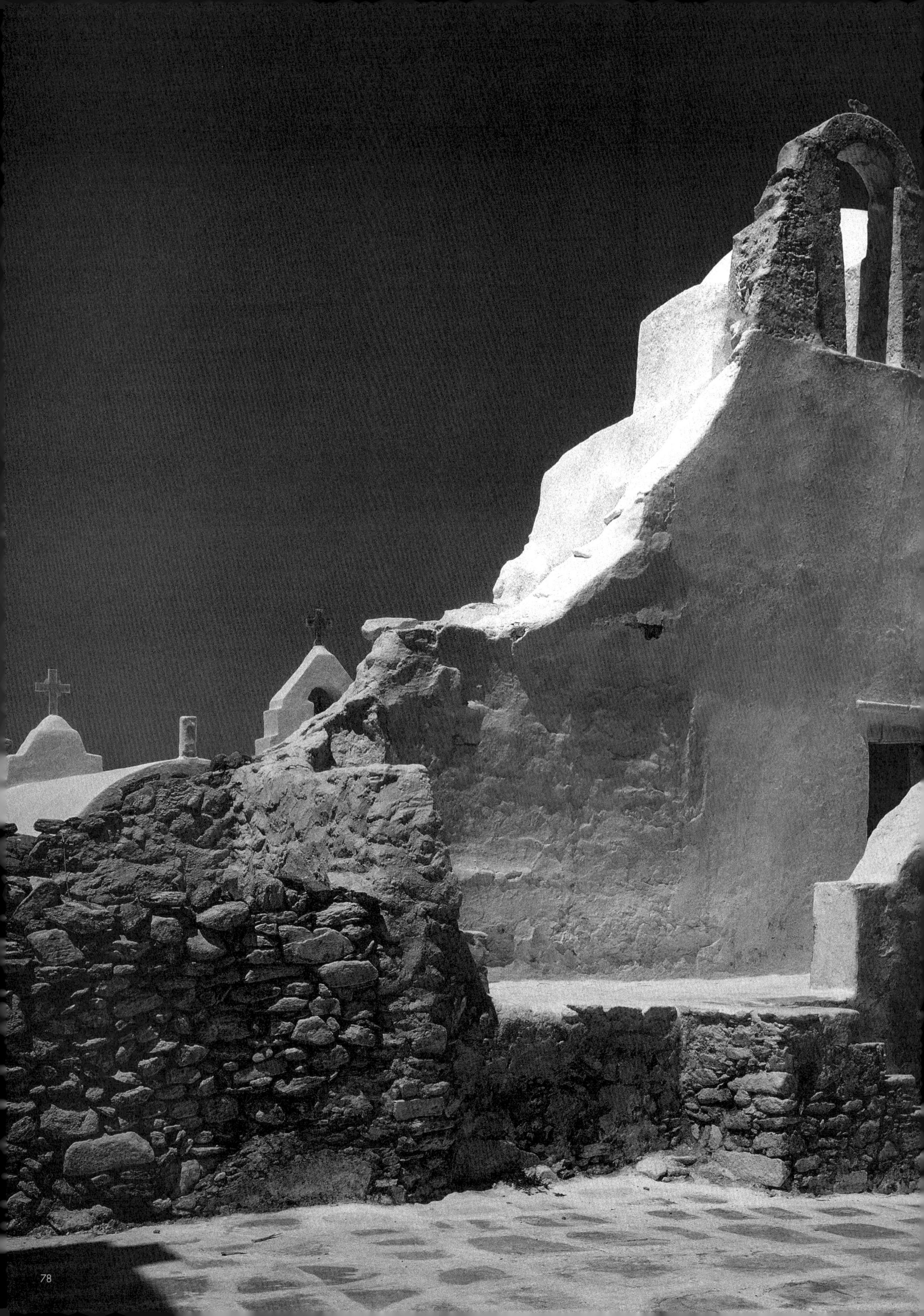

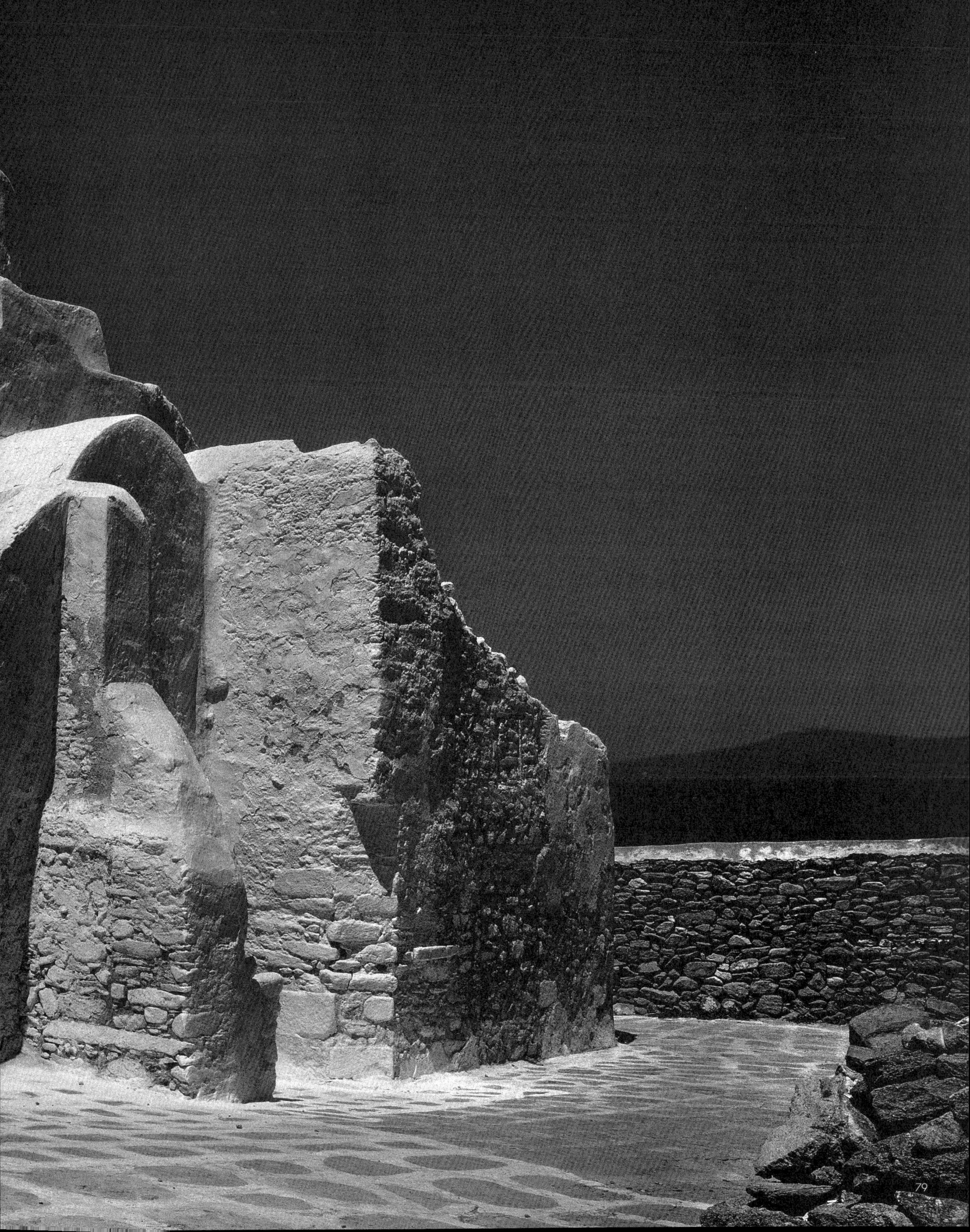

第2章〈サントリーニ島〉
SANTORINI

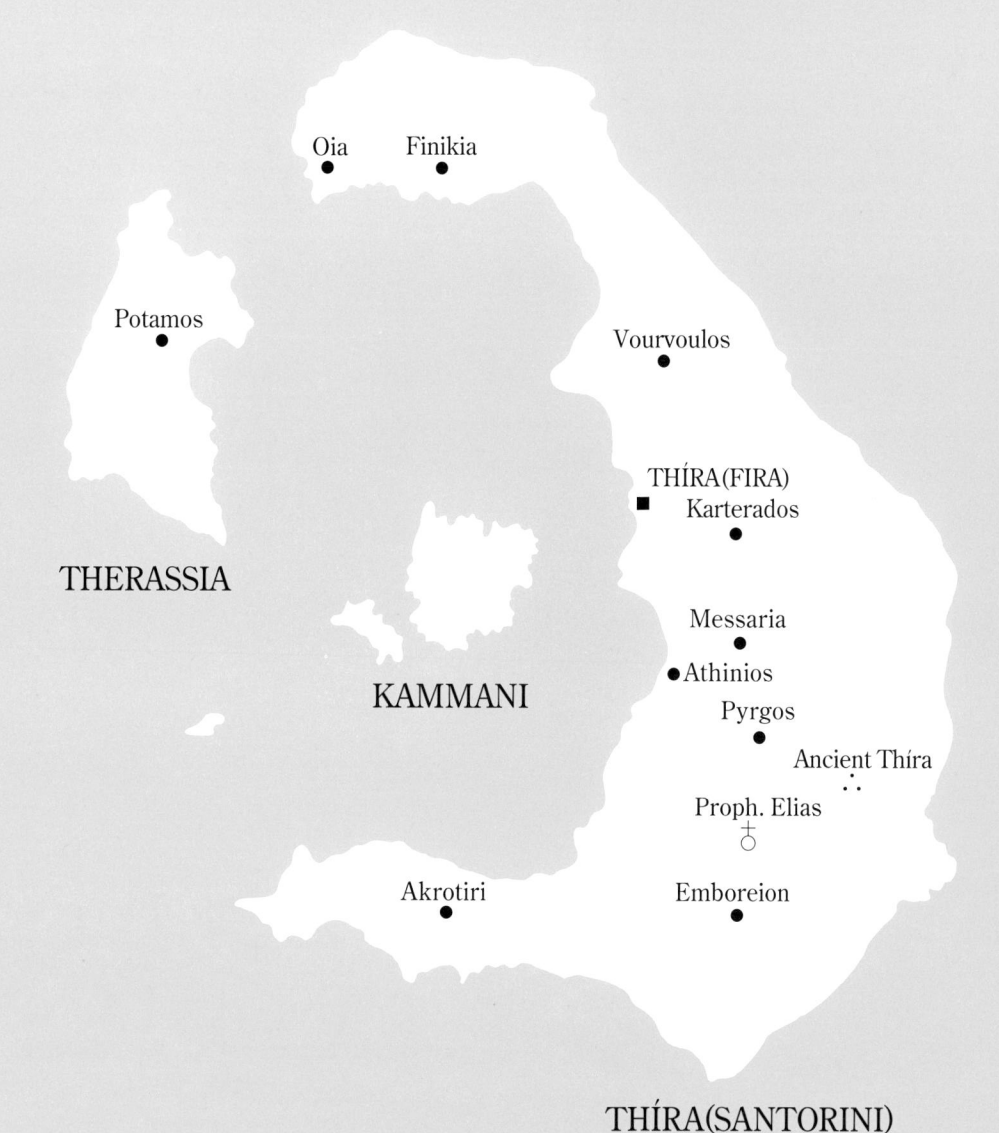

- Oia
- Finikia
- Potamos
- Vourvoulos
- THÍRA (FIRA)
- Karterados
- Messaria
- Athinios
- Pyrgos
- Ancient Thíra
- Proph. Elias
- Akrotiri
- Emboreion

THERASSIA

KAMMANI

THÍRA (SANTORINI)

サントリーニ —— 鈴木恂
Santorini *by Makoto Suzuki*

島の地殻は，フィラやオィアという，その島の山上にある集落の形を決めている。

　自然条件が，街や村の型に強い影響を及ぼすとき，島の社会や生活様式が，自然条件に沿うように組みかえられることを意味する。サントリーニは，キクラデス諸島中で最もその条件が徹底している島であり，その自然と生活は，常に極度な緊張関係をとりつづけてきたといってよい。

　この島の爆発と地震の歴史を，われわれがいま正確に辿ることはできないが，それらの自然変動が，断続的に，決定的に島そのもののかたちを変えていったことをその現場に立って見取ることができるだろう。

　われわれにとって，基本的に不動である大地が，ここでは天空に吹き消え，海底に崩れ落ちる消滅する大地としてあるのだ。考えてみると，街や村は自然を切り，それを抑えるところに開かれることが多い。しかしサントリーニのように根底的な自然条件に関わるときのみ，街は自然に沿い，それに従う，という数少ない例が生まれるのではないか。この島は，基本的にのどかではない景観をもっているのである。

紀元前1500年頃まで，この島は円形の島と呼ばれていた。プレ・ヘレニズムの時代を通してキクラデス文化に強い影響をもちつづけ，また特にミノア文明の重要な，あるときは3万人におよぶ人口をもった大都市があったと信じられている。島の大部分が噴火で消滅し，残る遺跡から全体を推理しなければならないにしても，天空に消えたアトランティスを説える人さえ居るほどなのだ。いずれにせよ，サントリーニは現在と全く違う形をした島であり，高度な文明がある期間続いたというのは事実らしい。

　知られている最も古い爆発は，このBC1500年まで遡る。この大爆発で，円い島は中央部を失い，三日月形になり，それ以後の爆発の繰返しを経て，そそり立つカルデラの円弧だけが海上に残ったといわれる。それでもなお，この島は常に活動を止むことなく，最近では，1956年の大地震で，カルデラの内側を大きく削り落した。フィラもオィアも，集落の20％近い範囲を失った地震がそれである。

　オィアの切断面を見て，その歴史と瞬間を，ヴィジュアルに重ねた生々しい記録盤を見る思いがするだろう。その断面がわれわれにレポートしていることは，自然に従って生活しつづけた

The island's earth crust defines the shapes of the hilltop settlements of the island, namely Fira and Oia.

　Natural conditions exerting powerful influences on the forms of towns and villages indicate that society and lifestyle on the island is subject to constant restructuring to suit the elements. Santorini is the best example in all the Cyclades, where nature and life have always been keeping a relationship of extreme tension.

　It is impossible for us to accurately trace back the island's history of eruptions and earthquakes. Nevertheless, we can still take in the consequences of nature changing the form of the island itself intermittently and critically through a visit to the actual scene.

　Here, what appears to be terra firma to us is vanishing earth that blows up into the sky and crumbles down to the bottom of the sea. As we come to think of it, towns and villages are often developed where nature is plowed down and controlled. But it is only in a case like Santorini where fundamental natural conditions are involved that rare examples of towns that follow and conform to nature are produced. The sceneries that this island has to offer are essentially far from idyllic.

Until around 1500 BC, it was called a circular island. All through the Pre-Hellenistic period it has exerted a significant influence on Cycladic culture. It is believed that there had been a huge, important Minoan city with a population of up to 30000 at its best. Although most of the island was lost in eruptions and we can only speculate on the entire picture from the remains, some people even claim its connection to Atlantis that vanished into thin air. In any case, it appears to be true that in the past Santorini had used to be entirely different in shape and that an advanced civilization had flourished there for a certain length of time.

　The most ancient eruption known to this day dates back to this 1500 BC. A huge explosion blew off the center part of the round island, making it crescent-shaped. It is said that after a series of subsequent eruptions only the arc of a towering caldera was left above the sea. Today, volcanic activities never ceases to shake this island: recently in 1956 a major earthquake scraped off a large portion of the inside of the caldera, to which both Fira and Oia lost nearly 20% of their land.

　Looking at the escarpment of Oia, one would feel like watching a visual, vivid recording of the moment and its

彼等の空間のメモリィなのだ。同時にそれが示す意味は村の荘厳であり、悲哀であり、村の時間のすべてではないか。

しかしながら、私には何故そこに村を繰り返しつくるのか解らない。崩れた住居の群の上に、何をおいてもまず、新しい生活の場を築こうとする姿を、われわれは真に理解することはできない。何故、人々はこの危険な断面にしがみついて生きようとするのか。いま崩れた村の暗い口をあけた廃墟の上に、同じ村の家を同じ形で、何故再びつくろうとするのか、われわれに解ることは無理なのだろうか。この答は理屈ではなく、不合理な範疇のことなのかも知れない。だから、そこに住むことは彼等の意図ではないのではないか、自然が村に与えた呪縛ではないのか、オィアの切断面の前で、われわれは、このように感動し、戸惑うのである。

西の海からこの島に近づくものにとって、長さ30kmにわたって円弧を描く300mに近い絶壁は圧倒的な景色である。近づくにしたがってその壁が、紫やピンク、茶色、そして灰色などの土が層を成しているのが識別できる。それは新鮮な切断面がもつ焼けた肉色か、削り取られた地殻の焦げた黒い縞模様である。

われわれが、一般的に感じる急勾配とは45°を越すことがないが、この壁は45°以上60°に近い勾配もあって、われわれの感覚でいう住居に不適当な勾配を遥かに上まわっている。もちろん、サントリーニを見た眼には、ミロス島もシフノスも、全く平坦な斜面に見えてくるだろう。

港はこの300mの壁の下、フィラの街の丁度真下にある。港から街まではジグザグの道をロバにまたがって登るのが一般的なようだ。街からは、まるで真下に港があり、旅行者待ちのロバの群が小さく動くのが判別できる。上から見た限りにおいて、この垂直の差は、街の防衛に有効な高さであったことが理解できるような気になるのだ。

この街も、最近になって旅行者が激増し、宿泊施設を含め大きな建築が多くなった。建物の規模がばらばらになり、強調されていた街のシルエットが変った。

フィラは、南北の陵線を境にして、西斜面と東斜面にひろがる街である。広く紹介されている部分は、もちろん西側の急斜面の街であって、東側はなだらかな傾斜で、街区をぬけると耕

history. What that cross section reveals to us is the spatial memory of those who have always lived in accordance with nature. At the same time, what it means is the glory, sorrow and all the moments and times of the village.

However, it is hard for me to see why they would build their village there again and again. We might never be able to truly understand their first and foremost urge to build a place for their new life on top of freshly collapsed houses. Why do people want to live clinging onto this danger-prone cliff? Will it be impossible for us to know why they would want to rebuild their houses of the same village in the same form on the ruins that opens a dark mouth in the crumbled village? The reason might be in the realm of the irrational, beyond any reason. So we cannot help being puzzled and deeply moved as we stand in front of the escarpment of Oia, wondering if living there might be against their will, a spell that nature cast on the village.

To those who approach this island from the western sea, the nearly 300 m-high cliff drawing an arc for as long as 30 km presents an overwhelming sight. Drawing closer to the sheer wall, one can identify the layers of purple, pink, brown and grey soil that make up the color of grilled meat of a fresh scarp or the black striped pattern of scraped, burnt crust.

Generally, our experience of a steep incline never exceeds 45 degrees, but this wall features gradients of over 45 degrees up to nearly 60, far beyond the figure deemed inappropriate for living in our sense. Needless to say, to the eyes that have seen Santorini, both Milos and Sifnos will appear as completely flat slopes.

The harbor is located at the foot of the 300 m-high wall, just below the town of Fira. People usually climb the zigzag road from the harbor up to the town on donkey-back. Looking down from the town, one can see the harbor right below and recognize tiny figures of donkeys moving around as they wait for tourists. From up the cliff, this vertical difference makes one feel capable of understanding how the height has been effective for the defense of the town.

Lately, as with other islands, this town experienced a sharp increase of tourists, and has a growing number of large buildings including accommodation facilities. Different scales of building are now mixed, resulting in the change in the emphasized silhouette of the town.

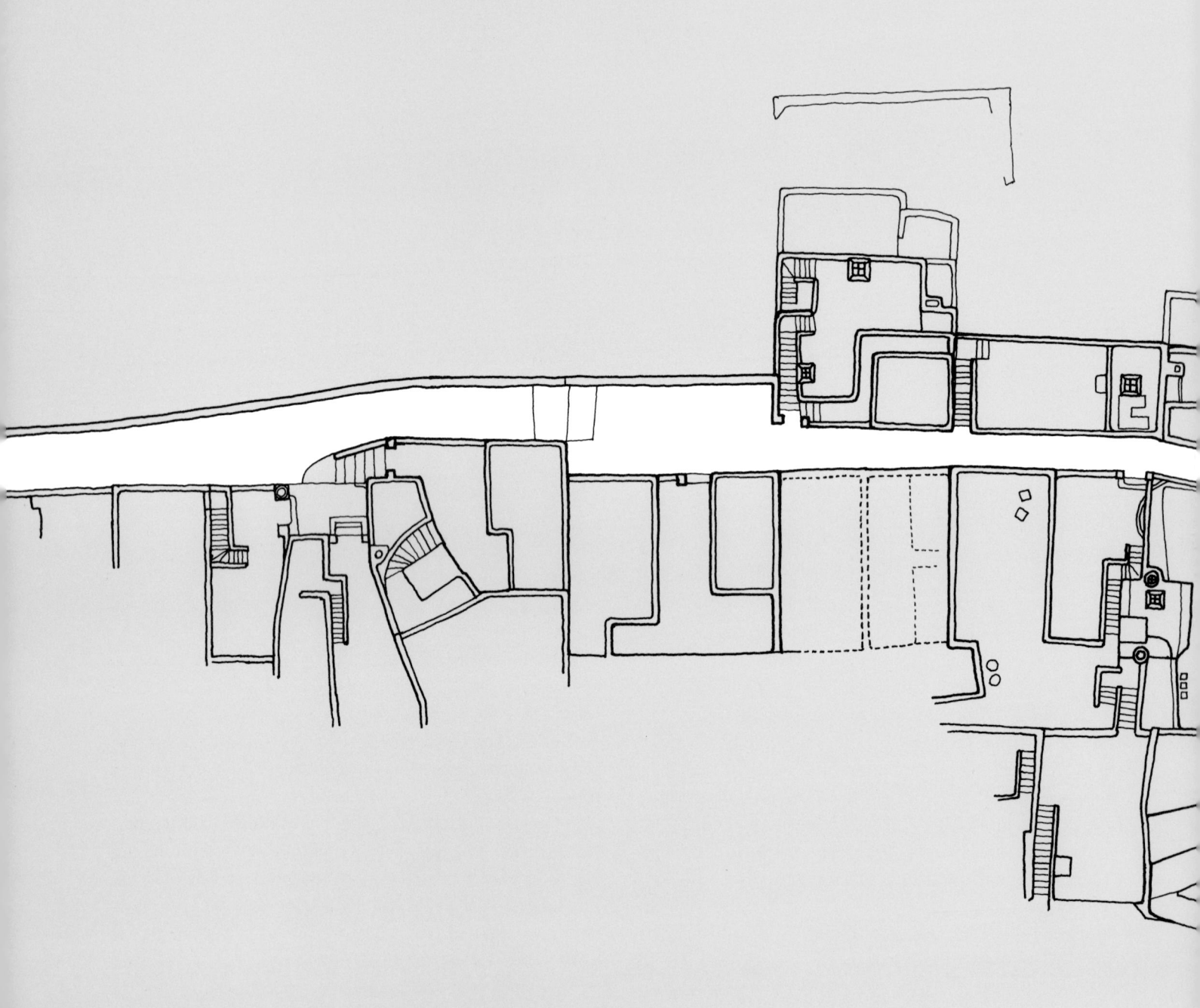

サントリーニの街路と住居群（部分）　Street and cluster of houses in Santorini (partial)

0　　　　　10m

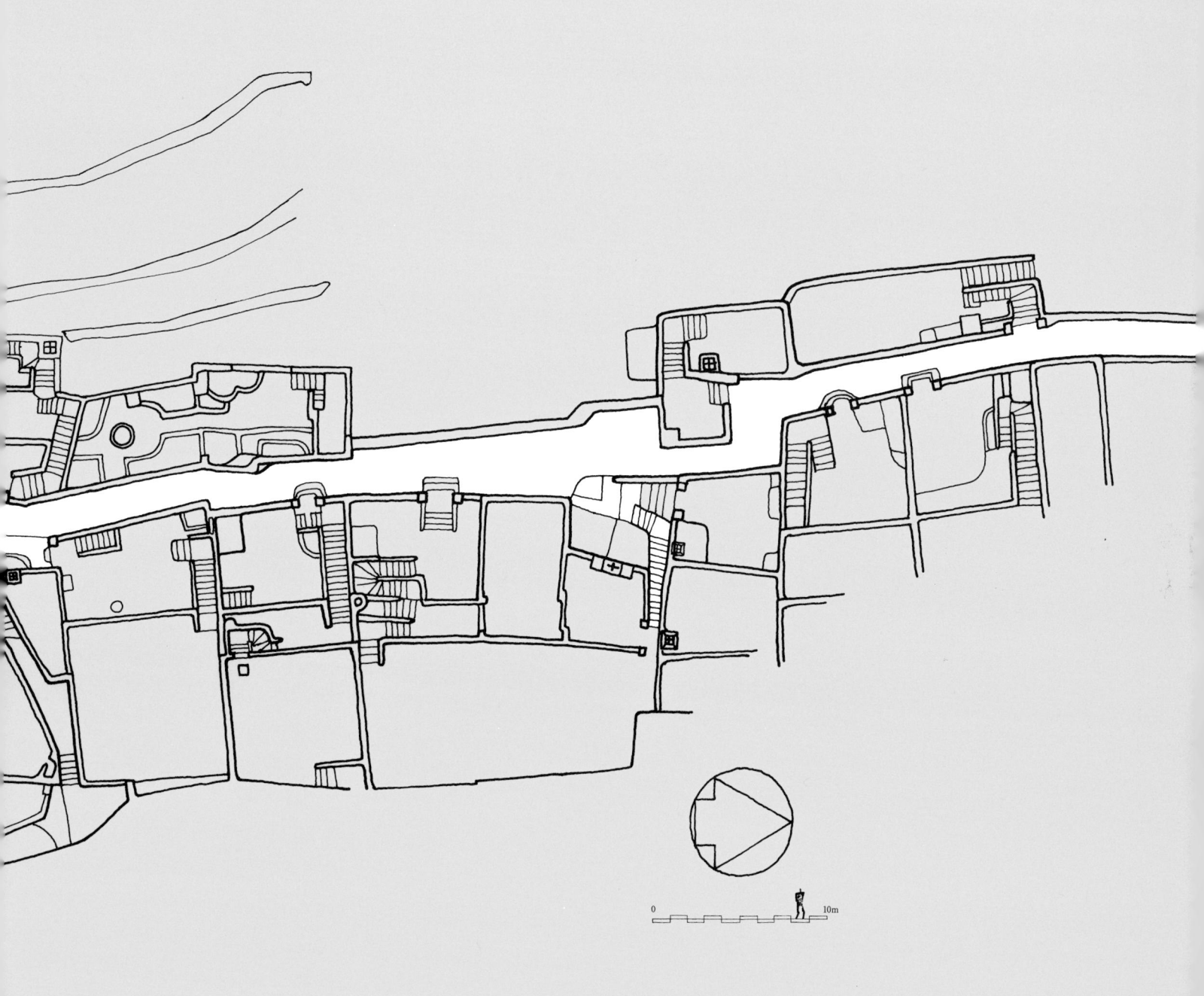

されand畑や葡萄畑が続き西側と全く異なった風景をもっている。

　西側にある街区は，東側にあるものに比較して旧い。しかし，実際に完全に近い形で残っている範囲は限られてくる。その範囲とは，現在の街の最も西側の低部，すなわち断崖に沿っている部分である。これは，その下の部分は崩れてしまい，またそれより上の街区は，旅行者のために造りかえられ，建て直された部分が多く，結果的に上下の変化から取り残された部分ということになる。

　ミコノスでは街が，道によって区切られた，不定形の住居グループによって形成された。住居は道を個化することでグループとなり，グループは，道を一体化することで，より大きな集合体になって，街全体がつくられた。サントリーニでも，特に西側にある街に限っていえば，それに近い関係の仕組みで個と全体が結びついていると云える。しかし，それら単位やコンポーネントといえるものを結ぶ媒体や，媒介する空間には差違がある。

　西斜面の街区は，立体的，断面的に，すでに重なり合い，堆積し合うことで，一体のものである。しかし平面的には，住居は各単位で完結したプランをもち，それほど緊密な相互の関係にはない。

　各家のパティオやテラスは，上に住む人々からはもちろん，上部の道を歩く人から，よく見えるが，この視界とは逆に，個人の領域として使用されている場合が多い。

　テラスやパティオをもつために，道は道として比較的厳密に区分されることになる。道の横断面を見ると，道の下が住居である場合が多いのであるが，平面上は明確に領域が別けられて使われていることに気付く。道がある程度住居を繋ぐものとして独立し，機能として単純化されてしまったのは，急勾配に対処する街路の取り方によるだろう。

　街路は垂直か水平か，つまり高低を繋ぐ階段やランプか，等高に沿った起伏のない道かに，はっきりと別けられる。階段やランプは大小種々のバラエティがあり，幹線になるものは別として，小型の階段は自由自在に，テラスを伝い，住居の間隙をぬって上下するフレキシビリティをもっている。しかし一方，水平方向の道は，通し方の難しさもあって，直線的であり，西側斜面で1，2の通路があるにとどまる。このことは，水平の道が常にメインの道として区別されることを意味するだろう。

Fira is a town that expands on both sides of a ridge line running north to south. The most famous being the area along the steep slope on the west, the eastern side is a gentle slope with a landscape that is totally different from the east featuring stretches of cultivated fields and vineyards beyond the town blocks.

The town blocks on the west are older than those on the east, though only a few still retains the original form, which are found toward the bottom of the western edge of the town, along the face of the cliff. In other words, because the area below has collapsed and the area above heavily transformed and rebuilt to cater to tourists, it was consequently left behind the changes of the areas above and below.

In Mykonos, the town was formed by irregular groups of houses divided by streets, and made up of houses that formed a group by privatizing a street and groups that gathered to form a larger ensemble by integrating the streets. In Santorini, a similar mechanism of relationships connects the individual with the whole, but that especially limited to the town on the west side. However, differences are found in the mediating spaces and elements that link such units and components.

Town blocks on the western slope are integrated through overlapping and accumulation in terms of three-dimensional and sectional aspects. But in terms of planar aspect, each unit of house has a self-sufficient plan and does not take part in such tightly-knit correlations.

The patio and terrace of a house is clearly visible from the upper-floor residents as well as from people walking the streets above, and yet contrary to such views, they are often used as individual private zones.

To allow houses to have terraces and patios, the streets come to be categorized as streets in a fairly precise manner. When we look at the cross section of a street, although in most cases houses are found beneath the street, we realize that the use of space is clearly divided into zones in terms of plan. The reason why the streets became independent as an element to connect houses to some extent and simplified as a function is probably due to the way streets were laid out in coping with the steep inclination.

Streets can be distinctly categorized into vertical and horizontal: stairs and ramps that bridge the height differences and flat, level streets along the contour lines. Stairs and ramps come in a variety of sizes and forms, and apart

傾斜は，すべての住居を西に向ける。それが互いに視界を遮らない程度の高さ，5,6mで，段状に積み重ねられるので，開口部は，必然的に西側にとられるということなのだ。したがって，住居は水平の道に開口部やテラスやパティオで接することになり，道の性格をより際立たせる結果になっているのである。このように急斜面がもつフィジカルな力が街の構成に大きな影響を及ぼしていることが解るだろう。

　前述したオィアや隣村であるフィニキアも，こうした断崖のシステムによって住居と集合の形態がきめられているが，地形に凹凸の変化があり，道にも住居にも，もっと複雑な展開とバリエーションが見られる。部分に見る造形的な配慮も，ビザンチンの遥かな影を素朴に残したりして，フィラよりももっと古い住居形式が残っているように思われるのである。

　ミコノスは視覚的には閉ざされているが，個と総体が常に重なり合っていることで，オープンな社会といえるとすれば，サントリーニは視覚的には開いて，解明しやすいが，個と全体は，いわゆる断崖のシステムの制約を受けて並列的または閉鎖的であるといえるのではなかろうか。

from those put to arterial use, small stairs have the flexibility of running freely up and down between terraces and through the gaps of houses. On the other hand, horizontal streets are, because of the difficulty of running them in that direction, rectilinear and few—only 1 or 2 of such exist on the western slope. This fact is an indication of horizontal streets being constantly distinguished from the main roads.

The inclination directs every house to face west. Houses are stacked in tiers of 5 to 6 m high so that neither of them block the view of others, hence their apertures facing west. Consequently, a house opens to the horizontal street through its apertures, terrace and patio, emphasizing the street's character. In this manner, we can see that the physical power of a steep inclination has a major effect on the composition of the town.

In the aforementioned town of Oia as well as in the adjacent village of Finikia, a similar system of cliffs defines the configuration of houses and aggregations, with bumpy and varied topography and more complex development and variation identified in their streets and houses. With the far distant Byzantine shadow still lingering artlessly in the formative details, it appears that these places have succeeded to keep some house types that are much older than those of Fira.

Whereas Mykonos, though visually closed, can be considered an open society because of the constant overlapping of the individual and the entirety, Santorini, while visually open and easily elucidated, is reclusive where the individual and the whole still remain juxtaposed due to restrictions imposed by the system of cliffs.

サントリーニの断面スケッチ　*Section sketch of Santorini*

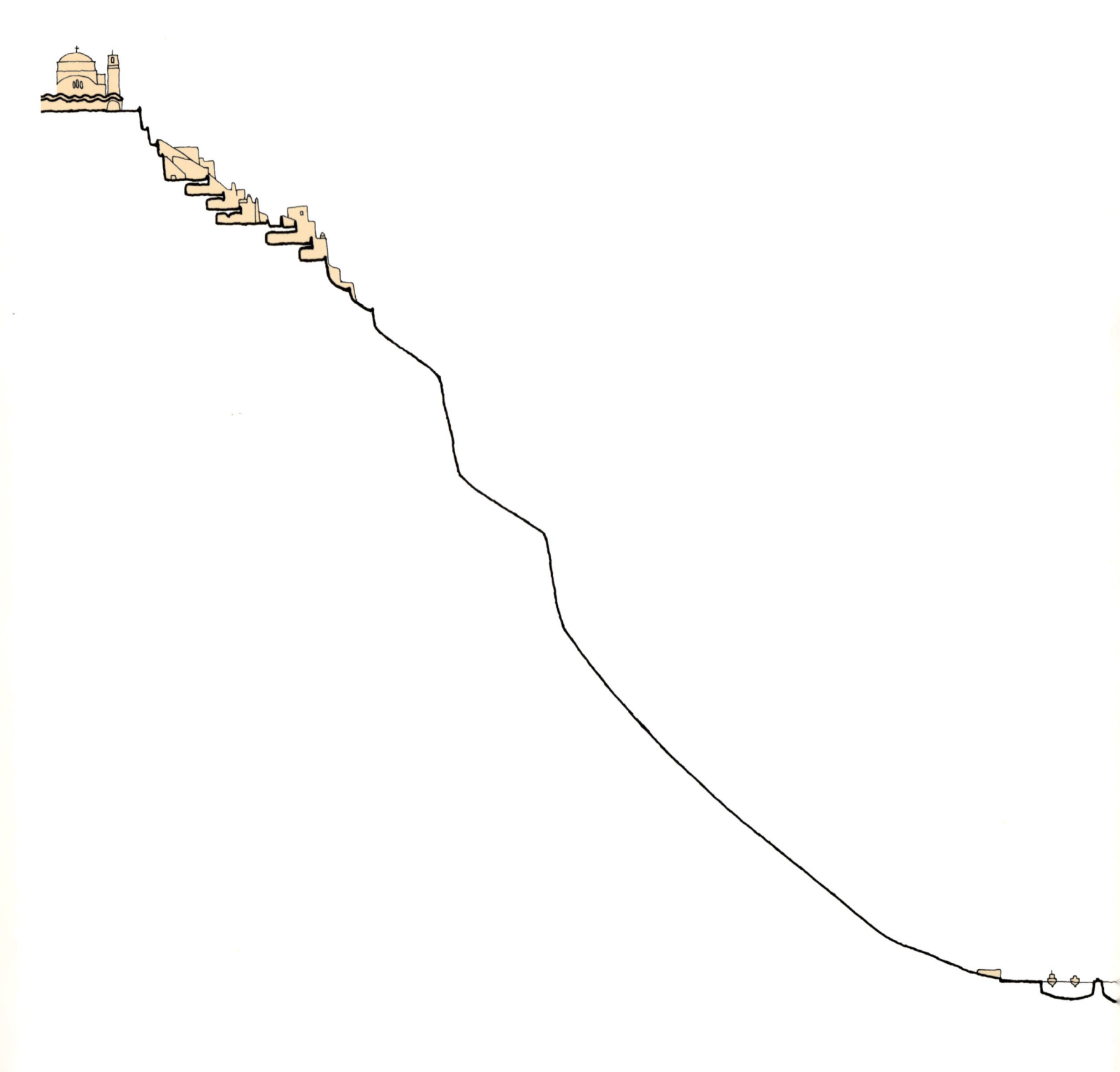

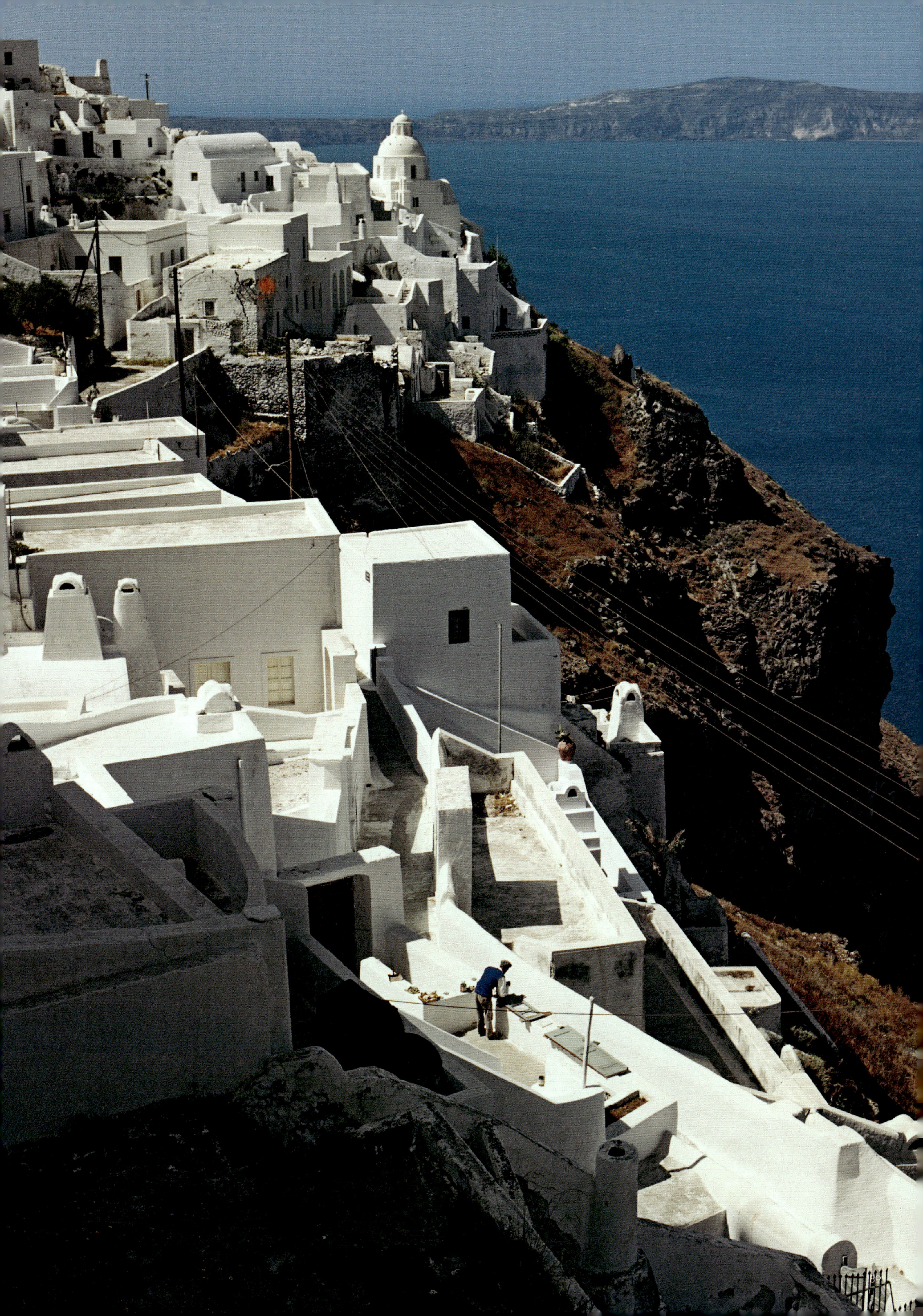

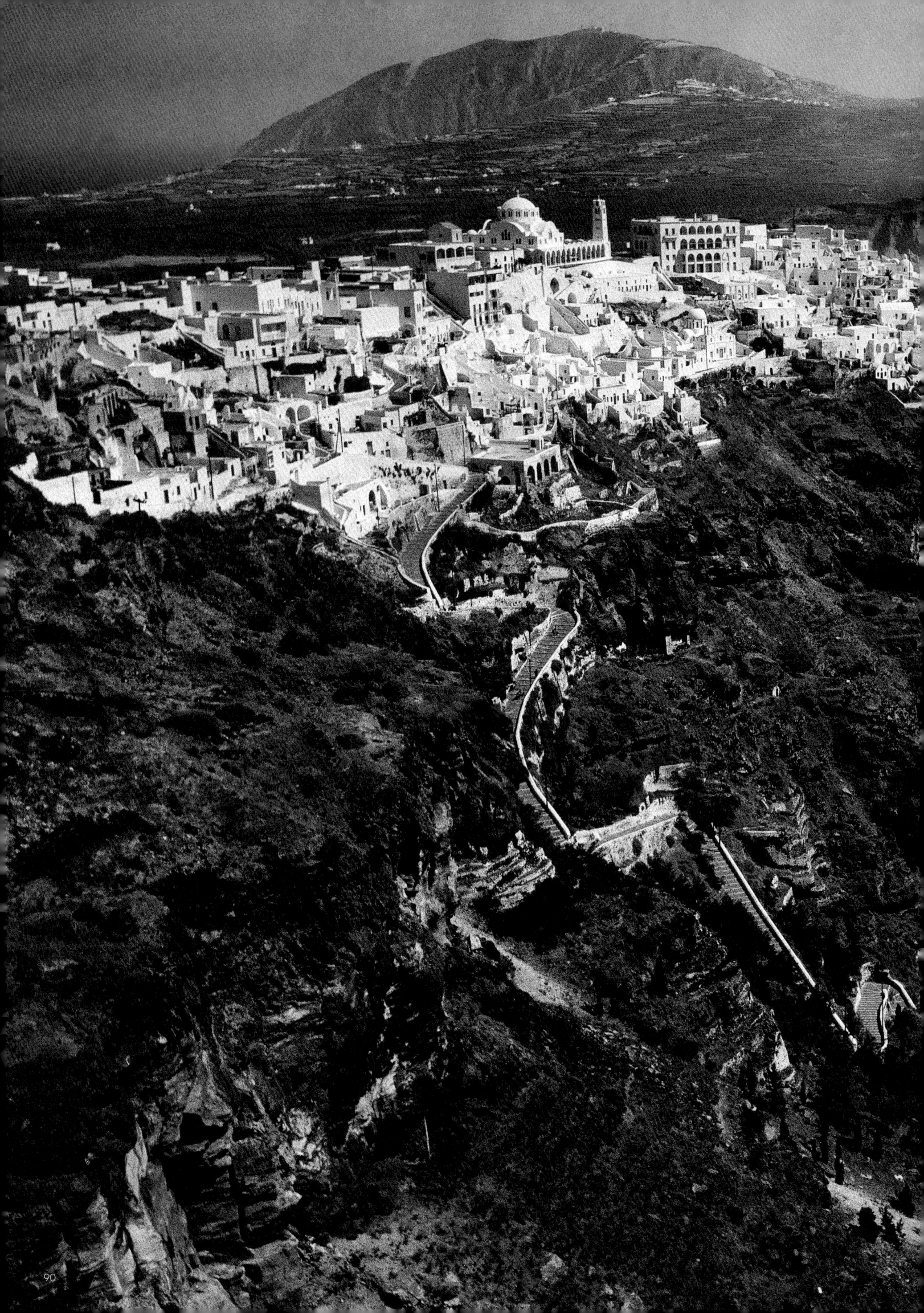

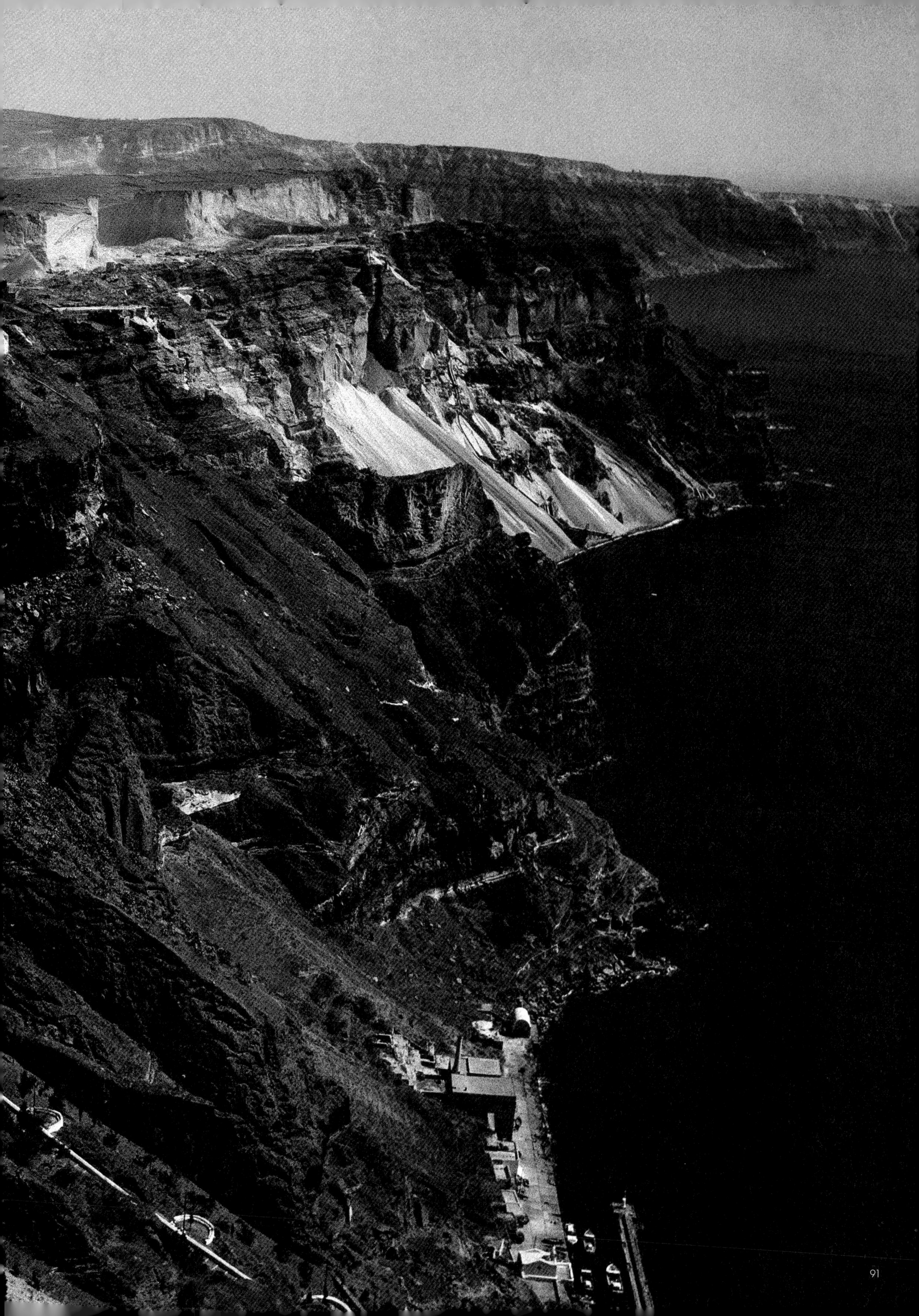

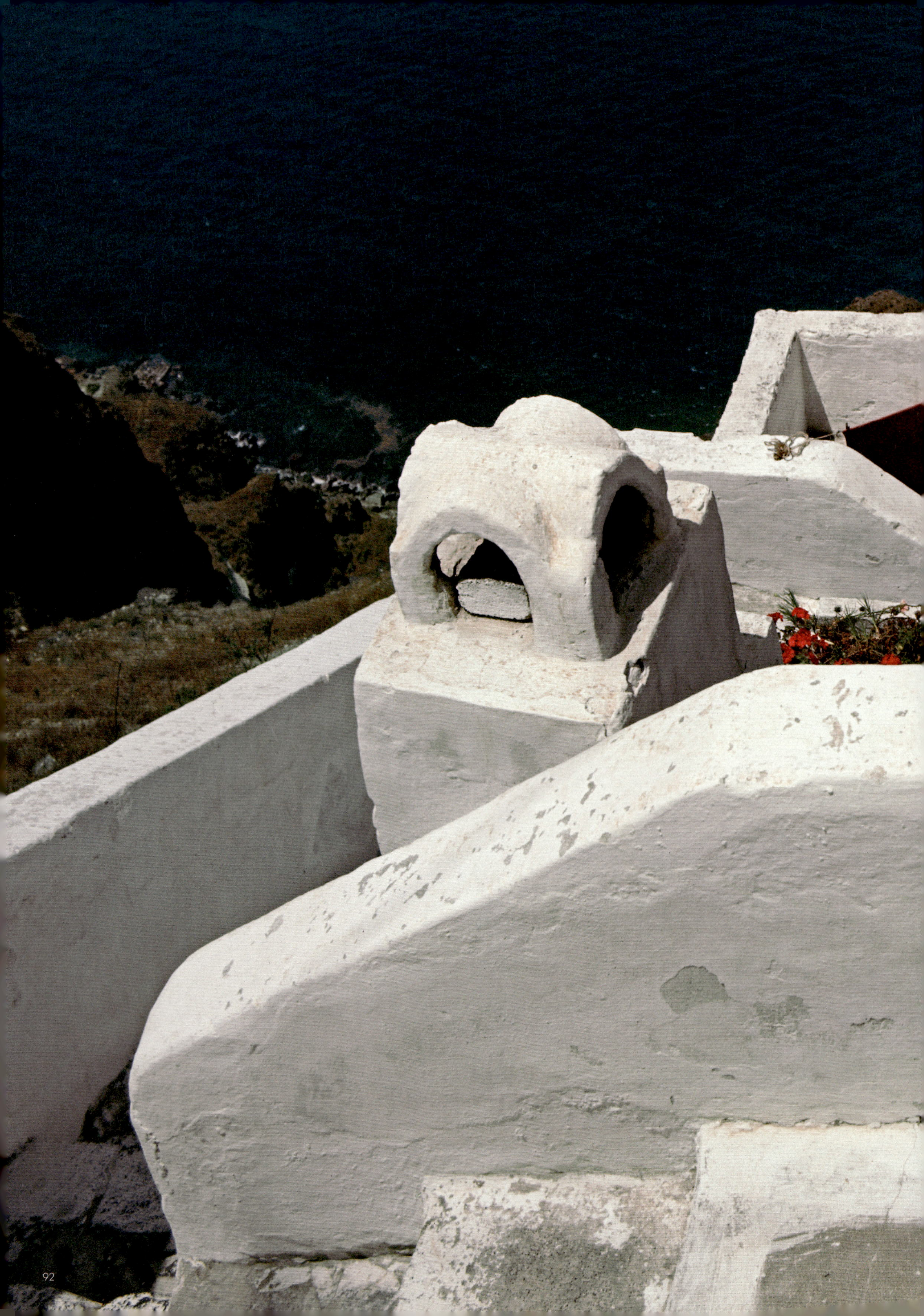

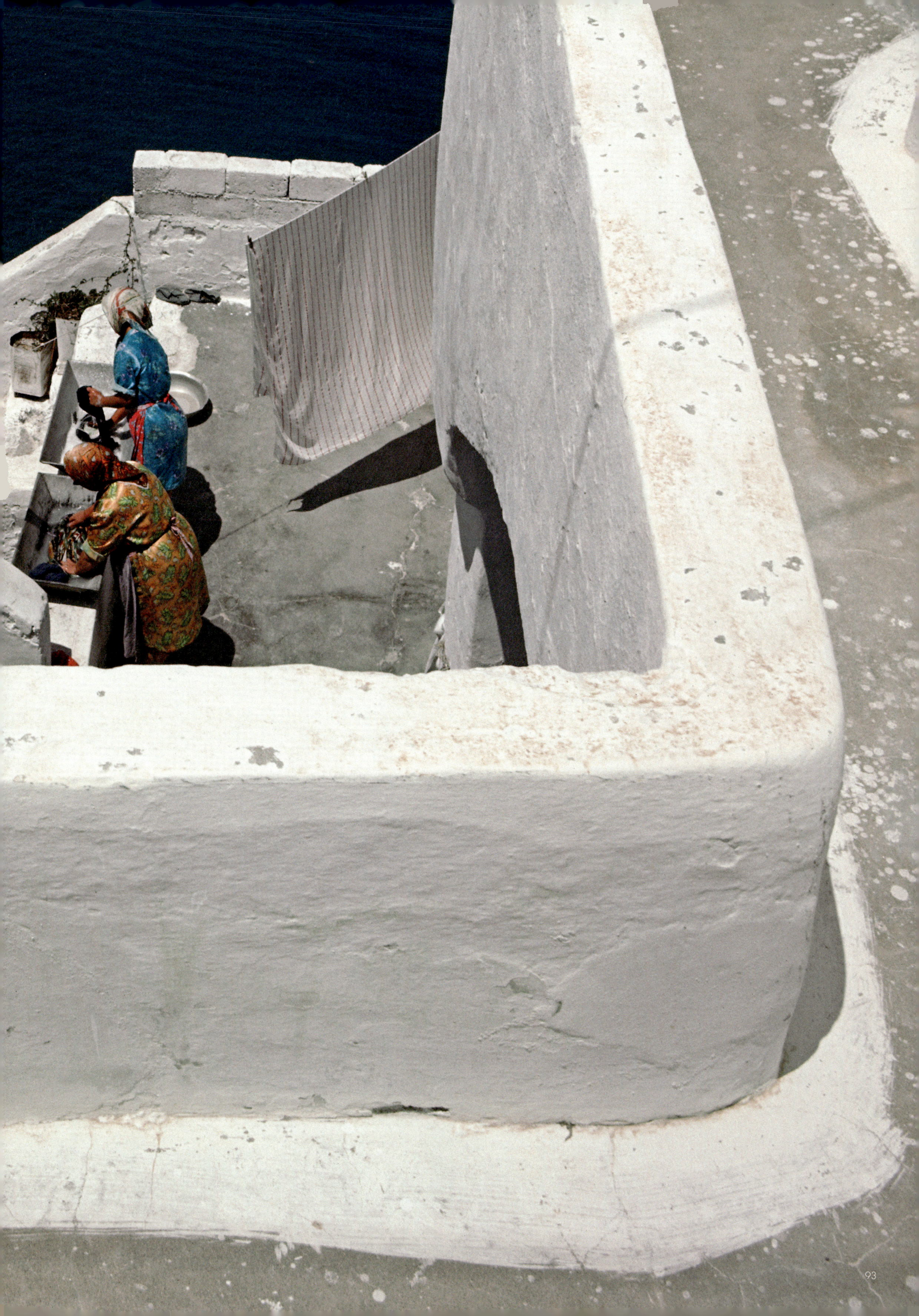

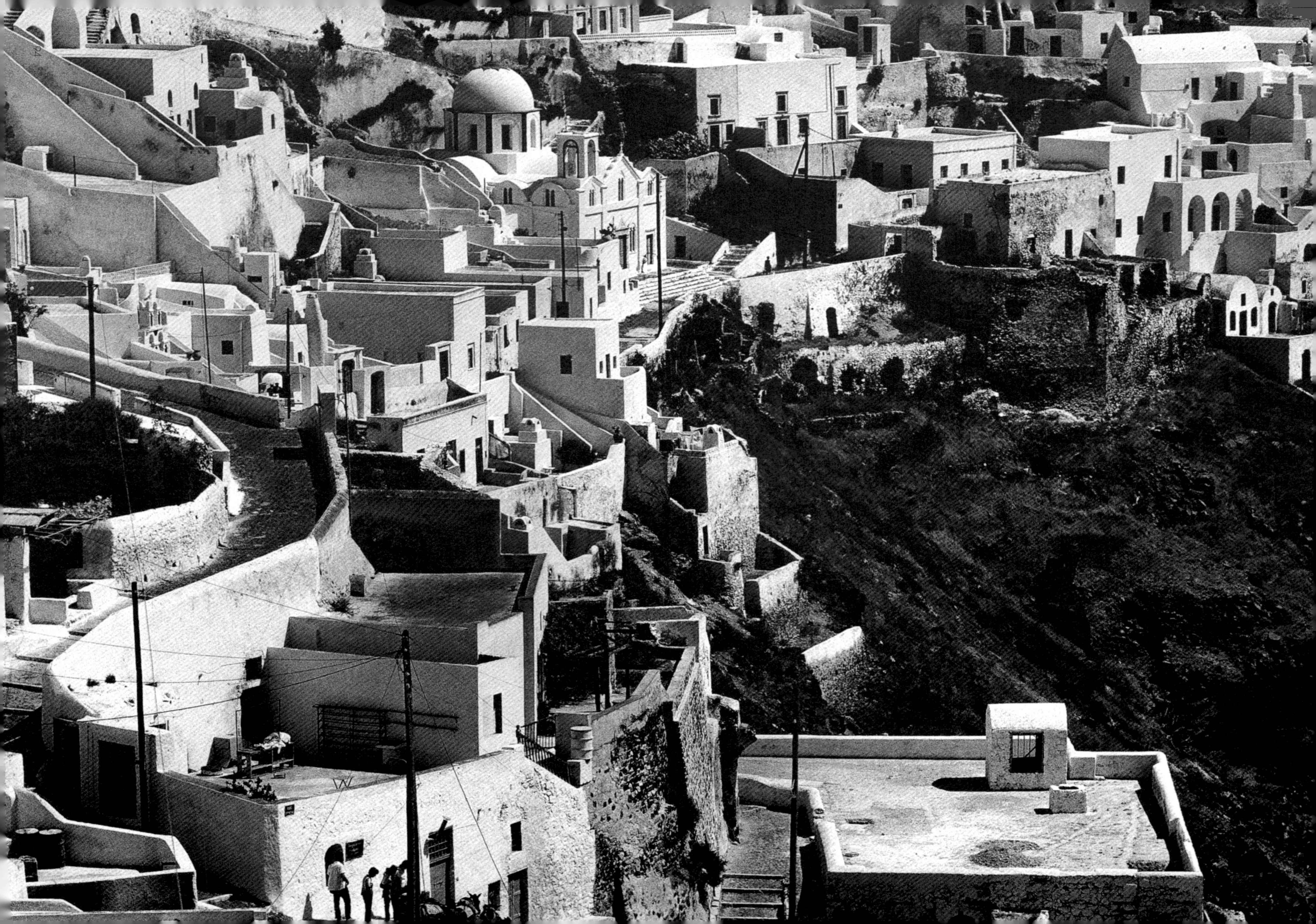

95

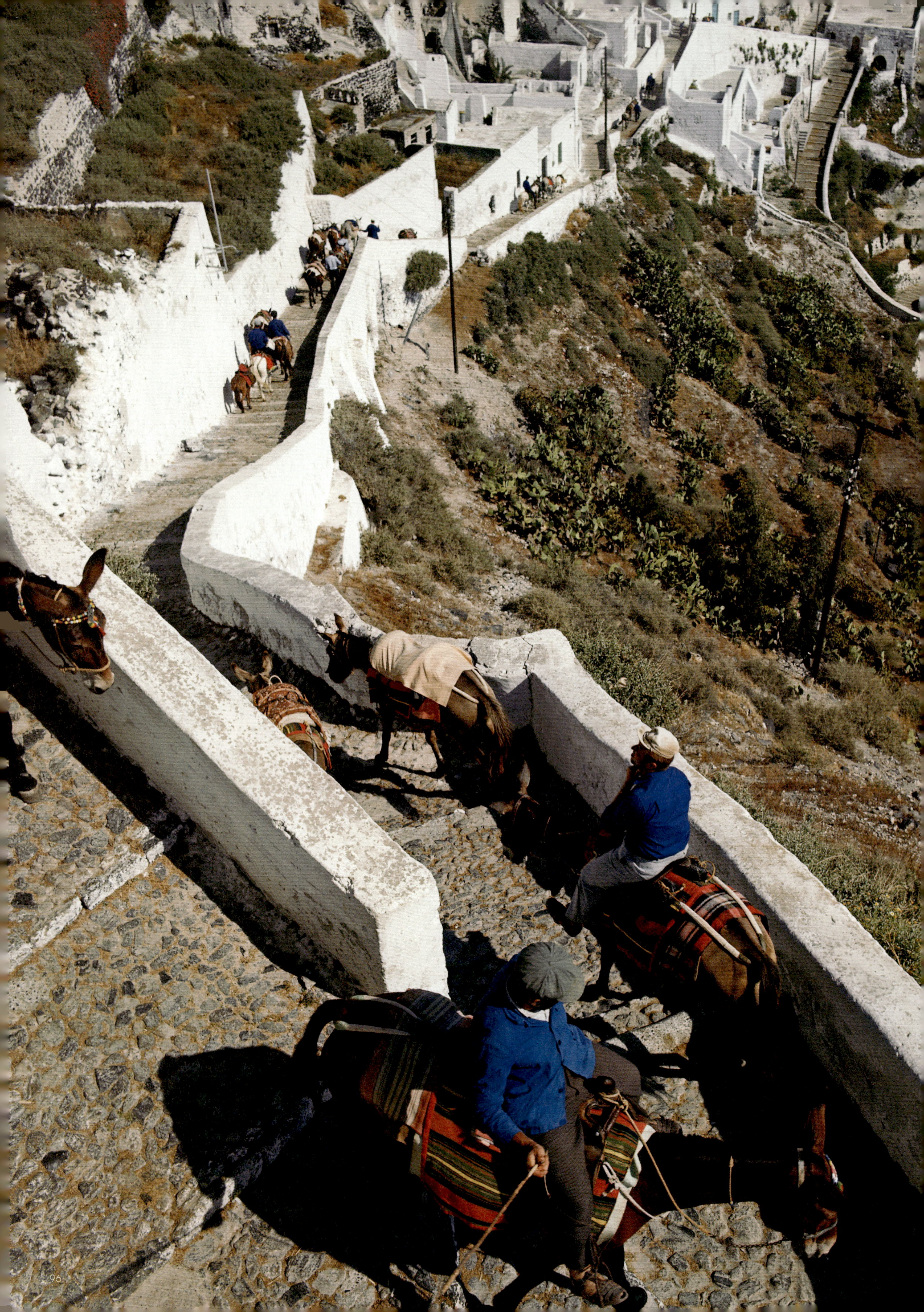

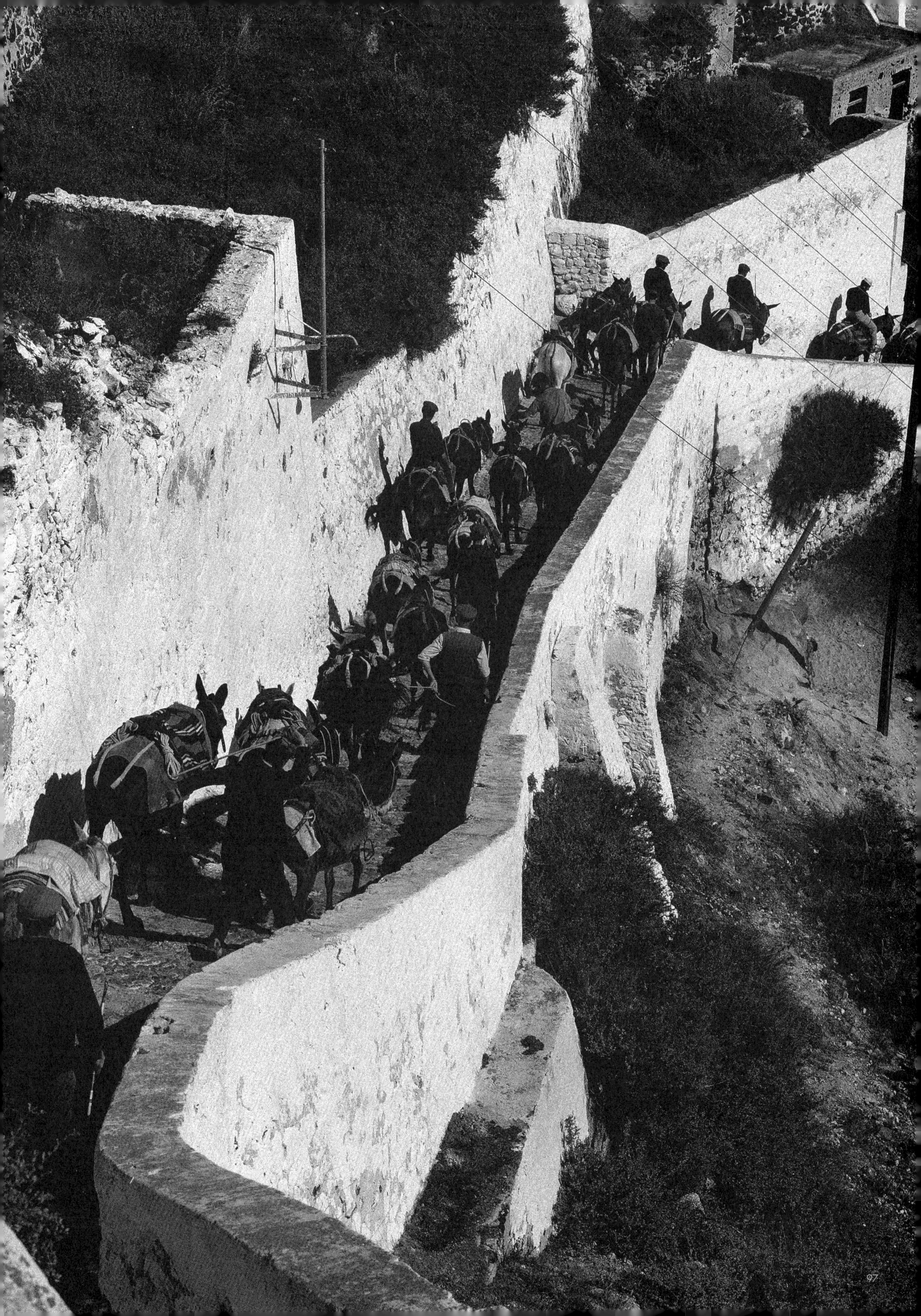

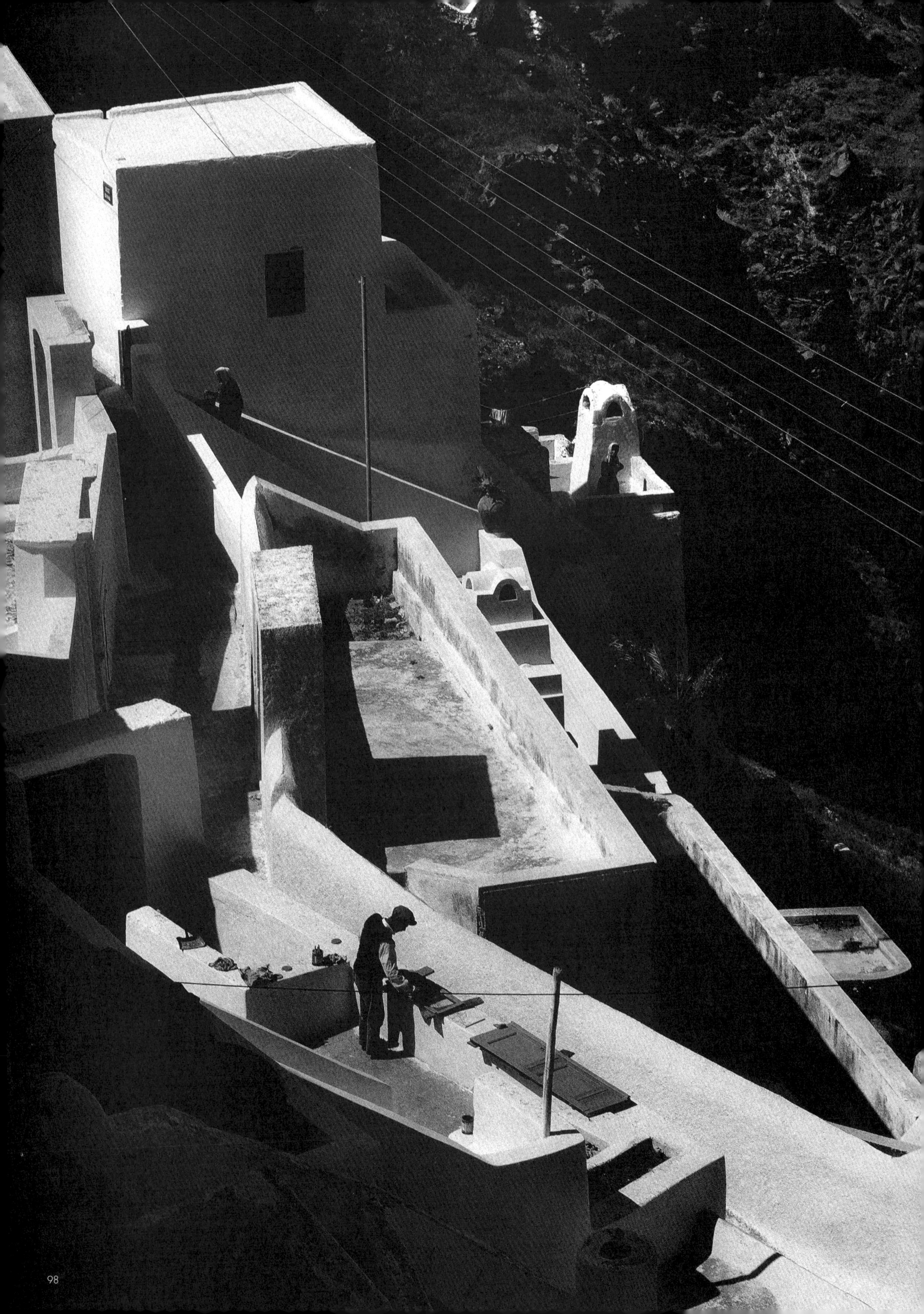

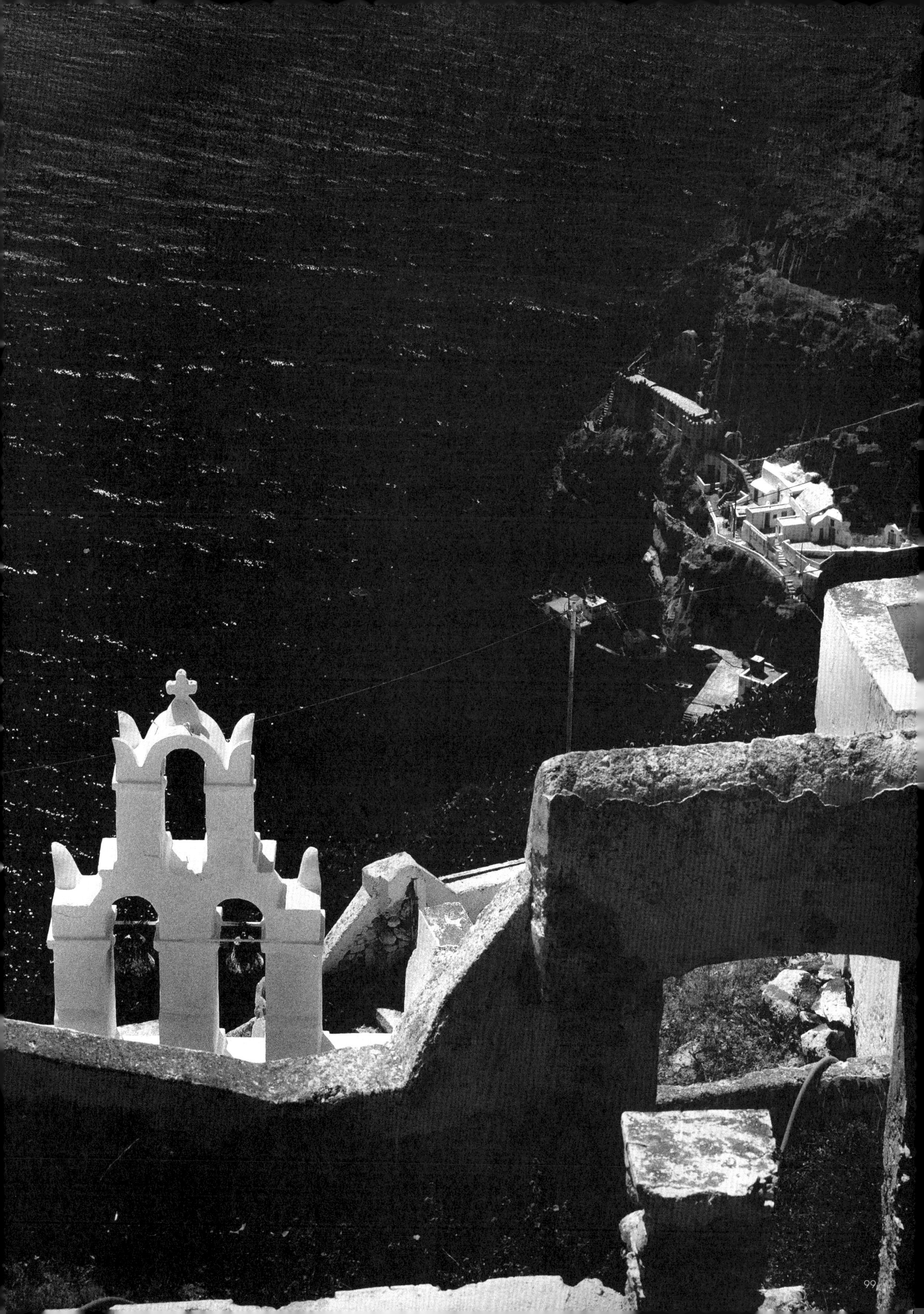

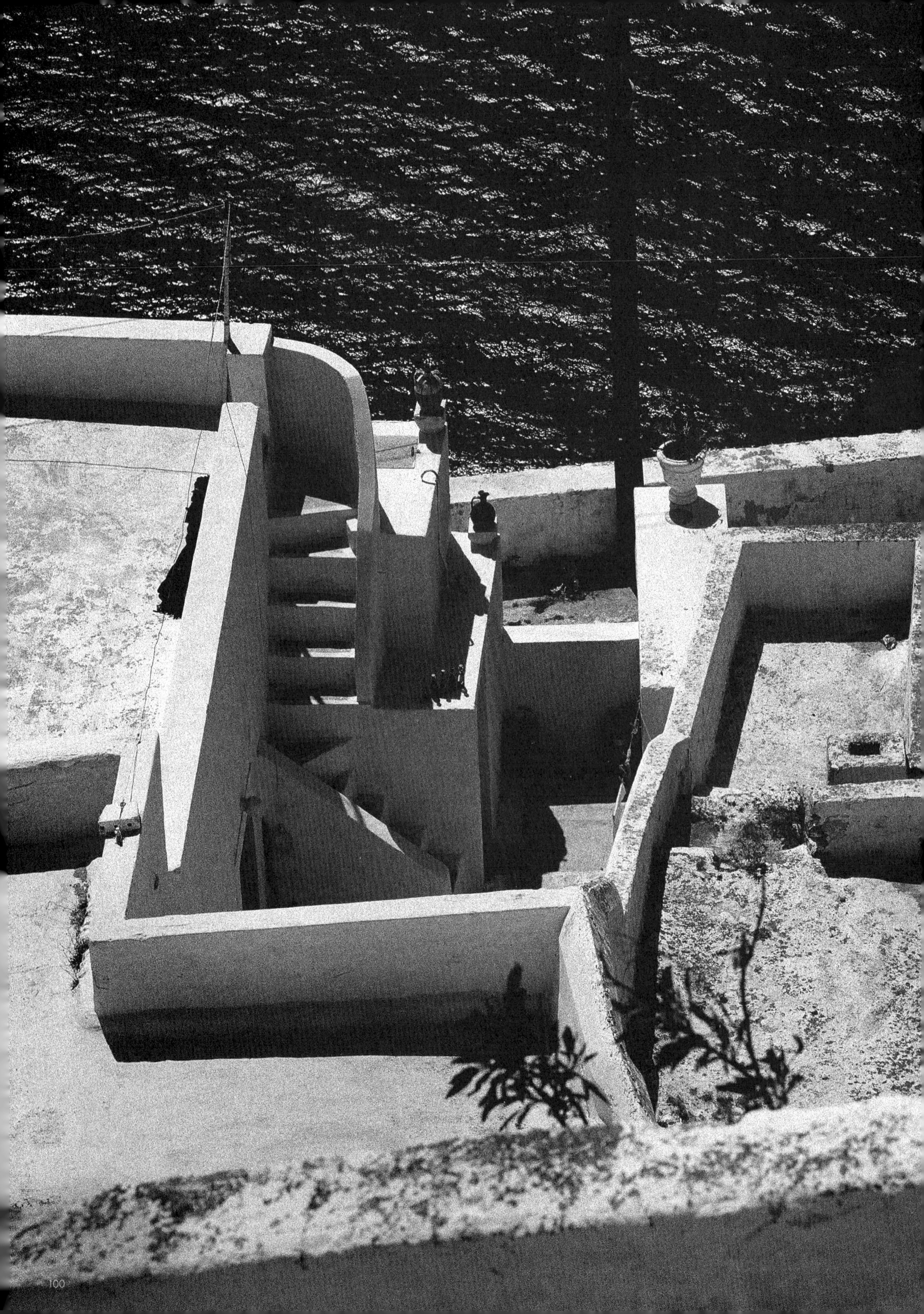

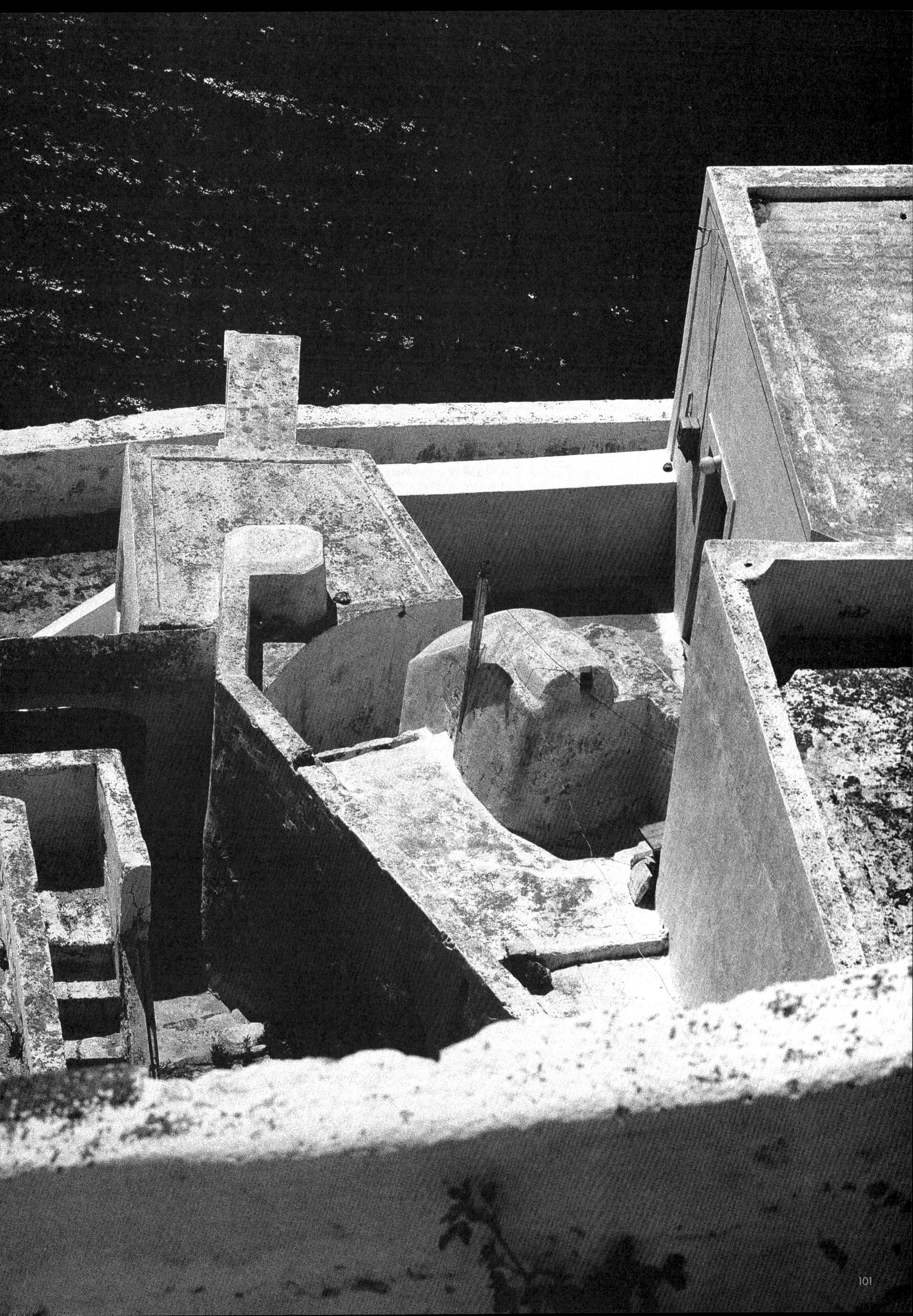

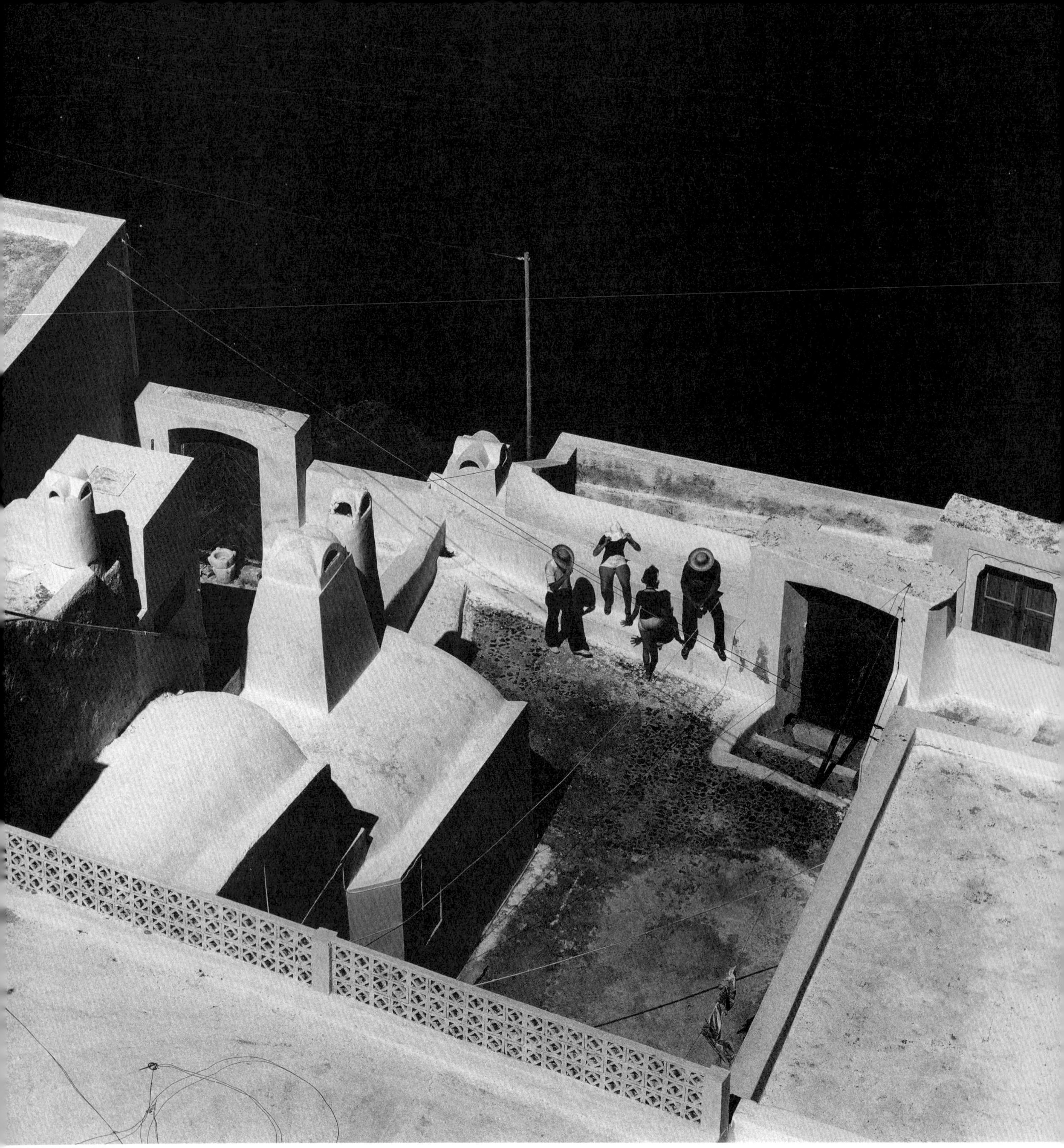

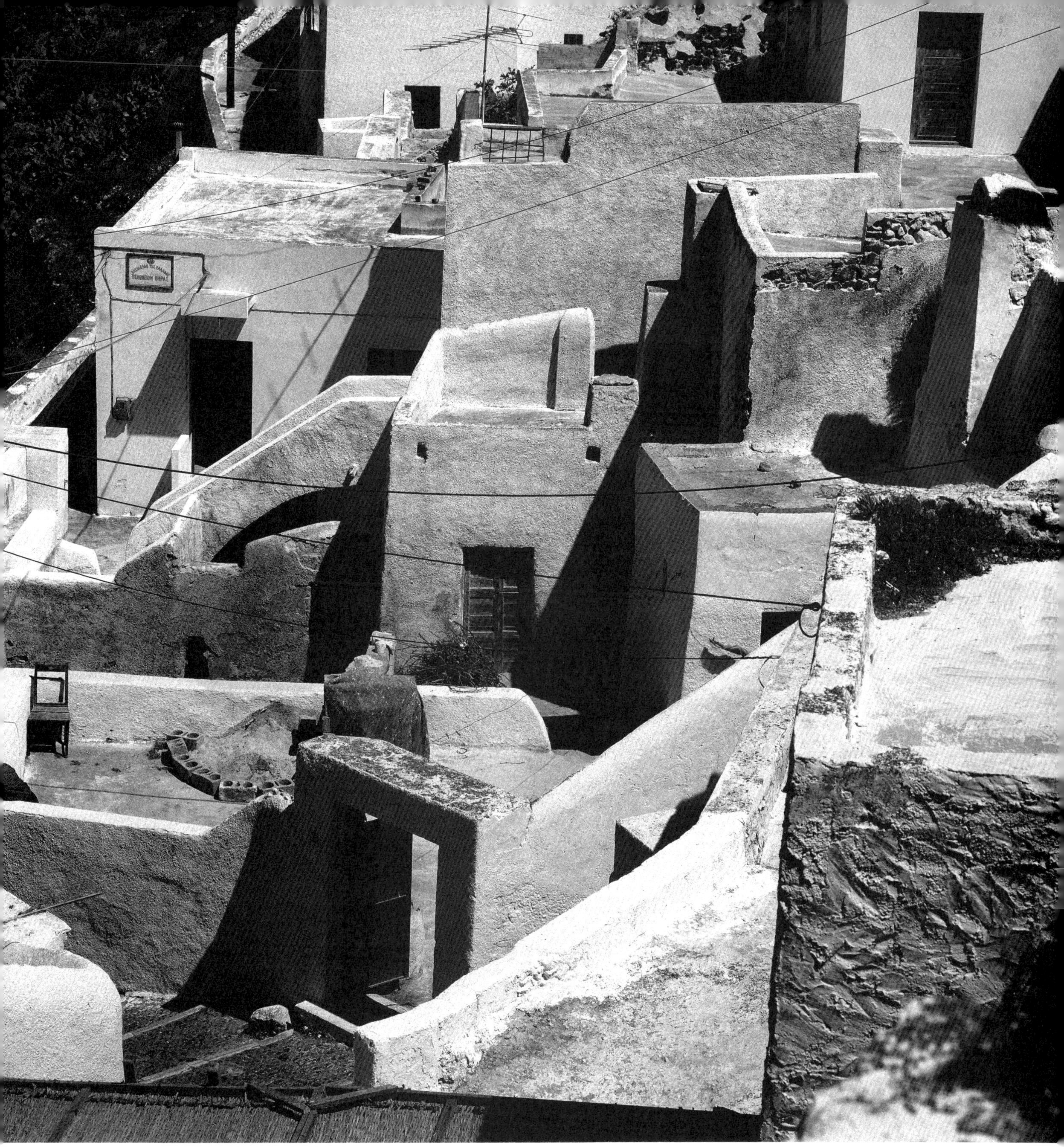

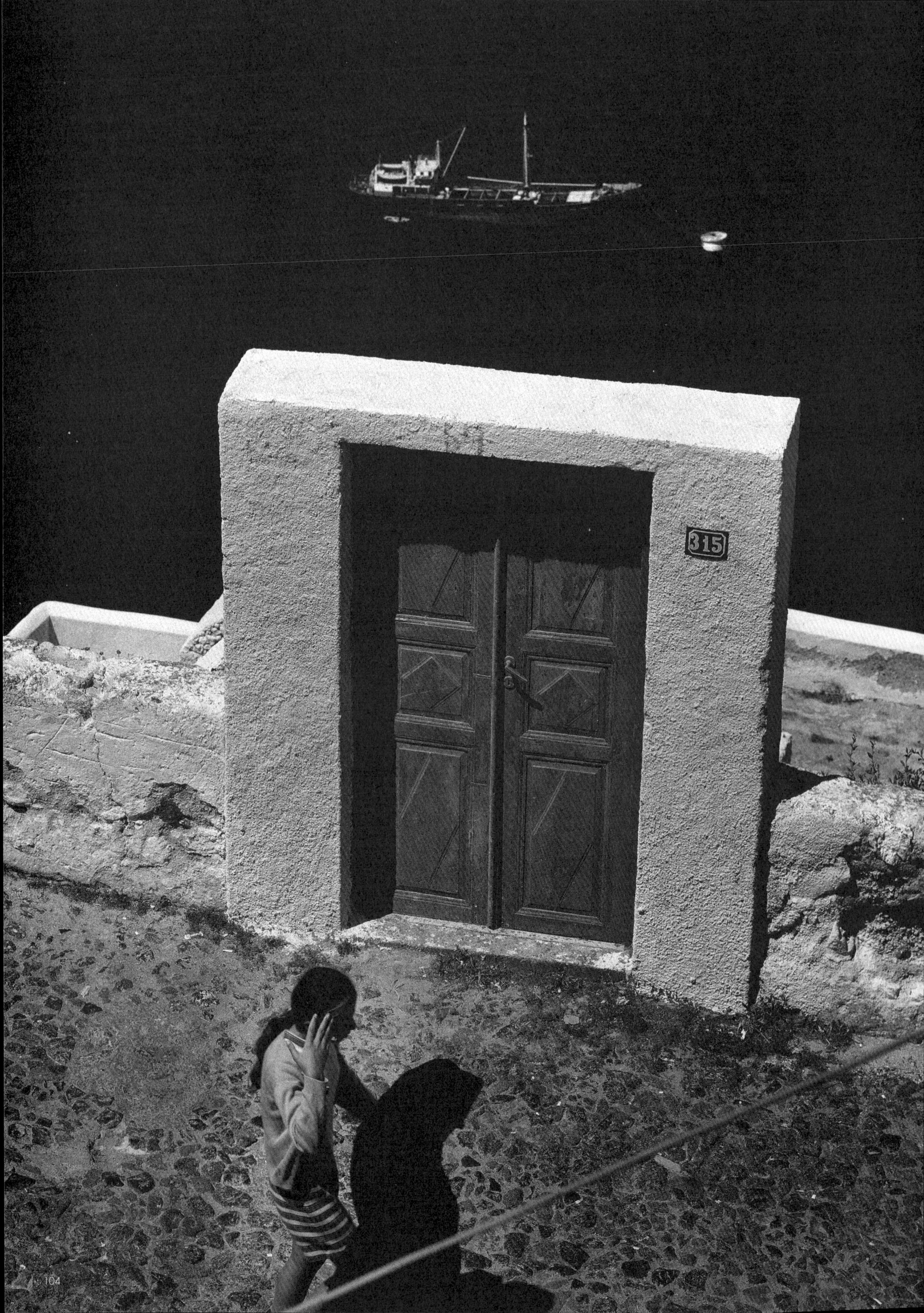
315

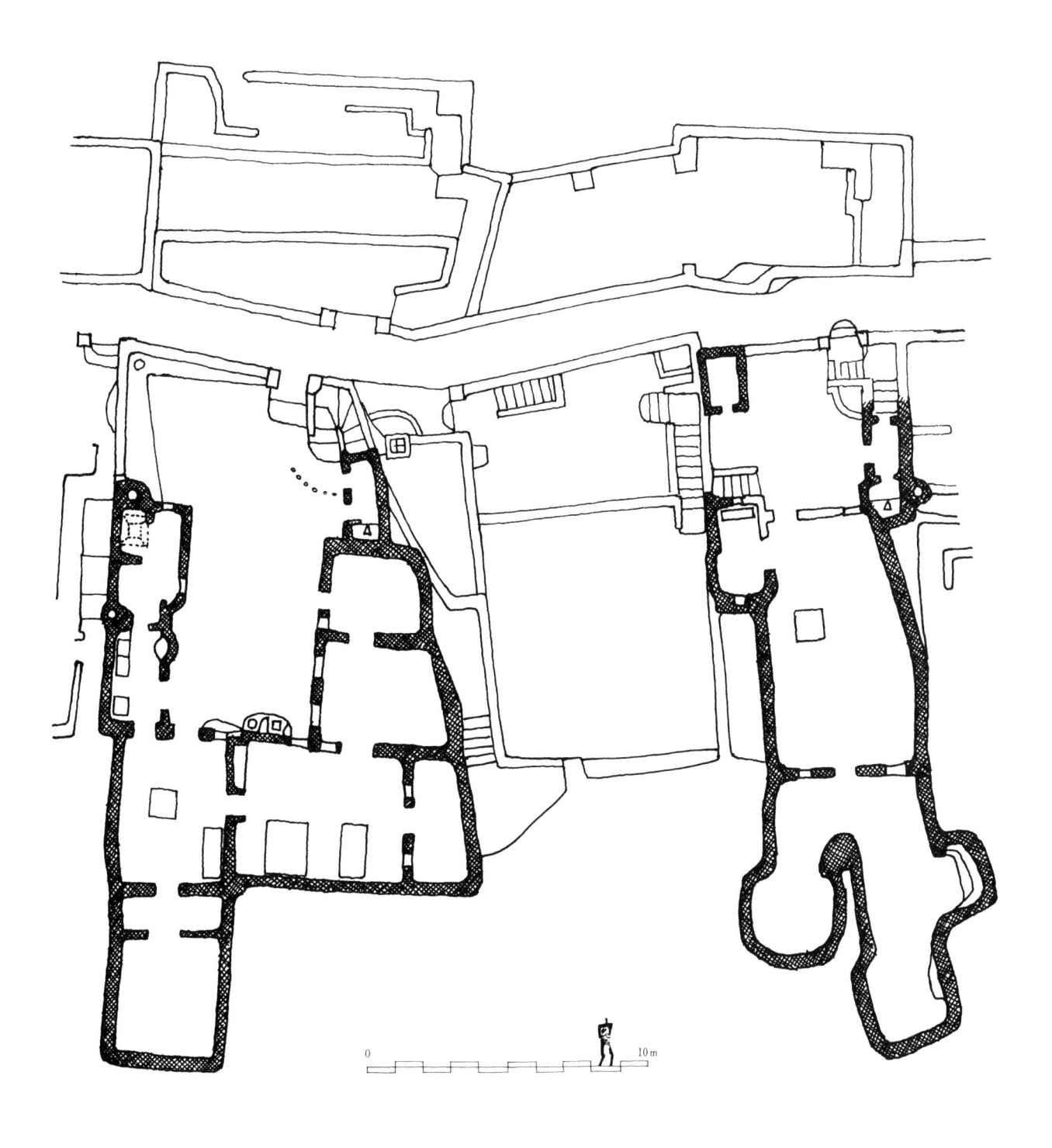

サントリーニの道, テラス, 住居　　*Streets, terraces and houses of Santorini*

Original
Santorin
Wein

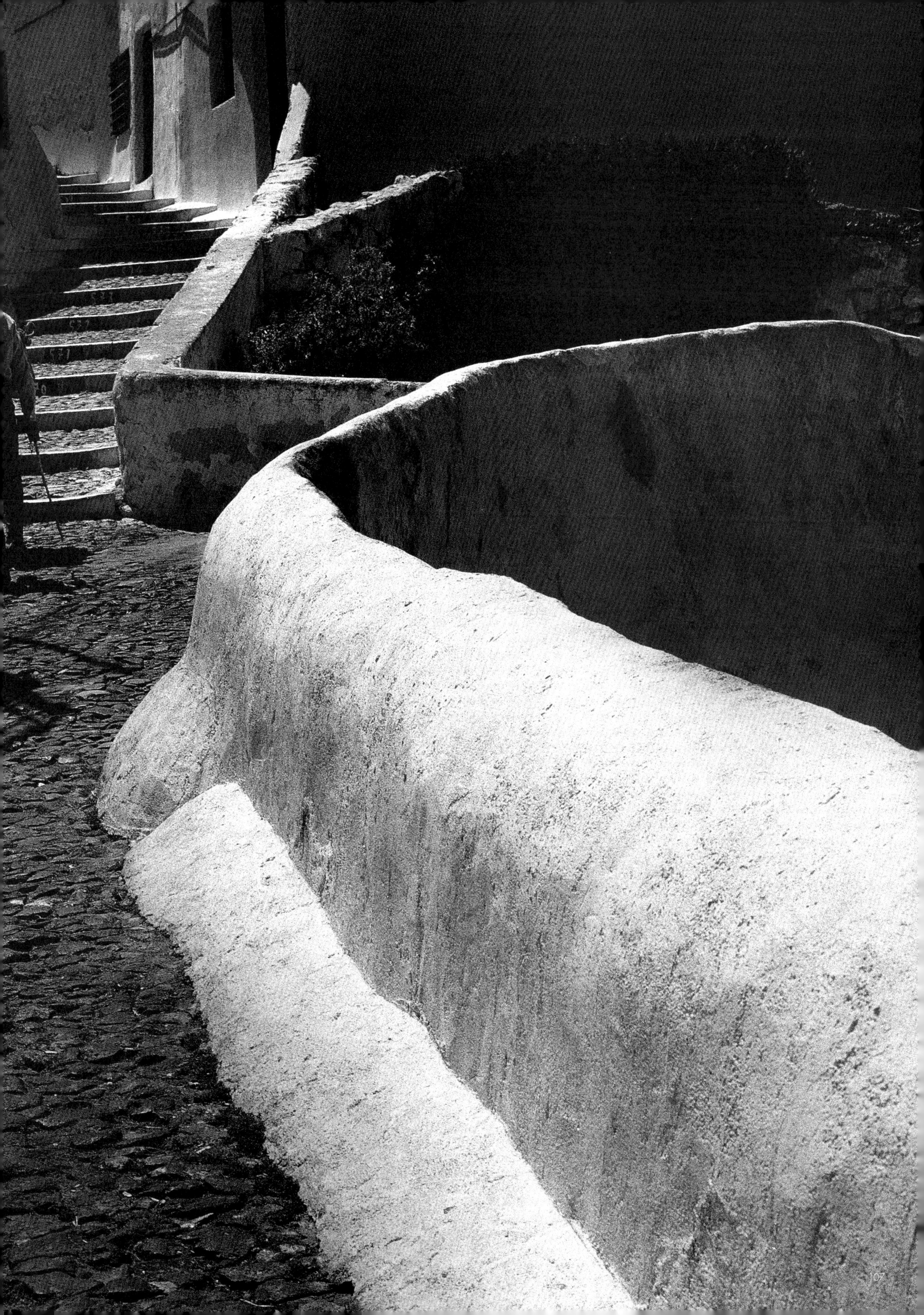

サントリーニのテラス───鈴木恂
Terraces in Santorini *by Makoto Suzuki*

ミコノスでは，バルコニーと階段が道を変えた。同時に道は，バルコニーや階段を変えている。同じような例を，サントリーニにとるなら，テラスということになるだろう。テラスはサントリーニの住居の断面を変え，と同時に断面はテラスによって生かされたと。一つのこうした生活の解法が，その生活を象徴的に示すような形をとるとき，われわれは，街のデザインに凝縮された生活をそこに見ることができる。当然それが個からも共同体としても使いよく，内部にも外部にもよい結果をもたらすものとして選び出され，街に定着することを認められた部分なのである。

しかし，ミコノスが，バルコニー，階段，物置きという生活のエレメントを，道に突き出して取り付けるシステムを普遍化したことと，サントリーニが，テラスやパティオを屋上につくり出していく方式を原則としたことの間には，その定着の仕方に次のような差を見付けることができるだろう。つまり，一つの原理が，生活の内側から押し出された場合と，外的な条件がそうであることを強いる場合とである。

これらの原理が土着化する過程は，街の匿名性や自発性に加えられる一種の共同体のオーダーの発生過程ということもできる。サントリーニとミコノスの街の差は，だからこのオーダーの対照的な差に顕著に現れているといってよい。そして，テラスはそのような過程を通して，サントリーニの住居に取り入れられていったものである。

一戸の住居は，斜面に突き立つ楔である。この楔型の，細長い平面をもつ建築によって，住居空間は壁のような崖に縫い付けられているようなものだ。楔型の家々が急傾斜で上下に重なっているので，勾配が急なほど，互いの家々の，重なりと縫い付けは強固になる。つまり全体が勾配を利用して一つの堆積構造になるような形をとっている。その堆積は多いところで6，7層，少ないところで4，5層であり，3，4層に一筋の等高に沿った水平の道が通っていることは前に述べた。1戸の住居がセット・バックしながら2，3層にわたることもあり，その場合屋上のテラスも含めて，3層のテラスやパティオが1戸の住居を示すことになる訳である。

以下は1967年に実測した1軒の家の記録であるが，この住居は，断崖がはじまる第1番目の道に面し，いわゆる旧い住居

In Mykonos, balconies and stairs changed the streets. At the same time, streets changed the balconies and stairs. If we were to look for a similar example in Santorini, it would be the terrace. Terraces changed the cross section of houses of Santorini, while cross sections were exploited by terraces. When a solution of living like this takes a shape that symbolizes that life, we are able to discover the living condensed in the town's design—obviously because such design was convenient for both the individual and the community, selected as something expected to bring good results both internally and externally, and allowed to take root in the town.

However, between Mykonos having universalized the system of installing elements of daily living such as the balcony, stairs and storerooms protruding into the streets, and Santorini having adopted the principle of creating terraces and patios on the rooftop, a difference can be observed in the way such methods came to be established: a case in which a principle was pushed out from inside the daily living, and a case in which it was forced by the external conditions.

It can also be said that the process of such principles being indigenized is the course of development of a type of collective order exerted on the town's anonymity and spontaneity. In other words, the difference between the towns of Santorini and Mykonos is prominent in the contrasting discrepancy of these orders. That is how the terrace came to be introduced to houses of Santorini.

A house is a wedge driven into a slope. It is as if living spaces are stitched onto the wall of a sheer cliff by wedge-like buildings with an oblong plan. Since these wedge-like houses are stacked up along a steep inclination, the steeper the inclination, the firmer the layers and stitches between houses. In fact, the entirety takes the form of a stratified structure that takes advantage of the inclination. The strata consist of 6 or 7 layers where it is thick and 4 to 5 layers where it is thin. As mentioned earlier, a horizontal street runs along the level line for every 3 to 4 layers. Some houses take up 2 to 3 layers with setbacks, in which case a house is composed of terraces and patios on different levels including the rooftop terrace.

The following is a measured record of a house from 1967. Facing the first street where the cliff starts, this house has an average scale and shape in the old part of the town.

が残る地区の平均的な規模と形をもつ住居である。この道は実測図にその部分を示したように，上下の景観がえられるサントリーニでは最も美しい道の一つである。

　住居は，道から奥に向って，道，門，パティオまたはテラス，前室またはサロン，奥室または寝室の順に縦に並べられた平面をもっている。間口が約6m，奥行きが約24mという非常に長いプロポーションの間取りだ。前庭のテラスは，視界を遮る程の高さの壁に囲まれ，プライベートなパティオまたはサーヴィス・ヤードであり，一般に，この両側に，炊事場，便所，物置き，洗濯場及び2階テラスへの階段がコンパクトに並んでいる。もちろん，炊事場はサロンに直接通じる位置に置かれている。前室は，ヴォールトの天井の高い部屋で，奥まで外光がとどくように高い位置に採光窓がある。しかし，その奥にある寝室へは仕切り壁があって，ほとんど光はとどかない。奥室は寝室であるが，それは岩を割り貫いた洞穴である。

　面積は1階で100㎡程度，40％がパティオ，60％が内部の割合である。従って住居の長手断面は，全体の30％ほどが上部の部屋やテラスと重なり，30％が土中にあたかも銛の先のように突きささっていることが解るであろう。

　そして，その横断面については，オィアの廃墟によって充分に語りつくされる。そこにはかつての居間や寝室が，無数に切口を露しているからだ。

　テラスと内奥の間にある住空間，光と影が結合した長い楔型の家，自然の形を優れて反映した住居，それはキクラデスのメガロンと呼ぶべき重厚な造形をもって岩に突き刺っているのである。

　テラスからは下にあるテラスの生活や，パティオで働く人々の動きがよく見える。ここから見る夕日はまた厳粛であり華麗だ。カルデラの円弧の岸が夕日に映えて，自分達を中心に置いて周囲を囲む黄金の屏風に思えるようだ。

　内海の中央にある溶岩の火口カメニ島を眺めるとき，そして重なり合うテラスがその火口に対して祭壇のように正しく向いているのを眺めるとき，自然と人間の異様な祭典が持続されているのをそこにイメージするのは，私だけではないだろう。

The street shown on the measured drawing is one of the prettiest in Santorini with a view of both up and down.

　Entering from the street, a gate, patio or terrace, front room or salon, and back room or bedroom are arranged in a row. With a width of approx. 6 m and depth of approx. 24 m, the plan of the house has a very elongated proportion. Enclosed in walls high enough to block the views, the front yard terrace is a private patio or a service yard. Everything is kept compact here, usually with the kitchen, toilet, storage room, laundry room and the stairs to the upper-floor terrace lined up on both sides of the front yard terrace. Understandably, the kitchen is directly connected to the salon. The front room has a high vaulted ceiling with a transom window to let external light deep inside. However, a partition wall mostly shields the light to the bedroom in the back. The back room is the bedroom which is a cave dug into the rocks.

　The first floor has a surface area of about 100 sq.m. with 40% of it occupied by the patio and 60% by the interior. We can see that about 30% of the longitudinal section of the house overlaps with the upper-level rooms and terrace and another 30% is stuck into the ground like a harpoon point.

　In terms of the horizontal section, much can be learned from the ruins of Oia, where countless cut surfaces of what had used to be living rooms and bedrooms are exposed to the elements.

　Living spaces between the terrace and the back room; long, wedge-like house where light and shadow are bound together; houses that superbly reflect the forms of nature—all of these are driven into the rocks within a massive form that may be called the Cycladic megaron.

　The terrace has a good view of the activities of the terrace below and the actions of people who work in the patio. Sunset from this terrace is solemn and gorgeous: the caldera's arched shore stands out against the setting sun, reminiscent of a golden folding screen that surrounds us.

　Looking at the lava crater of Kameni island in the middle of the lagoon and watching the overlapping terraces all facing precisely toward that crater as if it were an altar, I am certainly not the only one who sees there an imagery of an endless, bizarre festival of nature and humans.

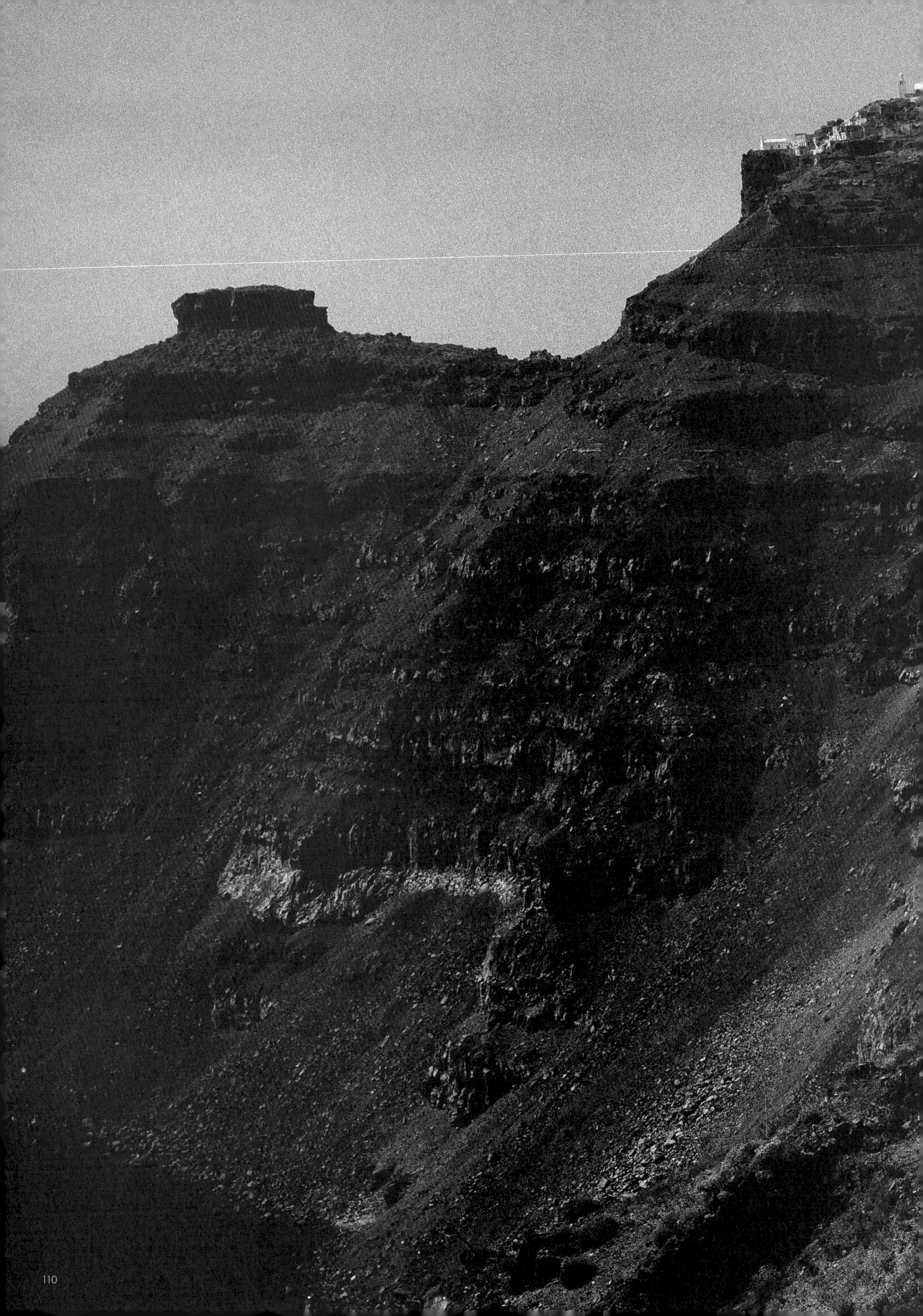

断面図　*Section*

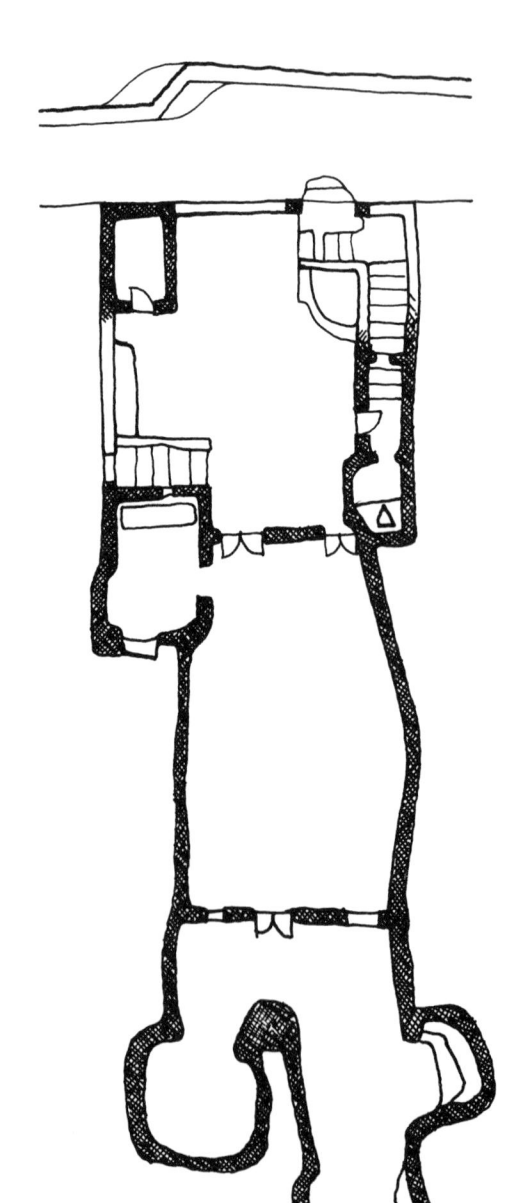

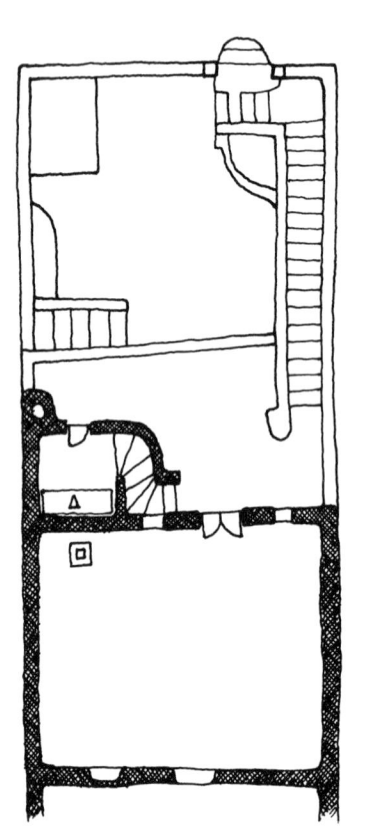

2階平面図　*Second floor plan*

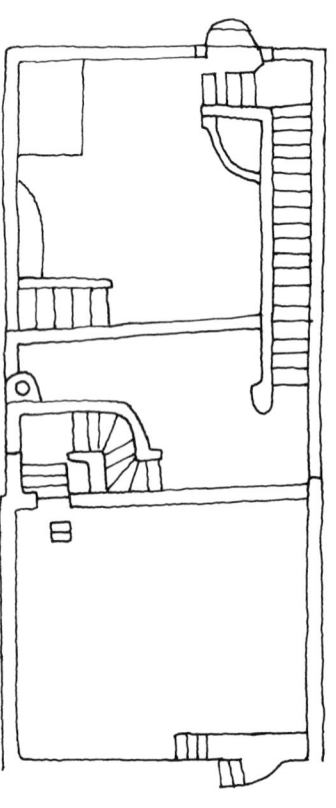

3階平面図　*Third floor plan*

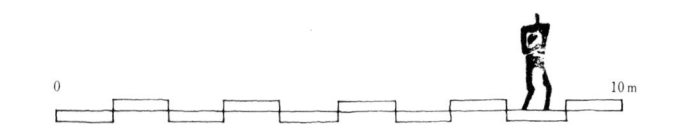

1階平面図　*First floor plan*

サントリーニの住居　*House of Santorini*

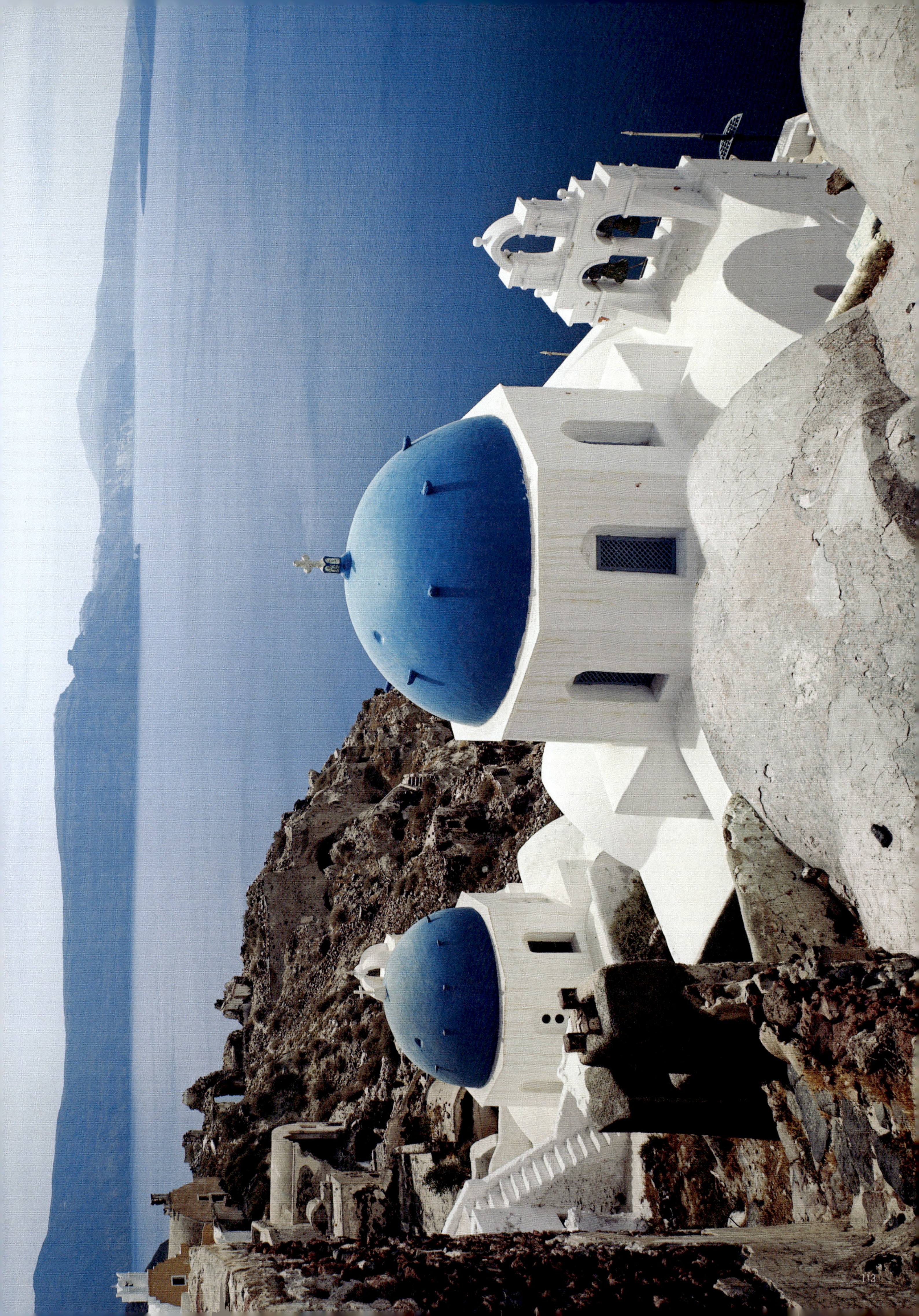

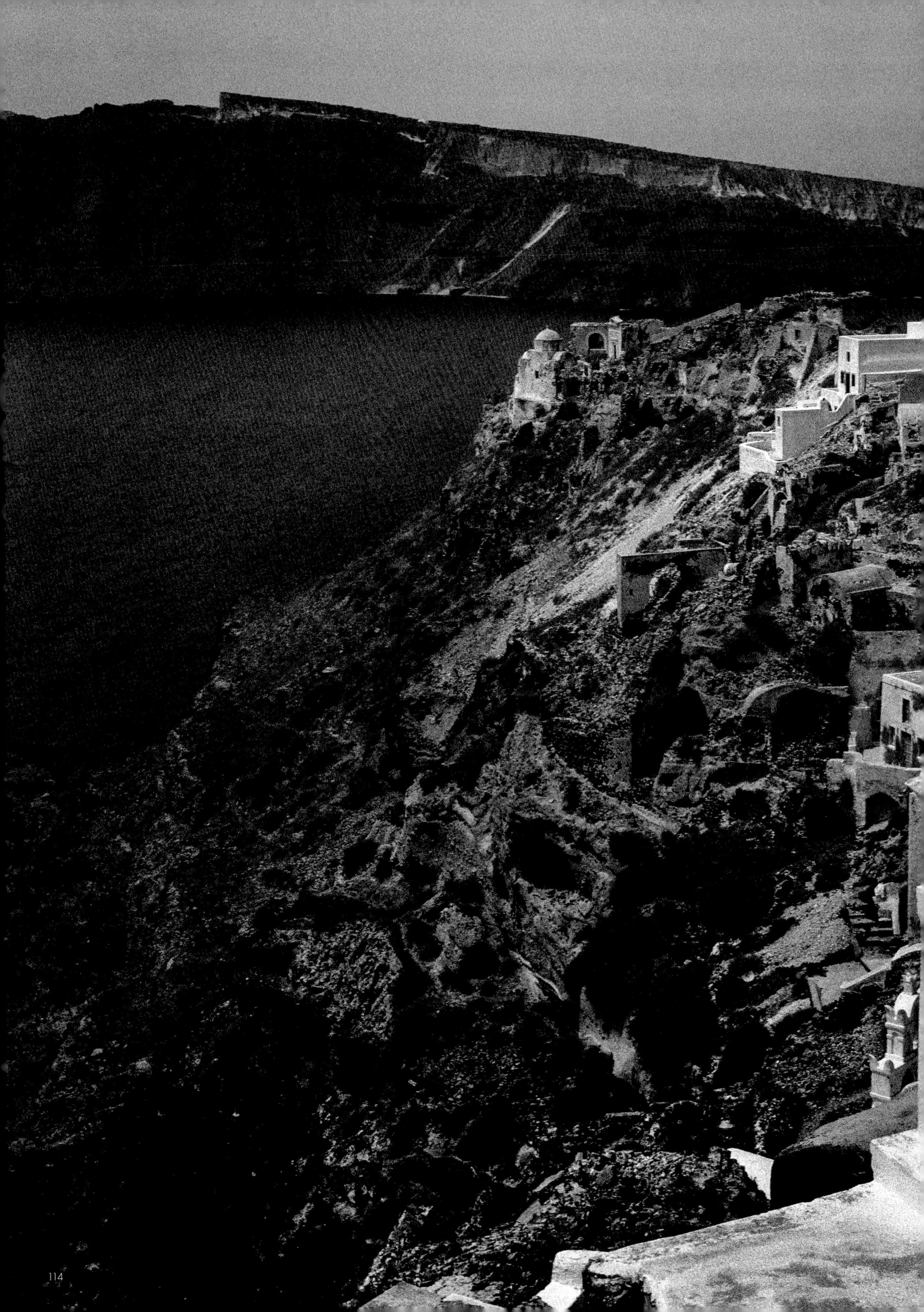

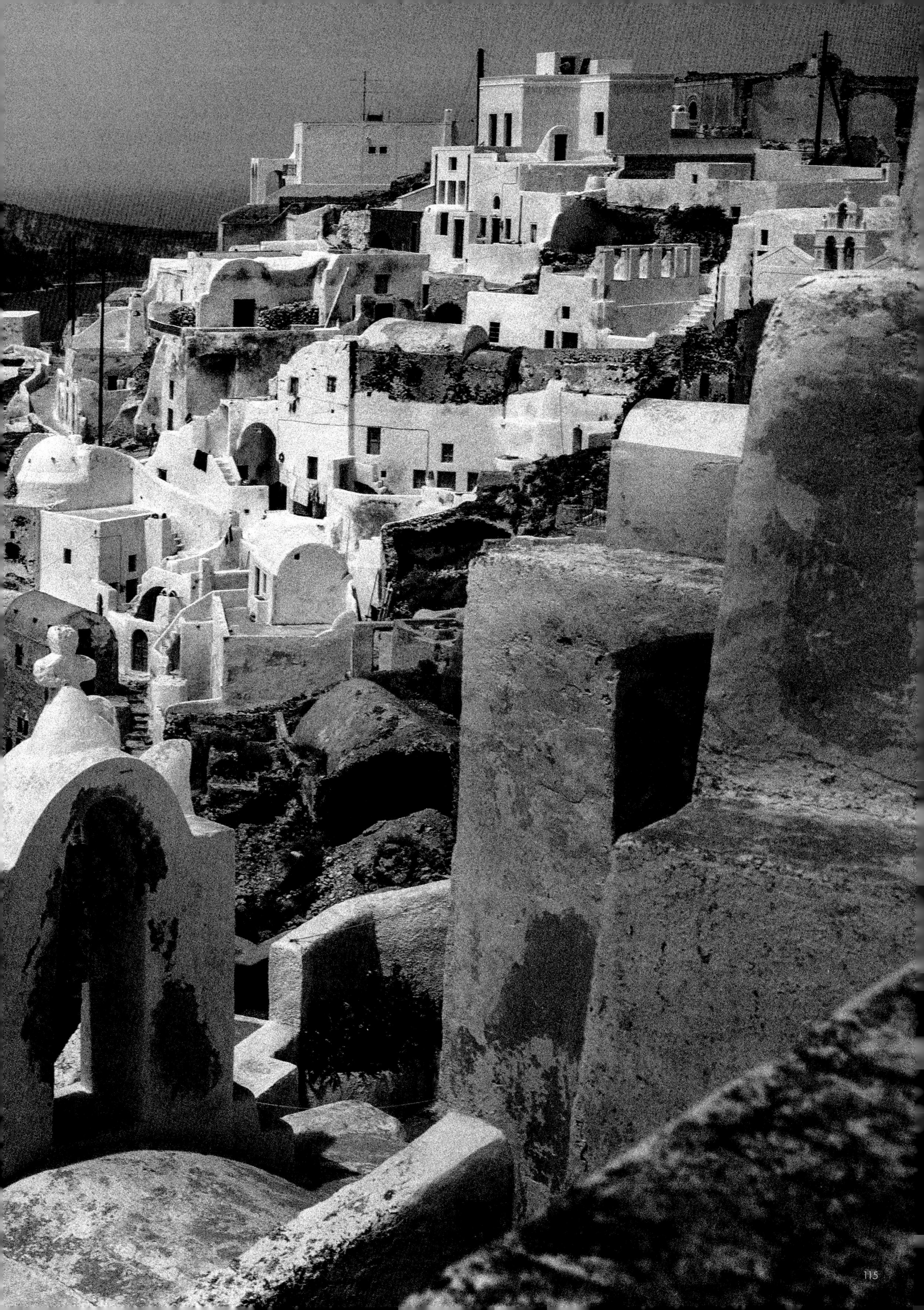

116

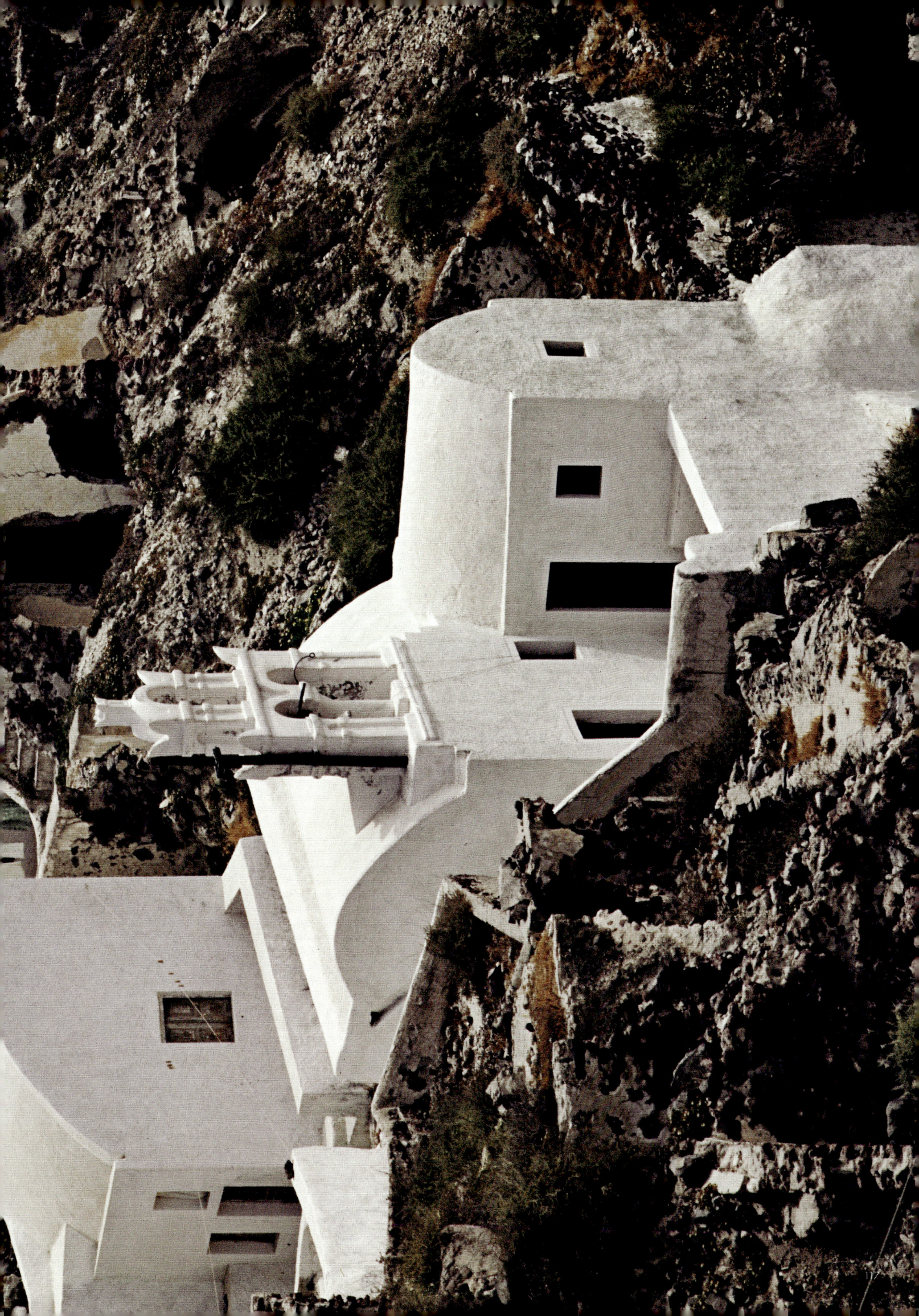

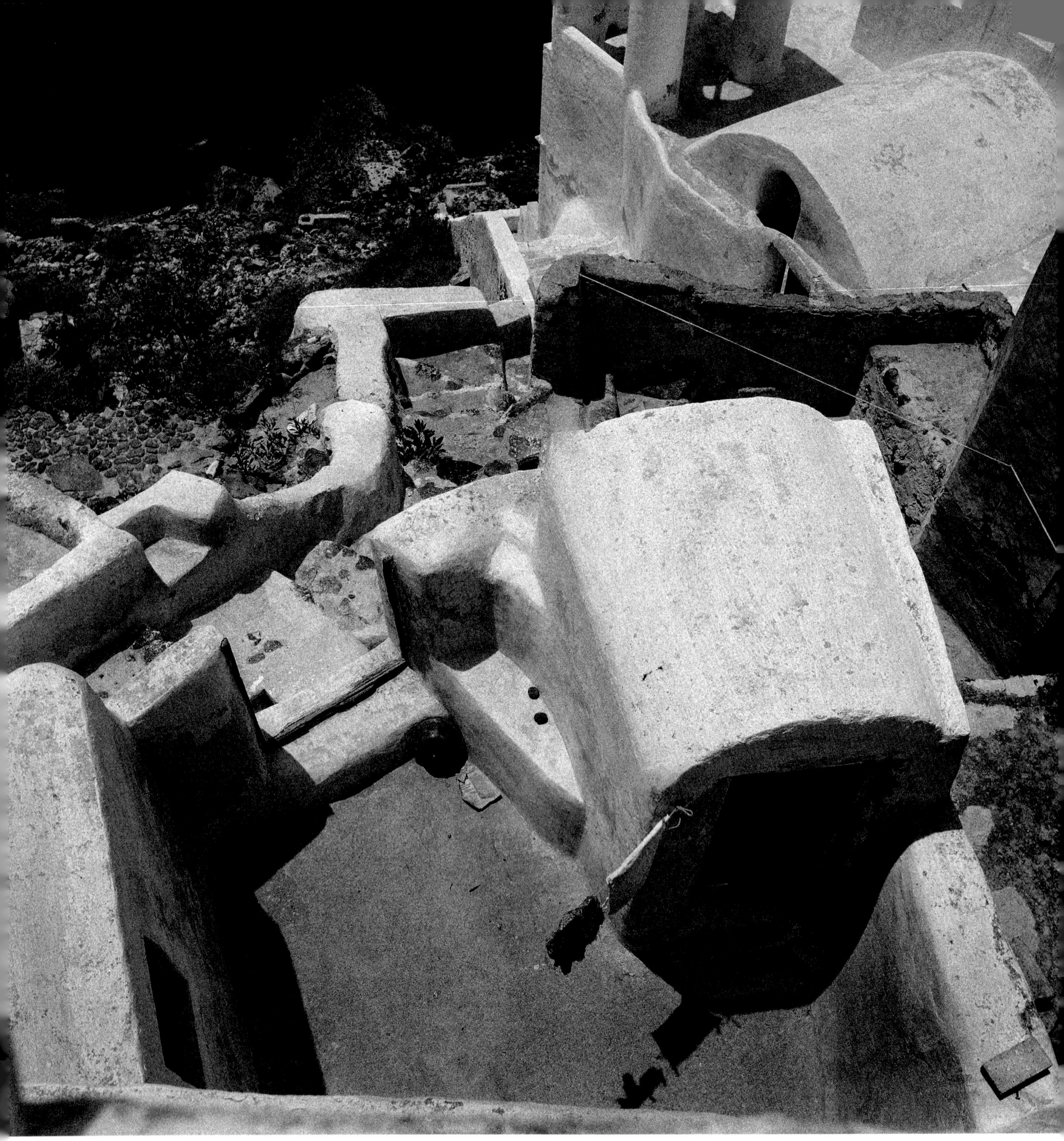

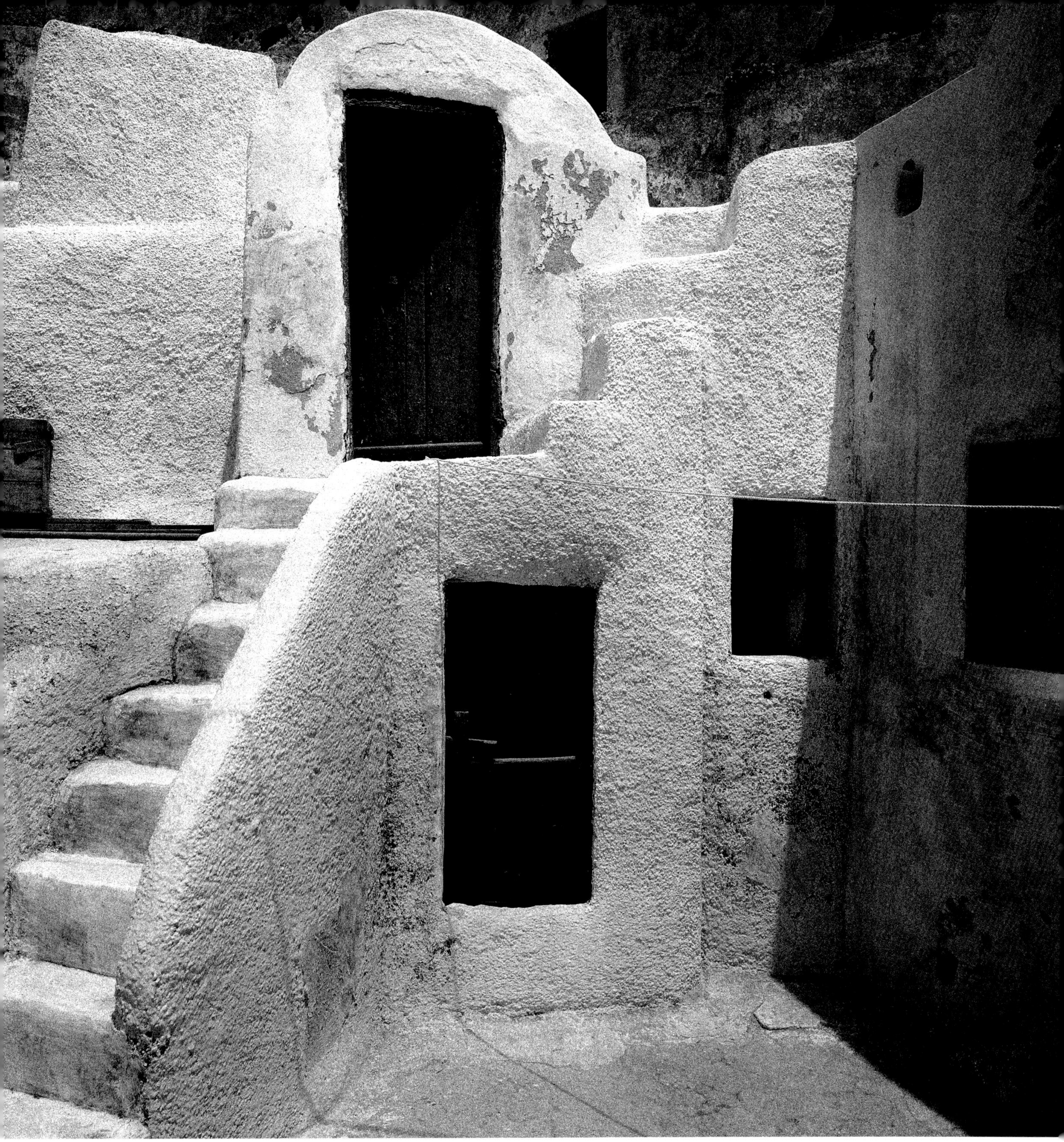

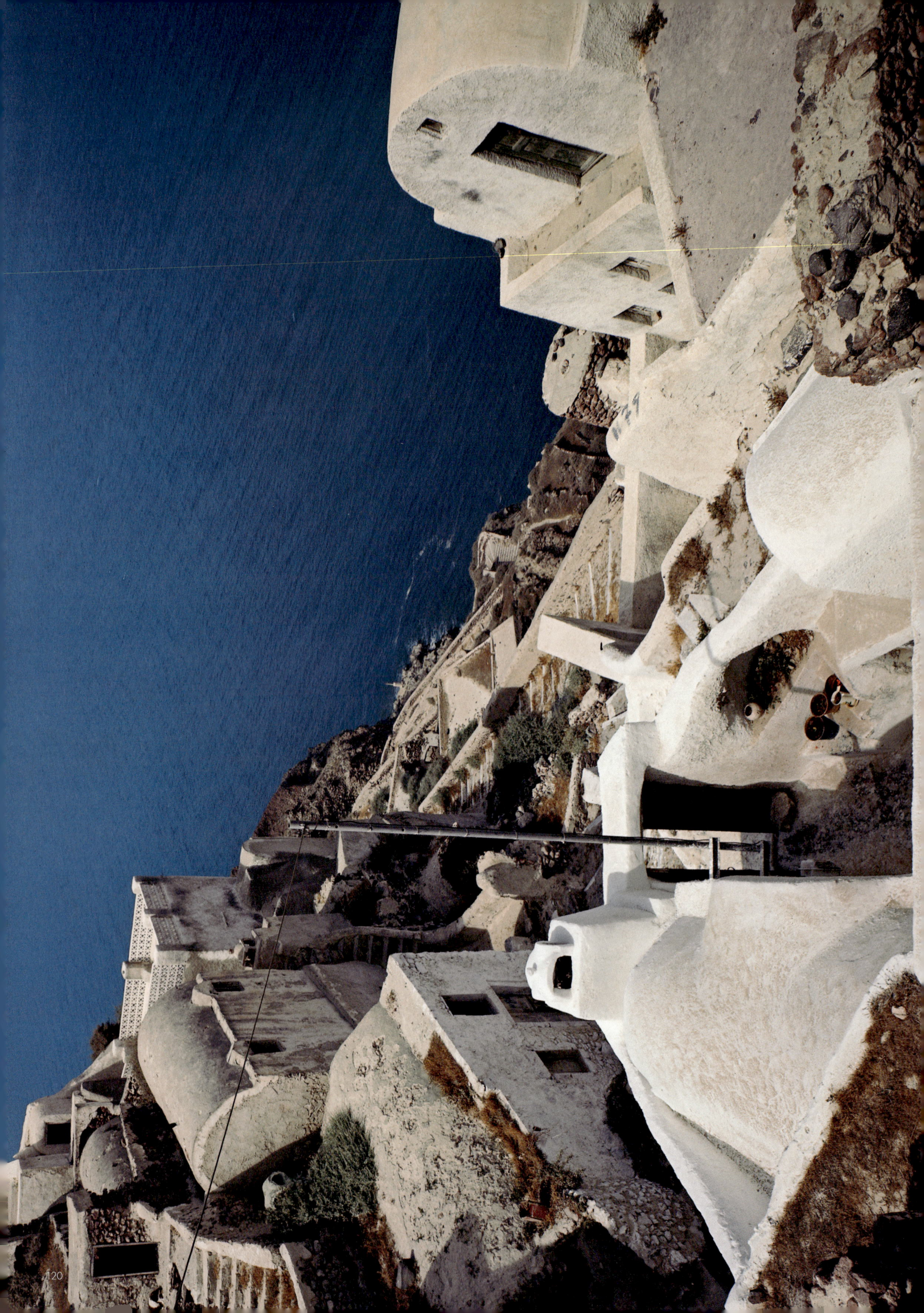

121

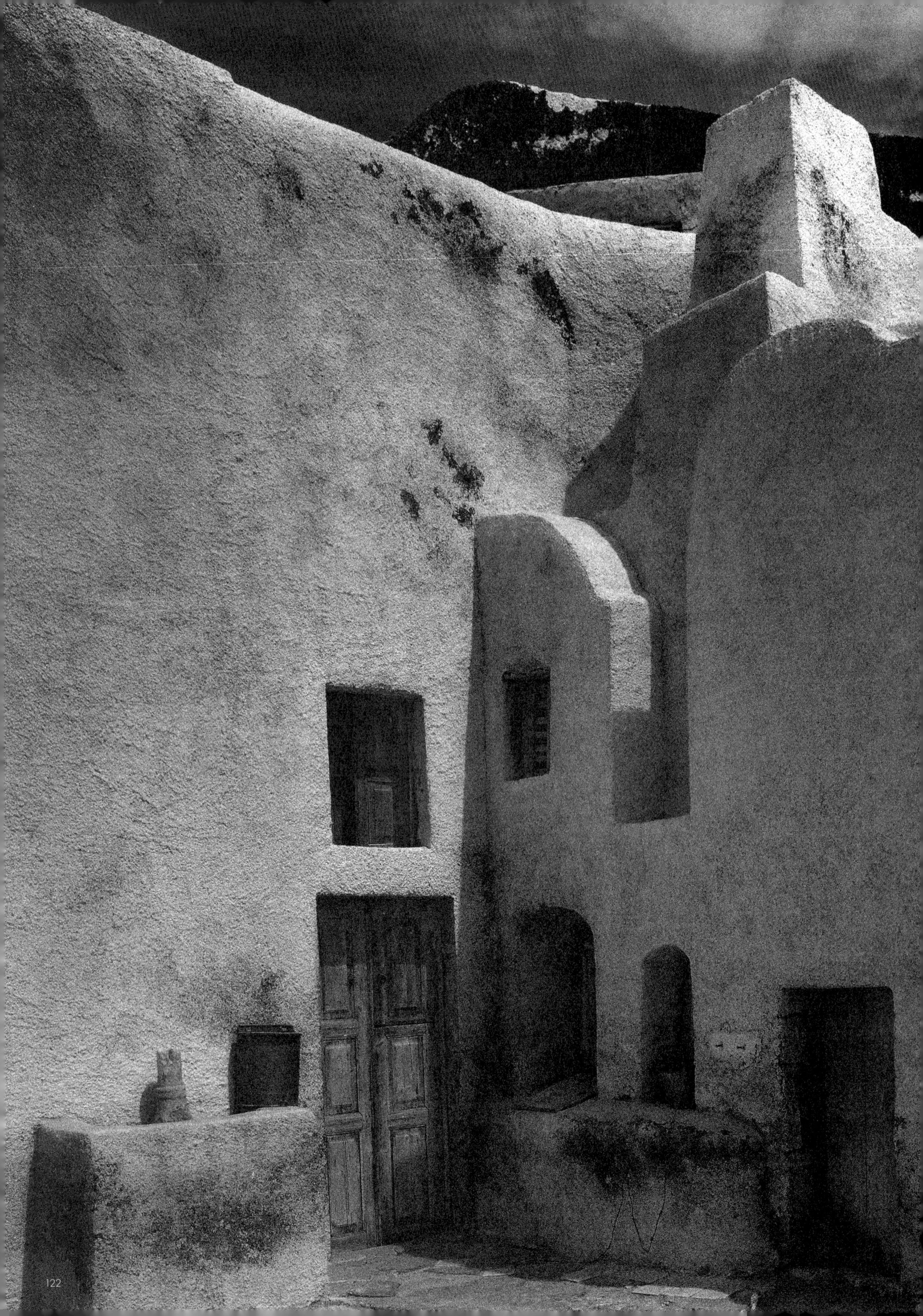

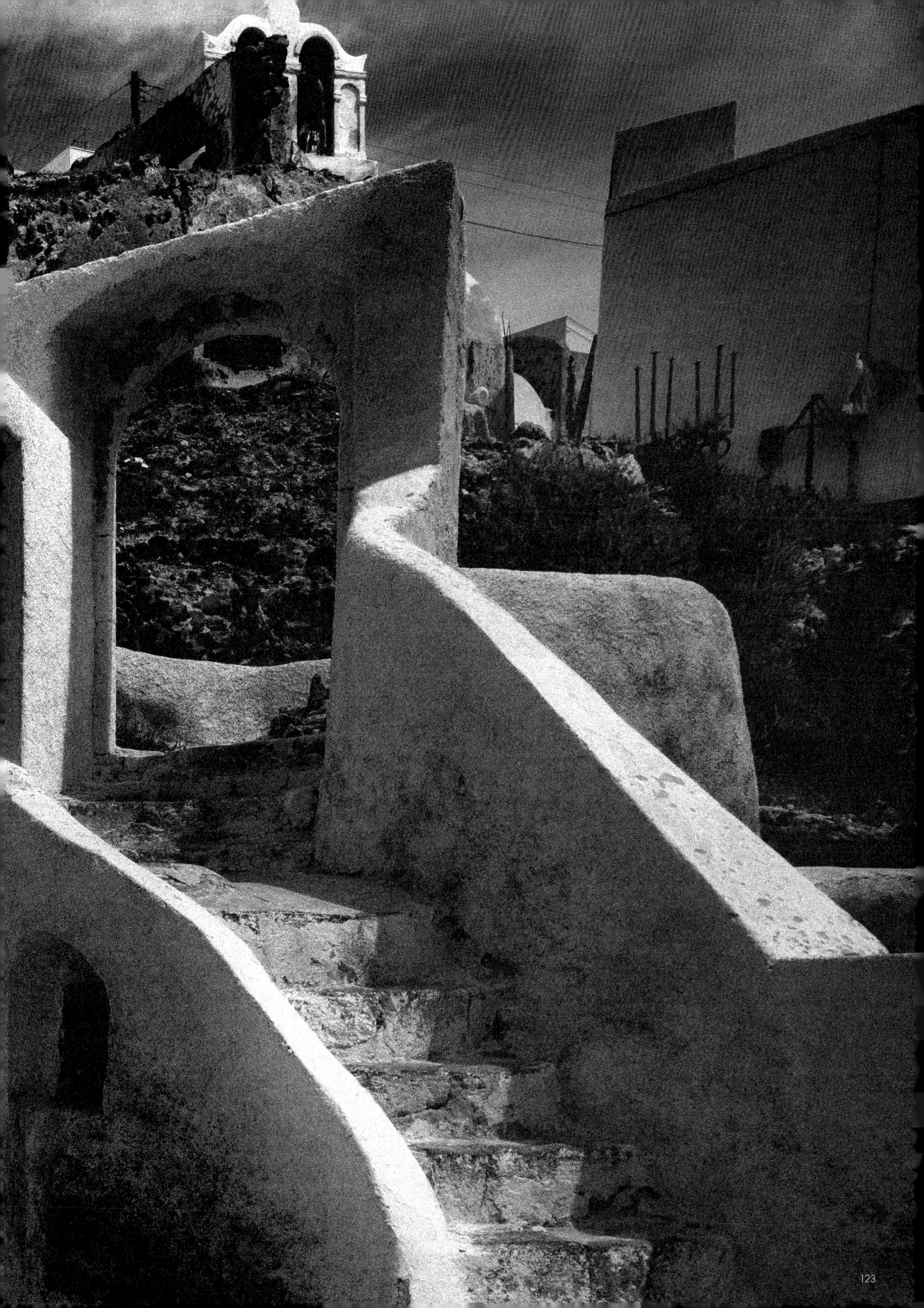

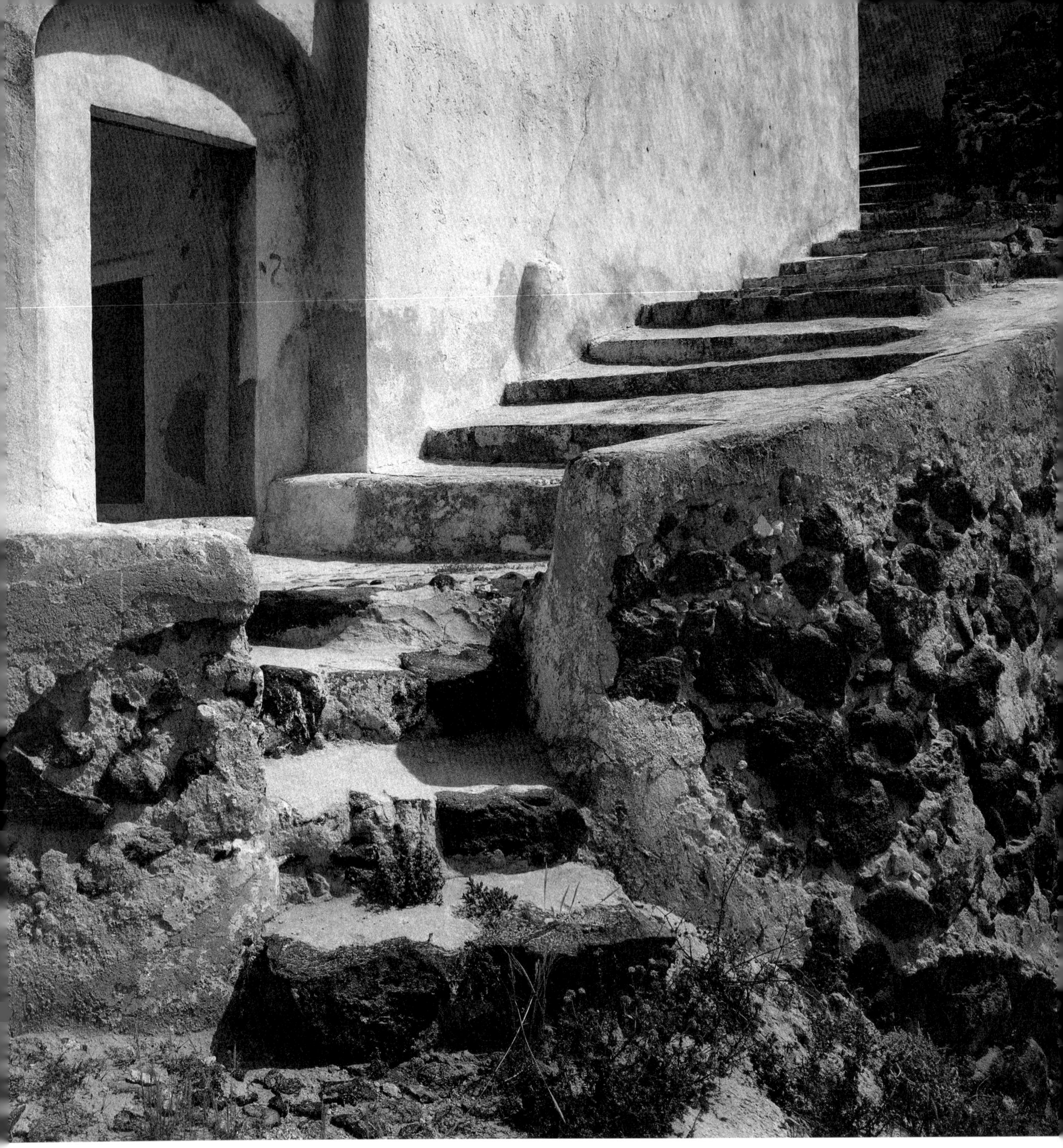

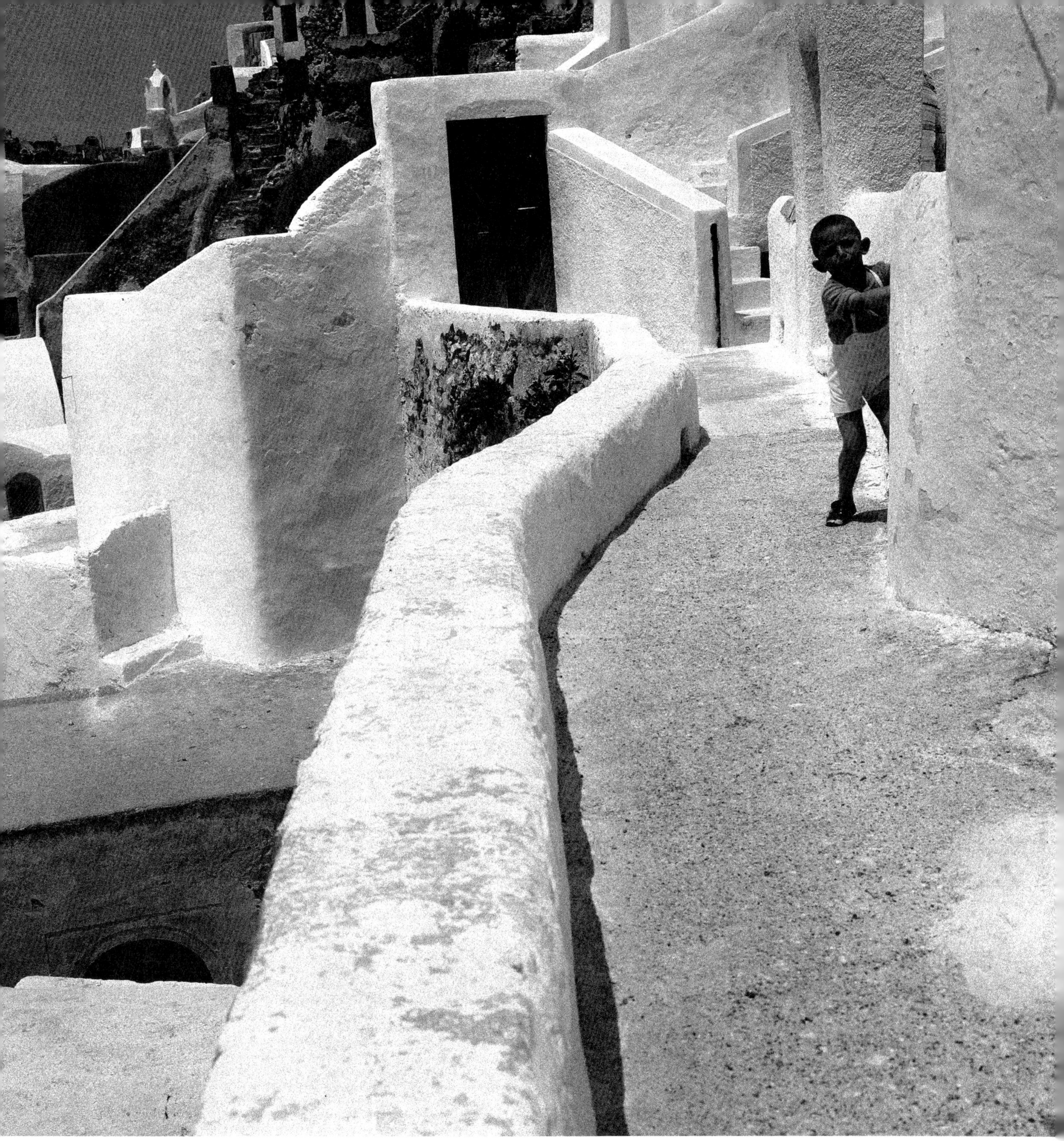

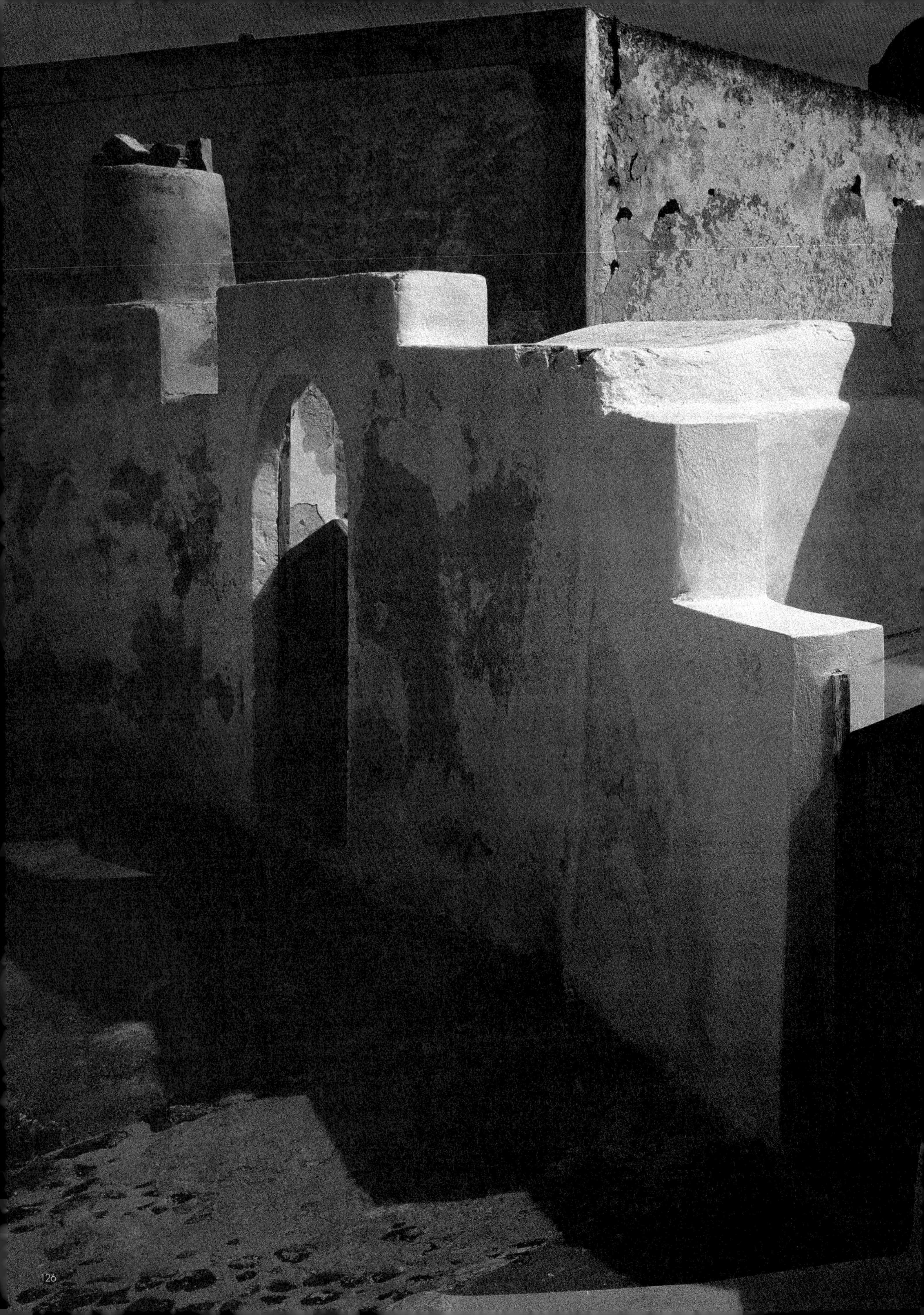

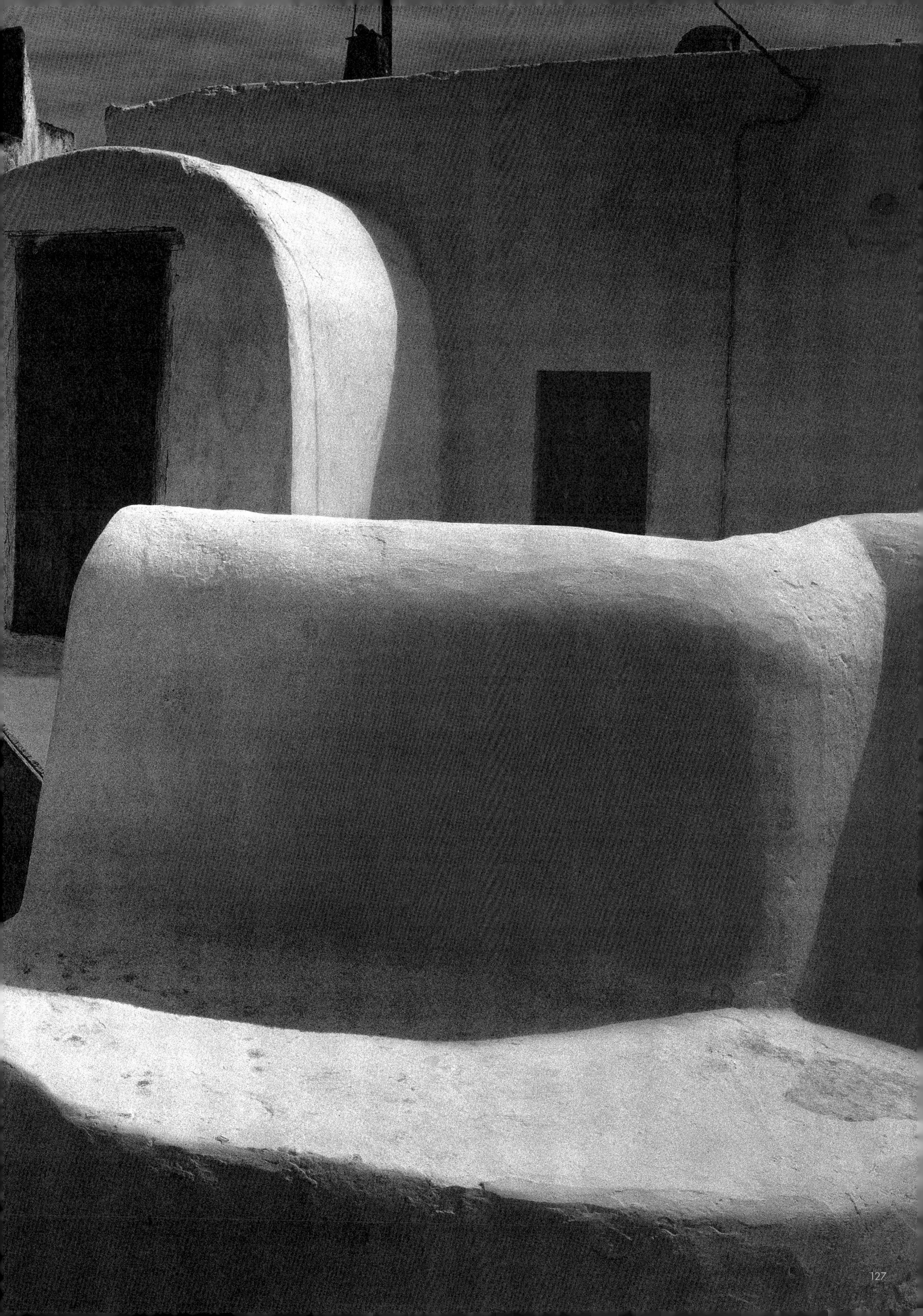

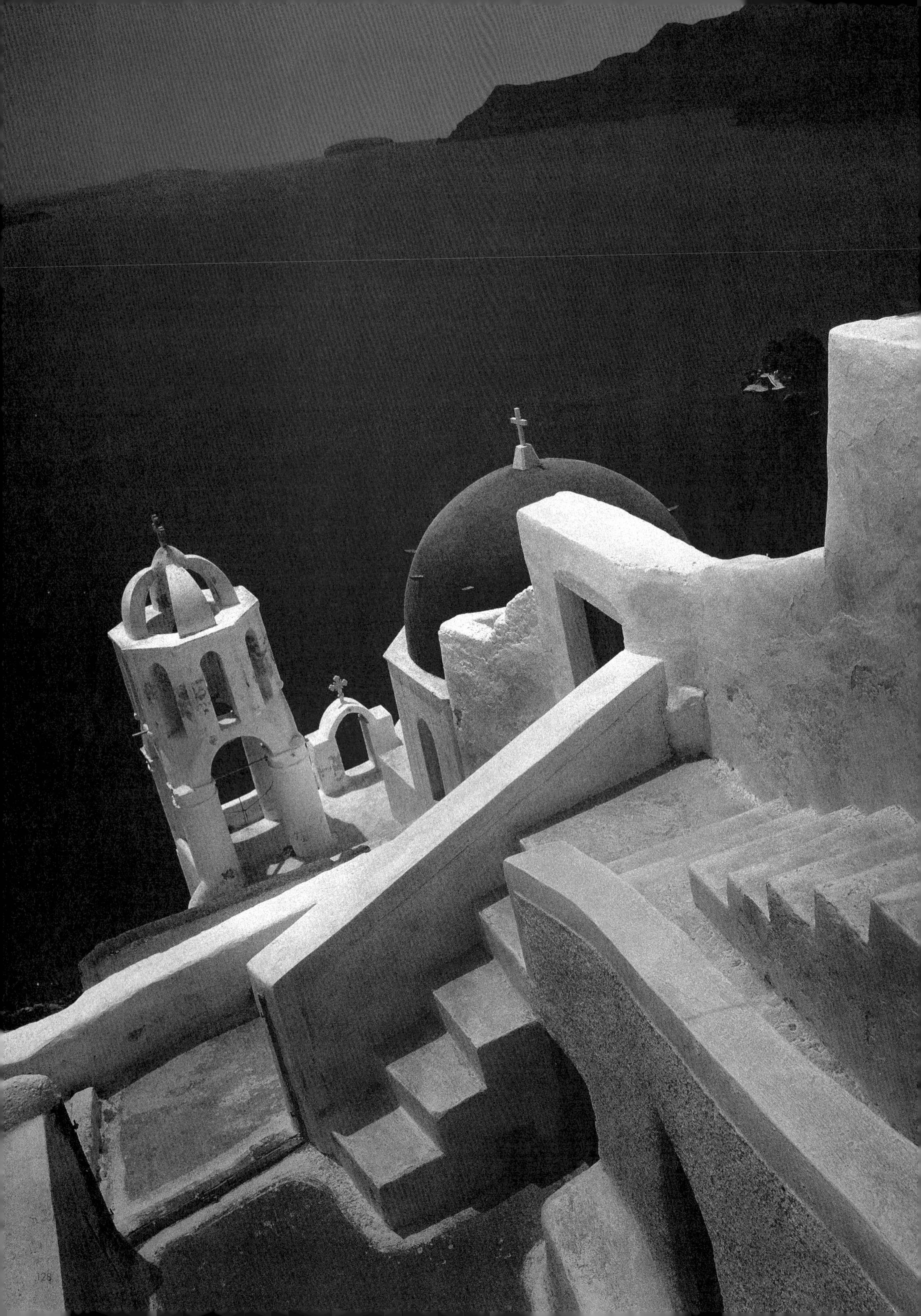

写真説明
Pictures and Explanations

P. 2〜3

船がサントリーニに近づくと
三日月形の島の北端にある漁村オィア(Oia)が強烈な印象で眼の前に立つ。

Boats approaching Santorini are greeted by a powerful sight of Oia,
a fishing village at the northern tip of the crescent-shaped island.

P. 6〜7

最近の地震で崩れた断崖は，オィアの切断面を生々しく露出したままである。
その上に新しい村が白くつくられていく。

Cliff failure caused by a recent earthquake showing freshly cut surfaces of Oia.
New village will be build on top of it in white.

P. 25

〈ミコノス島〉
南北10km，東西15kmの小島の西湾に面して街があり，
更に西の海上7kmにデロスの遺跡がある。

<Mykonos Island>
A small island 10 km wide north-south and 15 km long east-west.
Town faces the western bay, with ancient ruins of Delos 7 km offshore.

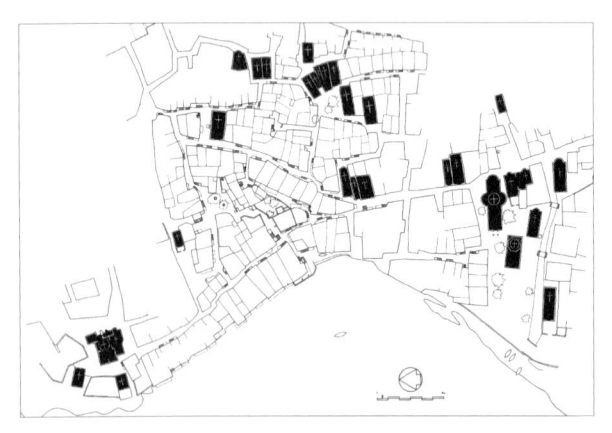

P. 28〜29

〈ミコノスの街路のネットワーク〉
住居グループと道のネットワークとの関係。
最も魅力的な2haほどの区域のプラン。

<Street networks of Mykonos>
Relationship between groups of houses and street networks.
Plan of the most attractive 2-ha area.

P. 32

〈ミコノスの港と街〉(部分)
港と岬と街の関係。旧い街区における迷路のシステムのスケッチ・プラン。

<Port and town of Mykonos> (partial)
Relationship between port, cape and town. Sketch of the old town's maze-like plan.

P. 33

のどかな漁港ミコノスの風景はロマンチックであるが，
最近では島内に車が急増してしまった。

Romantic view of Mykonos' peaceful fishing port.
Island is recently experiencing a sharp rise in automobiles.

P. 34〜35

ミコノスへのアプローチは楽しい。
岬の先端にあるパラポルティアの教会は、近づく船へのミコノスのサインだ。

Approach to Mykonos is a feast for the eyes.
Church of Paraportiani at the tip of the cape is a sign for boats approaching Mykonos.

P. 36

夏になると港は広場にかわる。
来る人、立去る人を見ながら、この夏の期間だけの海の広場は賑わう。

In summer the port turns into a plaza.
As people come and go, this temporary port plaza is busy all summer long.

P. 36〜37

数多い旅行者が集れる場所は街の中にはない。
港はテントがのび、レストランが張出すことの出来る唯一の空地だ。

The only space in town capable of accommodating flocks of tourists is
the port where restaurants stretch their awnings.

P. 38〜39

古くからミコノスの港は通商が栄であったといわれる。
外来者に開かれた空間が街中にある。

Port of Mykonos has been a trading center from old times.
Town is dotted with spaces open to visitors.

P. 40

幾つかの風車はまだ使われている。風車のある丘は、
風の関係から見晴らしの良い場所であり、外来者は好んでここに訪れる。

Some windmills are still in use. The hill where the windmills are is a
vantage point chosen in terms of wind that is popular among tourists.

P. 41

風車はミコノスのもうひとつのランド・マークであるが、
半分程が稼働し、残りは形骸だけになっている。

Windmills are another iconic landmark of Mykonos.
Half of them are in operation while the rest stand idle.

P. 42〜43

カテドラルの前の海岸から、旧い住区のある岬を見返すことが出来る。
左手にあるのがパラポルティアの教会。

View of the old town on the cape from the shore in front of the Cathedral.
Church of Paraportiani is seen on the left.

P. 44
道は細い迷路になっている。

Narrow maze of streets.

P. 44〜45
道は自然にふくらみをつくり出し,それが広場のように使われる。
道か広場か境界のない空間が連続する。

Streets naturally grow wider in places and are used as plazas.
A series of spaces of no boundaries between streets and plazas continues.

P. 46〜47
ミコノスの道は,塗り込められて部厚いテクスチュアをもつ。
これが道の暖かな感触を伝えるのだろう。

Streets of Mykonos have a texture of thick paint that adds a warm touch.

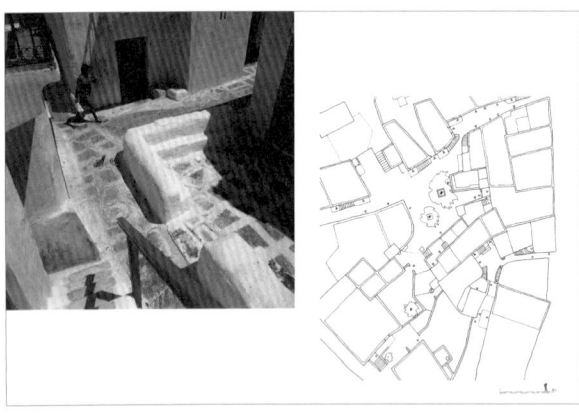

P. 48
住居はくっつき合ってグループをつくる。
グループの隙間は個人のものとも共有のものとも見別けがつかないまで同化する。

Houses cling to each other to form a group.
Gaps in a group are so integrated that the private and the public are indistinguishable.

P. 49
〈ミコノスの道と広場1〉
西にある小さな広場と道と家の関係を示す実測スケッチ。

<Streets and plaza in Mykonos 1>
Measured sketch showing the relationship between a small plaza,
streets and houses in the west area.

P. 50
広場らしい道のふくらみには木がある。
すべてが輝く街にさわやかな自然の影をおとしている。

Bulging area of a street looks like a plaza, with trees that offer
refreshing natural shades to the gleaming town.

P. 50〜51
自然のまま残された樹木の配置。
自然の木影があった部分に道のふくらみをつくったのかも知れない。

Natural placement of trees is preserved.
Maybe the street was widened where there were natural tree shades.

P. 54
道に突出された内部。
つまり外部に出された住居の階段やバルコニーは,ミコノスの道を演出する。

The interior protrudes into the street.
Stairs and balconies of houses placed outside characterize the streets of Mykonos.

P. 55
街は港のある高台から,序々に東の丘の斜面へ登って行く。
樹木がアトランダムに街から頭を出しているのが見える。

Town stretches from the port on a platform up along the eastern hillside.
Trees can be seen randomly poking their top out in the townscape.

P. 56

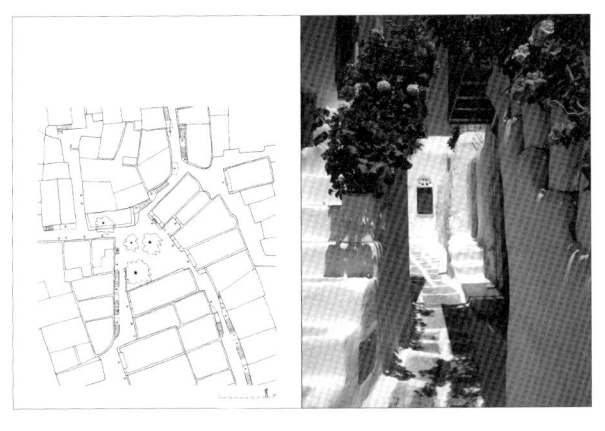

〈ミコノスの道と広場2〉
東にある広場と道，家と教会の関係を示す実測スケッチ。

<Streets and plaza in Mykonos 2>
Measured sketch showing the relationship between a plaza, streets,
houses and church in the east area.

P. 57

狭い道が，豊かな道であるために必要な道具がある。
自由な形，白い色，青いバルコニー，思い思いの草花。

Some tools are needed to make a narrow street a rich one.
Freedom of form, white color, blue balcony, haphazard flowers.

P. 58

六つの教会のある広場へ，南側から入る道。
住居と同じスケールの教会が，自然な形で街路の目印になっている。

Street leading to the plaza with six churches from the south.
Churches in the same scale as houses become landmarks in a natural manner.

P. 59

六つの教会のある広場から，南へ抜ける道。
光と影や道の幅が効果的にパースペクティブを強調している。

Southbound street from the plaza with six churches.
Light, shadow and street width work effectively to highlight the perspective.

P. 60

海寄りの広場へ北東から入る道は，港からここへ来る最もポピュラーな道だ。
道は広場のコーナーへ入るのが一般的だ。

Street accessing the plaza near the sea from northeast is the most popular route from the port.
Typically, a street enters at the corner of a plaza.

P. 61

ときとして，一つの階段を両側の家が使う場合も出てくる。
また，向かいの家の壁を利用して構造的に処理する場合もある。

In some cases a set of stairs is used by both houses on left and right.
Also, some are structurally managed by using the opposite house's wall.

P. 62

道の光と影は，白い囲みの空間の中では，
遠近や，方向を示す貴重な役割を果たしていることが解る。

Light and shadow in a street play precious roles in showing directions
and perspective within the enclosed white space.

P. 62～63

バルコニーは互いに繋がり合って道を覆い，トンネルをつくる場合がある。
公共と私有が自由に重なり合う。

Sometimes balconies join together to cover the street and form a tunnel.
The public and the private freely overlap with one another.

P. 64

道は明るく乾いている。
白い光が乱反射しあって，人々の顔を横や下から照らすことになる。

Streets are bright and dry.
Diffused white light illuminates people's face from below and from the sides.

P. 65

道は常に三叉路で交わる。
この迷路のシステムこそ，ミコノスの街の重要な空間のネットワークだ。

Streets always intersect as a three-way junction.
This maze-like system is the very spatial network that is essential to the town of Mykonos.

P. 66
道は公共的というより，もっとプライベートな場として意味をもち，
私的空間の複合として捉えられる。

*Streets are private rather than public in significance:
they may be interpreted as a combination of private spaces.*

P. 67
道と家は続いているのだという造形がここにある。
階段は道となり，道は家となる連続の手法がある。

*A figurative example of continuity between streets and houses.
A method of continuity in which stairs become streets, streets become houses.*

P. 68
はじめの数段が共用で，中間から各家の方向へ勝手に回り込んでいる。
階段というより，家自体が階段状であるといえそうだ。

*First few steps are shared. The rest of stairs run around each house arbitrarily.
Not so much a stairway as a house built in tiers.*

P. 69
白い階段は自由にずれて住居に近づく。
人の歩く部分だけ石の面のままわずかに塗り残されている。

*White stairs shift aside freely and approach houses.
Area where pedestrians walk is left unpainted, showing the stone surface.*

P. 70
上：60cmに充たない狭さも，隅やコーナーも光に同化してしまうのは白い色の最大の効果だといえる。
下：自由な形で道に出る階段。

*Above: Best effect of the color white is its ability to integrate
widths less than 60 cm, angles and corners with light.
Below: Stairs giving onto a street with a freedom of form.*

P. 70〜71
道が段となり，ベンチになり，犬走りになる。
構造体も壁も，汚水管も，同じテクスチュアに塗りこめられて一体となる。

*Street turns into steps, benches and scarcement.
Structure, walls and waste pipes are all painted in the same texture to become one.*

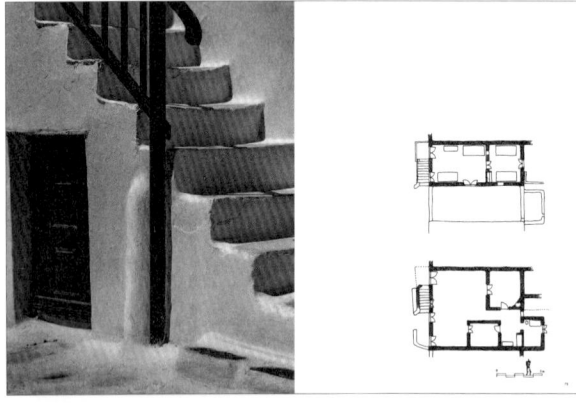

P. 72
最も重要なエレメント。道，階段，バルコニー，手摺，物入れ。
これがミコノスの住居のファサードのオーダーだ。

*The most important elements are: street, stairs, balcony, handrail, storage.
This is the order in the facade of houses in Mykonos.*

P. 73
〈ミコノスの住居〉
1階が居間，2階が寝室，外部階段など標準的住居に見られる間取り。

*<House in Mykonos>
Floor plan of a standard house with living room on 1st floor, bedrooms on 2nd floor and exterior stairs.*

P. 74〜75
ミコノスの住居のスタイルには色々な地方や年代の影響が認められる。
これはサハラ的ともいえる要素の濃い，しかし新しい家になるだろう。

*House styles in Mykonos display influences from various regions and time periods.
This one with heavy Saharan influence will be a new type of house.*

P. 75
教会の鐘楼は大袈裟なものではなくスケールも扱いも住居と同じだ。
これでも装飾の多い方である。

*Church belfries are far from extravagant, with scales and attitudes similar to those of houses.
The one shown here is more ornamental than others.*

P. 76〜77

〈ミコノスの街路立面及び平面図〉
港から街へ入って東寄りの道。約40mの区間における道の立面と平面スケッチ。

<Elevation and plan of a street in Mykonos>
Street near the port in the eastern part of town.
Sketches of street elevation and plan for a 40 m-segment.

P. 78〜79

パラポルティアの教会は、幾つかの教会が凝固して出来たものだ。
このプラスティックなフォルムがそれを物語る。

Church of Paraportiani is a conglomeration of several churches.
Its origin is demonstrated in this plastic form.

P. 81

〈サントリーニ島〉
三日月形の島は、南北18km、最高地が568mの急峻な火山そのものだ。
サントリーニはThíra(Thera)島のニックネームであり、Thíraの町はFiraとも呼ばれる。

<Santorini Island>
Crescent-shaped island measuring 18 km from north to south and
reaching a height of 568 m is virtually a precipitous volcano.
Santorini is a nickname for the island of Thíra (Thera),
and its town Thíra is also known as Fira.

P. 84〜85

〈サントリーニの街路と住居群〉(部分)
フィラの西側の最も海寄りの道と住居群の関係を示すスケッチ。

<Street and cluster of houses in Santorini> (partial)
Sketch showing the relationship between a cluster of houses and a
street on the east closest to the sea in Fira.

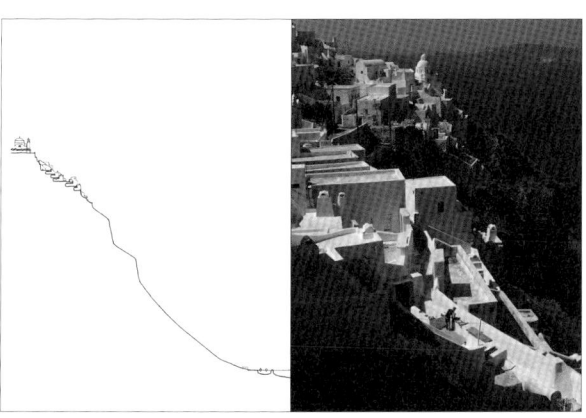

P. 88

〈サントリーニの断面スケッチ〉
港と街、住居群の堆積した位置関係を示す島の断面のイメージ・スケッチ

<Section sketch of Santorini>
Sketch picturing the section of the island shows positional
relationship between port, town, and accumulation of clustered houses.

P. 89

南端のアクロティリが見える。
テラスは日常生活の重要な機能を果す西に開いた居間である。

Distant view of Akrotiri at the southern tip.
Terrace is a living room open to the west that serves an important function in daily life.

P. 90〜91

フィラの全景。港と街をつなぐジグザグの道，
西の斜面，急峻な断崖，東南のなだらかな斜面など。

*Full view of Fira: meandering street connecting the port to the town,
western slope, precipitous cliff, gentle southeastern slope.*

P. 92〜93

絶壁寄りの水平街路からテラスを見る。
フィラの街で最も西側の海に突き出した印象的な家だ。

*Looking down a terrace from a horizontal street by the cliff.
An impressive house projecting to the sea at the western end of Fira.*

P. 94〜95

自然地理が決定する堆積の方法。
堆積する住空間がつくり出す様々な景観がすべてサントリーニのものなのだ。

*Nature and geography defined the way of accumulation.
Diversity of sceneries created by accumulated living spaces is all that Santorini has to offer.*

P. 96

街と港を結ぶ石畳の道はメインの道であり，水平の道はこの道から分岐して住居区に入る。

*Stone-paved street linking the town and the port is the main road,
from which horizontal streets branch off into residential areas.*

P. 97

200m下の港への道はロバの歩き易いようにつくられている。
今日もロバの一群が旅行者を迎えに下りてゆく。

*Road to the port located 200 m down allows donkeys to move easily.
Yet another group of donkeys climbing down to fetch tourists.*

P. 98

テラスの中で，人々は思い思いの作業をしている。
テラスの中の出来事が上からよく見える。

*People performing daily chores on the terraces.
From above, activities on the terraces are in plain view.*

P. 99

テラスから西を見ると眼下に港が見える。
テラスや鐘楼は常に光る海を背景に眺められることになる。

*Looking toward east, the port can be seen right below.
Terraces and belfries are always viewed against a gleaming sea in the background.*

P. 100〜101

地中に深くささり込んでいる住居は，幾重ものテラスとなって外部に表現される。
この一帯は実測図で示した部分だ。

Houses anchored deep into the ground are expressed on the outside as layers of terraces.
This is the area shown in the measured sketch.

P. 102

前庭のテラスは，左側にある炊事場，右側の便所や収納のユニットで，不定形なアルコーブをつくり出す。

A front terrace, together with the kitchen on left and toilet and
storage unit on right, creates an irregular-shaped alcove.

P. 103

テラスは見た目にはオープンであるが，使われ方はプライベートだ。
上下のテラスは自由に細い階段で連結されている。

Terraces look publicly open to the eye, but their uses are private.
Upper and lower terraces are freely connected via narrow stairs.

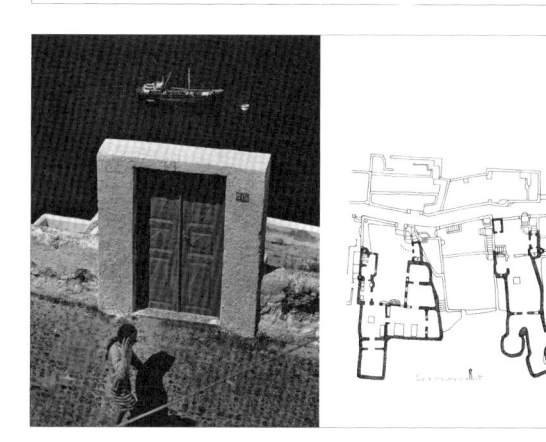

P. 104

水平の道から下にある住居への入口。大きな門構えだけが，下にある住居の大きさを示している。

Entrance to a house located below the horizontal street.
Its massive gate is an indication of the house's large size.

P. 105

〈サントリーニの道，テラス，住居〉
住居群から二つの平面を取り出して道とパティオ，テラス，階段，厨房，居間等の関係を見る。

<Streets, terraces and houses of Santorini>
Two plans are extracted from the house cluster to examine the relationship
between street, patio, terrace, stairs, kitchen, and living room.

P. 106〜107

港からの道を登りつめて街に入る。右は水平の道に繋る。
サントリーニの場合も三叉路が道のジョイントの基本になる。

Uphill road from the port leads to town. Course to the right connects to the horizontal street.
Also in the case with Santorini, streets basically intersect in a three-way junction.

P. 110〜111

南のクリフからフィラの街を見る。
頂上にある教会はフィラの最も高い場所にあり，何処からでも良く見える。

Viewing the town of Fira from the southern cliff.
Church at the top is the highest point of Fira, visible from anywhere in the island.

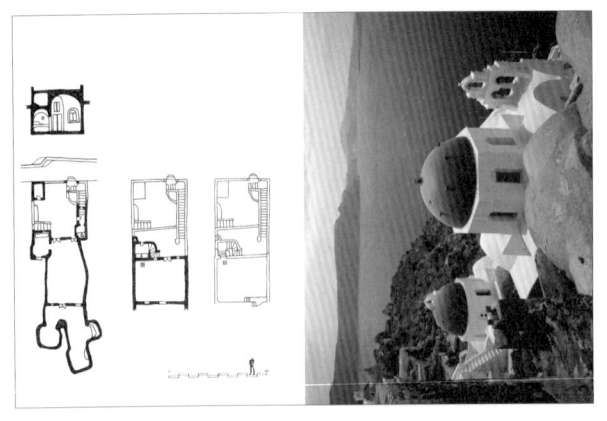

P. 112
〈サントリーニの住居の実測によるスケッチ・プラン〉
住居は斜面に深くささり込んだ楔型の平面をもつ。

<Measured sketch of floor plan of a house in Santorini>
Floor plan of the house is wedge-shaped, anchored deep into the slope.

P. 113
西の斜面は，夏は涼しく冬は暖かい。
円弧で囲まれたサントリーニの内海は穏かだ。

Climate of the slope on the west is cool in summer and warm in winter.
Surrounded by an arc, Santorini's lagoon stays calm.

P. 114〜115
オィアはフィラよりももっと劇的な景観を残す。
失われた住居の生々しい廃墟が眼前にひろがる。

Oia retains a scenery that is much more dramatic than Fira's.
Fresh ruins of lost houses spread across the area.

P. 116〜117
かつての住居の切断面をそのままにして，その上に，新しい生活を続ける。
新しい石の家が白く輝き出す。

Leaving the old sections of the houses intact, a new life continues on top of them.
New stone houses begin to shine white.

P. 118
フィラよりもっと土俗的で，すべてが部厚く，不定形だ。
地形は家々の並びをフィラとは別のものにしている。

Compared with Fira, everything is more indigenous, thicker, and more irregular.
Topography differentiates the layout of houses from that of Fira.

P. 119
家の形はどこか東方を思わせる。歴史の通り道であって，
色々な影響があったが，ビザンチンが最も強く残っているという。

Forms of houses are somewhat reminiscent of the Orient. Having been part of a historical corridor,
it has been subject to a variety of influences, the strongest being the Byzantine.

P. 120
最も優れた漁村として栄えたオィアの港に下りる道も，今は荒れたままになっている。
灰色のままで残された家も多い。

Road climbing down to the port of Oia, once the most prominent of fishing villages,
is now left to devastation.
Many houses remain gray, without paint.

P. 121
瓦礫の上を水平にはしる道は人通りがない。
自然の脅威を眼前にして，しかし白い村が活動しはじめている。

Street running horizontally above the rubbles looks vacant.
Despite its vulnerability to natural threats, the white village is coming back into action.

P. 122〜123

古い家は廃墟に繋がってあり，新しい家もまた廃墟の上にある。
サントリーニが常に繰り返してきた自然と人のヴィジュアルな歴史である。

Old houses are connected to the ruins, while new houses are built on top the ruins.
A visual history of nature and humans as it has been repeated in Santorini.

P. 124

垂直の村において，階段の形は数限りない。
上下，左右，地形に合わせて自由奔放にふられる。

In a village of verticality, forms of stairways are countless.
They deliberately drift up and down, left and right along the topography.

P. 125

オィアの道は，フィラよりも複雑である。
それは曲がりくねった斜面にある迷路なのだ。

Street of Oia is more complex than Fira's.
It is a maze set up on a meandering slope.

P. 126〜127

オィアの最も古い建築の様式を残している。
厚く，太く，粗く，大まかであり，石と土の感触が生である。

Vestige of Oia's oldest architectural style.
Heavy, thick, coarse and rough, with a raw touch of stone and soil.

P. 128

垂直の村にあって，視界は常に下へ向けられる。
この塔も，海の色を背景にあることを意識してつくられたのであろう。

In this village of verticality, eyesight is constantly directed downward.
The same is probably true to this tower, created against the color of the sea in the background.

後記――二川幸夫
Notes and Remarks *by Yukio Futagawa*

エーゲ海の数多い島の中から，ミコノス島，サントリーニ島を選んだ理由は，この両島の集落が持つ性格が，今日きわだった個性を持っているからである。またその集落の姿はほぼ完全に保たれ，街並としては格調があり，生活のちえの中から生れたデザインとしては世界第一級のものである。現代人が忘れ去ろうとしている自然のイメージが，青い空と青い海にサンドイッチされた純白の島の姿に明確に生きている。しかし，これらの島々が観光の資源となり徐々にであるが，崩されていく姿を見ることは否定できない。

〈ミコノス島〉
アテネからミコノス島までは，約150キロ，船によって所要時間は異なるが5時間から7時間の船旅である。われわれが5月に利用した船は，朝アテネのPiraévs港を発ち，Sounion岬の南を通ってKéa島とKithnos島の間に航路をとり，穏やかなエーゲ海の上をすべるように進んで行った。途中，Síros島へ寄港し，Síros島から2時間で青い海の波方にミコノス島の細長い白い帯が横たわっているのを発見することができる。まぶしいばかりの太陽を反射した白いミコノスの街が近づくにつれて，あの特徴ある風車が一つ二つ三つとゆっくりと回っているのを見ることができる。われわれは長い船旅を忘れて，ただあまりにも美しい風景に茫然とするばかりである。港のまわりは，忙しそうに漁船が行きかい，その船腹に塗られた原色と，青い海と，白い家々とがあざやかな色彩のコントラストをなしていた。ミコノス島の大きさは約90km²で，島はおしなべて平坦で，島のほとんどの人々は港の附近で生活し，海で採れる蛸，海老，各種の魚，海綿などが特産物である。またミコノスの向かいには，ギリシア時代の有名な遺蹟Delos島がある。

アテネからミコノスへの便船は，毎日就航しているOia号と，日，水，土に就航しているMimia号があり，料金は1等片道7.60ドル，往復15.25ドル，2等片道5ドル，往復10ドル，デッキ片道2.50ドル，往復5.35ドルである。

〈サントリーニ島〉
サントリーニ島へ行くにはアテネからの直行便と，途中の島々に寄港して行く便がある。われわれはミコノスからOia号でSíros島に引返し，ここでアテネからきたElli号に乗変えてサントリーニに向った。午後4時にSíros島を発った船は，Paros島，Naxos島，と寄港し，途中Ios島で一泊し翌朝6時すぎ断岸絶壁の立ちはだかるサントリーニに到着する。朝日が昇った直後の逆光気味の眩しい光の中

The reason why I chose Mykonos and Santorini from the myriad of islands in the Aegean is the characteristics of both islands and their marked individuality as we know them today. Also because their installments were kept completely intact, their streets are elegant, and they present first-class designs that sprouted from the wisdom of living. Imagery of nature that modern people are about to dismiss from their minds is alive and well within the picture of whitewashed islands sandwiched between the blue sky and the blue sea. There is however no denying that these islands are being destroyed, though gradually, as resources for tourism.

<Mykonos>
Approximately 150 km away from Athens, Mykonos may be accessed by a 5 to 7-hour cruise depending on the type of ship. The one we boarded in May departed the port of Piraévs in Athens in the morning, steered past the south of Sounion cape and between Kéa and Kithnos islands and glided over the quiet Aegean sea. Stopping at Siros island on the way and cruising for another 2 hours we discovered the long, white belt-like island of Mykonos beyond the blue sea. As we approached the white town of Mykonos reflecting the glaring sun, the so typical slowly turning windmills came into view one by one. All that we could do was to forget the long ship ride and get lost in the all too beautiful scenery. The area around the port was busy with fishing boats, as the primitive colors painted on the ship belly, the blue sea and the white houses created vivid, colorful contrasts. Mykonos measures about 90 sq.km.. The island is overall flat. Most islanders live in the vicinity of the port. Local specialty is octopus, shrimp, a variety of fish and marine sponge. Facing Mykonos is Delos island famous for its Greek ruins.

Regular connection from Athens to Mykonos is assured by the Oia daily and the Mimia serving every Sunday, Wednesday and Saturday. First class one-way fare is 7.60 dollars, round trip fare is 15.25 dollars. Second class one-way fare is 5 dollars, round trip 10 dollars. Deck seat one-way fare is 2.50 dollars, round trip 5.35 dollars.

<Santorini>
There are two routes to Santorini from Athens: nonstop direct and stopping over at other islands. In our case we left Mykonos and came back to Síros island on the Oia, then boarded the Elli which has arrived from Athens and traveled to Santorini. Leaving Síros at 4 pm, the ship stopped at Paros island and Naxos island before spending a night at Ios island and arriving at the precipitous bluffs of Santorini shortly after 6 am the next morning. As the volcanic island of Santorini made its appearance gleaming black against the glaring sunshine just after dawn, the paradise

に，黒々とした火山島サントリーニがわれわれの目前に出現したとき，ミコノスで経験した楽園のイメージは吹きとび，自然の厳しさをまざまざと見せつけられた。サントリーニは，ティラ（Thíra, Thera）島のニックネームで，BC 9世紀ごろの大地震でほぼ今の形になったが，このようなことは消えたアトランティス大陸がサントリーニであるという説を生んだ。

船はThíra(Fira)の街の沖に碇泊し，そこから艀で上陸し，そこからロバの背に揺られて，5キロの道を頭上の街Thíraへ運ばれてゆく。またフェリーの着接できるPorto Athemosに着く船もあり，その場合はタクシーでThíraへすぐゆける。Thíraから車で20分の北の岬にOiaがあり，ここは1956年の地震で廃墟になった街であるが，都市空間や建築の造形はすばらしいものがある。

サントリーニの集落の特徴は，海を望む急峻な岸にあるため，ミコノスの街が平面的なのに対して立体的である。個々の家はエーゲ海を一望に見渡せるすばらしいテラスをもち，そのテラスの陰影がより一層この島の集落を立体的に見せる役目をはたしている。またミコノスの家々が連続的な空間を持っていて，デザインに一体性があるのに対して，サントリーニの家々は1軒1軒が個性にあふれている。われわれが5月に滞在している間にも何日か強い風が吹きまくり，海を伝わってくる風はようしゃなく山頂の集落を包み，より一層，深い孤独感にさそいこんだ。青い海に太陽がふりそそぐ微風吹くエーゲ海は，ホメロスの唱ったように暗く，また荒れた海でもあった。

サントリーニ島からは，クレタ島へもゆけるが，アテネに帰るには，直行便と，多くの島に寄港する便がある。急ぐ時は直行便のElli号がよく，ゆっくりと時間をかけてキクラデス諸島巡りをするにはEvaggelia号が良く，途中碇泊する島々は，サントリーニ島のThíra, Oia, Folegandros島, Síkinos島, Ios島, Iraklia島, Skhoinousa島, Káros島, Amorgos島のKatapolaとEgiali, Dhenoúsa島, Naxos島, Síros島, アテネのPiraévs港で，所要時間は26時間である。料金はアテネ，サントリーニ間1等片道10.50ドル，往復22ドル，2等片道6ドル，往復12.50ドル，ツーリスト・クラス片道5ドル，往復10.50ドル，デッキ片道3.25ドル，往復6.80ドルである。料金，船名は1972年調べ，所要時間は天候で大巾に変更する。また船のスケジュールは，シーズンによって変わるので，アテネのダウンタウンのアメリカン・エクスプレスを調べると良い。

＊ 1973年初版時の文章をそのまま収録

imagery experienced at Mykonos was blown off by the graphic representation of nature's harshness. Santorini is a nickname for Thíra or Thera. It eventually took its present-day shape after the great earthquake that occurred around 9th century BC, thus the speculation that Santorini was Atlantis, the vanished continent.

After the ship dropped its anchor off the shore of the town Thíra (Fira), we stepped onto a barge for disembarkation. Then we were carried on donkey-back for 5 km until we reached the town of Thíra towering above. Some ships arrive at Porto Athemos where ferries can be docked, offering direct access to Thíra via taxi. From Thíra, a 20-minute car ride took us to Oia on the northern cape, a ruins of a town destroyed by the 1956 earthquake where we can admire some wonderful architectural forms and urban spaces.

A typical settlement in Santorini is three-dimensional, compared to that of Mykonos which is flat, due to its location on the precipitous bluffs overlooking the sea. Each house has a magnificent terrace with a panoramic view of the Aegean. The shades and shadows of these terraces contribute in making the settlements on this island look even more three-dimensional. In contrast with the houses of Mykonos that have continuous spaces and integrated design, every one of those of Santorini is full of individual characteristics. During our stay in May, there were instances when strong wind from the sea swirled for several days, brutally enveloping the clifftop settlement and bringing them to deep solitude. Aegean imagery of blue sea, pouring sunshine and gentle breeze turned out to be dark and stormy as depicted in Homer's verses.

From Santorini, one may continue onto Creta island or return to Athens either non stop or with many stops at other islands. When in a hurry the direct route of the Elli is the best option, but if one were to spend some time touring the Cyclades the Evaggelia is better suited, with stops at Thíra and Oia on Satorini, Folegandros island, Síkinos island, Ios island, Iraklia island, Skhoinousa island, Káros island, Katapola and Egiali on Amorgos island, Dhenoúsa island, Naxos island, and Síros island before arriving at the port of Piraévs in Athens and the total cruising time of 26 hours. Cost between Athens and Santorini are: First class one-way ticket for 10.50 dollars and 22 dollars round trip, Second class one-way ticket for 6 dollars and 12.50 dollars round trip, Tourist class one-way ticket for 5 dollars and 10.50 dollars round trip, and Deck seat one-way ticket for 3.25 dollars and 6.80 dollars round trip. Fares and ship names are as of 1972, and cruise time depends largely on the weather. Ship schedule varies with season, so visitors are advised to inquire at the American Express desk in downtown Athens.

This afterword was written for the first edition published in 1973.

エーゲ海地図　*Map of Aegean Sea*

Aegean Sea

- Lésvos
- Bergama
- Khíos
- IZMIR
- Andros
- Tínos
- Síros
- Mykonos
- Sámos
- Ikaria
- Prine
- Miletus
- Didyma
- Naxsos
- Paros
- Dhenoúsa
- Íos
- Skhoinoúsa
- Iráklia
- Amorgós
- Kos
- Folégandros
- Síkinos
- Thíra (Santorini)
- Ródhos

Kikladhes (Cyclades)

- Kárpathos
- CRETE (KRÍTI)
- IRÁKLION
- Cnossus
- Hagia Triada

世界の村と街 No.1
〈エーゲ海の村と街〉

1973年1月25日初版発行
2016年3月25日改訂新版発行

企画・撮影　二川幸夫
　　　　文　磯崎新
解説・作図　鈴木恂
　デザイン　細谷巌
　　　和訳　谷理佐
　　発行者　二川由夫
印刷・製本　大日本印刷株式会社
　　　発行　エーディーエー・エディタ・トーキョー
　　　　　　151-0051 東京都渋谷区千駄ヶ谷3-12-14
　　　　　　TEL.(03)3403-1581(代)

禁無断転載

ISBN978-4-87140-454-9 C1372

AEGEAN SEA

Lésvos

Bergama

Khíos

IZMIR

Andros

Tínos

Síros   Mykonos

Ikaria   Sámos

Prine

Miletus

Didyma

Paros   Naxsos

Dhenoúsa

Íos   Skhoinoúsa
Iráklia   Amorgós   Kos

Folégandros

Síkinos

Thíra (Santorini)

Ródhos

Kikladhes (Cyclades)

Kárpathos

CRETE (KRÍTI)

IRÁKLION

Cnossus

Hagia Triada

143

世界の村と街 No.1
〈エーゲ海の村と街〉

1973年1月25日初版発行
2016年3月25日改訂新版発行

企画・撮影　二川幸夫
　　　　文　磯崎新
解説・作図　鈴木恂
　デザイン　細谷巖
　　　和訳　谷理佐
　　発行者　二川由夫
印刷・製本　大日本印刷株式会社
　　　発行　エーディーエー・エディタ・トーキョー
　　　　　　151-0051 東京都渋谷区千駄ヶ谷3-12-14
　　　　　　TEL.(03)3403-1581(代)

禁無断転載

ISBN978-4-87140-454-9 C1372